# THE PARABLES OF JESUS IN THE
# LIGHT OF THE OLD TESTAMENT

# THE PARABLES OF JESUS
## IN THE LIGHT OF
## THE OLD TESTAMENT

Claus Westermann

*Translated and edited by*
Friedemann W. Golka
*and*
Alastair H. B. Logan

T&T CLARK
EDINBURGH

T&T CLARK
59 GEORGE STREET
EDINBURGH EH2 2LQ
SCOTLAND

First Published 1990

ISBN 0 567 29162 6

British Library Cataloguing in Publication Data.
Westermann, Claus
The Parables Of Jesus in the Light of the Old Testament
1. Bible. O.T. Parables – Critical studies
I. Title
II. *Vergleiche und Gleichnisse im Alten und Neuen Testament*
English
223′.207

Typeset by Barbers (Highlands) Ltd, Fort William
Printed and bound in Great Britain by Billing & Sons Ltd, Worcester

# Contents

# Abbreviations

| | |
|---|---|
| ATD | Das Alte Testament Deutsch |
| BEvTh | Beiträge zur Evangelischen Theologie |
| BK | Biblischer Kommentar |
| CTM | Calwer Theologische Monographien |
| EvTh | Evangelische Theologie (Sonderheft) |
| FRLANT | Forschungen zur Religion und Literatur des Alten und Neuen Testaments |
| GA | Gesammelte Aufsätze |
| Gosp.Thom. | Gospel of Thomas |
| IDB | The Interpreter's Dictionary of the Bible |
| JTS | Journal of Theological Studies |
| RGG | Die Religion in Geschichte und Gegenwart |
| THAT | Theologisches Handwörterbuch zum AT (Jenni-Westermann) |
| WMANT | Wissenschaftliche Monographien zum Alten und Neuen Testament |

# Editors' Preface

This book developed from a paper read by Professor Westermann at the Summer Meeting of the Society of Old Testament Study held in Exeter, 19–22 July 1983, under the presidency of Professor the Reverend Canon J. R. Porter. It was in fact Professor Porter who encouraged the editors to render the book into English.

It has always been characteristic of Professor Westermann's scholarship that he has sought to point out the connections between the Old and New Testaments. Similarly, he has always been concerned to emphasize the relevance of biblical exegesis for the theology and preaching of the church today. These seeds sown earlier in his working life the author has now reaped in this present book, written in his seventies.

Quotations are generally from the Hebrew Bible. However, where a verse is quoted in English, the RSV reference has been added in brackets where it differs. German books have been quoted in the original, but English translations where they exist have been listed in the bibliography. Professor Westermann regards his book as a preliminary study and, as he frequently points out, expects others to take up the task which he has begun. We hope the seed thus sown will not fall on barren ground.

Friedemann W. Golka
Alastair H. B. Logan

# INTRODUCTION

# Task and Terminology

As far as I know, a connected treatment of comparisons in the OT has never been undertaken. This is probably due to the fact that they were generally considered insignificant. They were regarded as an 'indirect' form of discourse over against a 'direct' form, as a pictorial form of speech in the way that in the Gospel parables a distinction was made between the 'image' and the 'subject at issue'. This in turn is based on Aristotle's earlier distinction between *res* and *ornatus* (cf. Part II on E. Jüngel, *Metapher*, p. 174).

The underlying assumption was that discourse in which comparisons were made was by definition pictorial and illustrative speech, as e.g. in the articles on 'Gleichnis' in RGG³ (see below p. 163 f.) and on 'parable' in IDB III p. 650: 'The parable saying is illustrative'. This explains why no-one was ever tempted to ask whether the comparisons themselves had anything to say. Equally no-one was driven to question more precisely the function of these comparisons, since it was automatically assumed that as forms of 'pictorial speech' they all had the same function, as is clear from the IDB quotation. (It was only after my investigation was virtually completed that I discovered from a work on German literature that in extra-theological research on metaphor the understanding of comparisons as pictorial speech has long been disputed; see below p. 179). But the simple fact that comparisons are virtually or completely absent from some parts of the OT while occurring frequently in others, points to the specific function of the comparison which is determined by the context.

I came upon this problem in a study of the interpretation of the parables of Jesus. I noticed that in the scholarly treatments of the parables so much emphasis was laid on the interpretation that the parable itself, i.e. its plain text, was not allowed a proper hearing. After having found the interpretation or the supposed interpretation one discarded the parable as no longer necessary. What was of theological use was only the intellectual extract of the parable, the so-called *tertium comparationis*. This made me very uncomfortable. I noticed that in the three groups of profane comparisons in the OT (see below p. 7) the comparison in each case had a significance in its own right. The function of these comparisons was different in all three groups, but never a matter of illustration or clarification. I attempted in a seminar on 'Proverb and Parable' (1977/78) to prove on this basis the independent meaning of the parable itself. Then it became clear to me that in order to understand the pre-history of the parables of Jesus it would be necessary to investigate the comparisons in the OT in their entirety in cases where the parables are regarded as extended comparisons (as by R. Bultmann *et al.*). Contrary to the opinion dominant among interpreters of the parables of Jesus that the function of parables is to illustrate (some even say: 'to illustrate the spiritual reality'; see below p. 164), an investigation of the comparisons in the OT shows that parables have different functions. These functions result from their context. An event in one sphere is juxtaposed with an event in another. The intention of this juxtaposition is in each case clear from the context. It is left to the judgment of the hearers to discover this intention. That the function of the comparisons in the OT is determined by their context is shown primarily by the fact that they are assigned to certain speech forms. They do not just occur anywhere; very rarely in the historical books, almost never in the legal corpora, in abundance in the prophetic books and the Psalms. They also occur in three non-theological complexes: in the tribal sayings in Gen. 49 and Deut. 33, in the Song of Songs, and in the comparisons of Proverbs.

Considerable confusion reigns over the question of terminology. However this can be resolved by proceeding on the assumption that all forms are based on the linguistic process of comparison and that for distinguishing between these forms one can only use formal and objective criteria. The comparison occurs most frequently in a single sentence (or two, at most three) which is part of a larger unit. It can be expanded into a parable which would then form an independent self-enclosed unit, a brief narrative. The explicit comparison consisting of a single sentence can also be reduced to an implicit comparison consisting of only one (or two or three) word(s). This implicit comparison reduced to one word is usually a metaphor (e.g. 'the earth opened its mouth', 'the arm of the LORD'). All three forms are comparisons inasmuch as they reflect a process of comparing or inasmuch as they are based on such a process. Although transitional forms exist, these three can nevertheless be clearly distinguished: the comparing narrative (parable) – the single sentence comparison – the comparison in just one word. To undertake a comprehensive investigation of the comparison one must take all three forms into account. (A similar distinction between these three forms can be found in C. H. Dodd, *Parables*, p. 16).

As we still have no comprehensive study of the comparisons in the OT (an investigation of the comparisons in the Psalms is under way at Tübingen), I can only provide a preliminary rough survey which would need more thorough elaboration. For this reason I have omitted discussion of the metaphor and have referred to secondary literature only in a few places, since otherwise this study would have exceeded all bounds. I am using this study also to demonstrate the possibility of co-operation in Old and New Testament exegesis. This is the intention of Part II where I indicate by reviewing a number of well known studies of the parables of Jesus what the investigation of the comparisons in the Old Testament contributes to our understanding of the parables in the New. Needless to say, these first hints have to remain very tentative.

I am aware of the importance of comparing the parables

of Jesus with early Jewish parables (e.g. Flusser). This would require a separate study, but I comment briefly on it in my review of M. D. Goulder (see below pp. 165 f.).

# COMPARISONS IN THE OLD TESTAMENT – THE PRE-HISTORY OF THE PARABLES OF JESUS

## The Profane Comparison

### Comparisons in the Tribal Sayings

The Tribal Sayings in Gen. 49 and Deut. 33 form a special genre (see C. Westermann, *Genesis 37–50* on Gen. 49). They go back in part to the period of the Judges. They arose and were transmitted orally at the meetings of the tribes or their representatives on various occasions. Depending on the occasion, the tribal sayings arose and were passed on individually or in small groups; the collections embracing all twelve tribes belong to a later stage. The tribal sayings serve to characterize a tribe by pronouncing praise or censure over it. (This is particularly clear from the earlier form without comparison in the Song of Deborah, Judg. 5.) This is done either by means of a wordplay or comparison (cf. the table in *Genesis 37–50*, p. 242). These are mainly comparisons with animals, on one occasion with a plant: Gen. 49.9, 14, 15, 16 f., 21, 22, 26; Deut. 33.17, 20, 22. The tribe of Judah is compared to a young lion, 49.9:

> 'Judah is a lion's whelp;
> from the prey, my son, you have gone up.
> He stooped down, he couched as a lion,
> and as a lioness; who dares rouse him up?'

The comparison is developed in three statements: he has snatched a prey, goes up with it, and couches in his den, 'and nobody dares to rouse him up'; cf. Hos. 5.14. There is no description of the lion, but we are told what he does.

The tribe of Judah is not compared with the *appearance* of the lion, but with what he does and achieves. This is true of all comparisons. This is why e.g. the comparison of Dan with a serpent lurking on the path which 'bites the horse's heels, so that his rider falls backward', v. 17, is significantly different from that of Judah with a lion, because it precisely describes the situation and the very limited opportunities of the tribe of Dan. Rather than comparing a characteristic of the tribe of Dan with one of the serpent, a process is narrated. What the serpent does is compared with what the tribe of Dan does. Also when Issachar is compared with a beast of burden, vv. 14–15, a story is told about the ass: '. . . he saw that a resting place was good, and the land was pleasant; so he bowed his shoulder to bear, and became a slave at forced labour'. Note the particular subtlety that the subject remains ambiguous, it is both the ass and the tribe signified by it. This shows that the comparison needs no interpretation. Frequently the distinction between comparison and what is being compared is blurred: the comparison is an allusion which is meant to be comprehensible by itself. When in the case of this comparison – as also in the case of the one of Judah with the lion – the simple comparison ('a lion', 'a serpent', 'a beast of burden') is continued with a relative clause and then a further main clause with two parts, then we have a transition from the comparison to the parable. This confirms that the parable is, or can be, an expansion of the comparison.

If it is the case that in *all* tribal sayings the comparison has the function of praise or censure, this proves that this is one of the earliest and original functions of the comparisons as such. The creature known to all and familiar to all, which always remains what it is, serves to form a judgment about a historical entity which changes in the course of history. This comparison is a very early form of historical judgment, which is expressed in this comparison. The changing nature of historical judgment is shown in such comparisons: Hosea compares God in his action against his people in similar words to a lion, he becomes a devouring

beast of prey for his people, Hos. 5.12–14: 'Therefore I am
. . . like a lion to Ephraim . . . I, even I, will rend and go
away, I will carry off, and none shall rescue.' It is the same
comparison in a different situation. The comparison (= the
image) has remained the same, what is being compared has
changed: in the case of the tribal saying it is an expression of
praise for the courageous fighters of the tribe of Judah, in the
case of Hosea an intensifying expression of the announcement
of judgment, God as judge attacks like a lion. This shows that
such a comparison is tied to the situation in which it arises. It
undergoes a fundamental change when it takes on continuing
and lasting significance. The appearance of animals (particularly a lion) in coats of arms is based on the linguistic
comparison e.g. in the tribal sayings. But change is no longer
possible. The animal comparison has lost its original function.
The comparison functioning as praise has another application
in Gen. 49, namely the praise of the king, 49.11–12: '. . . his
eyes shall be red with wine, and his teeth white with milk'.
This comparing of members of the body, eyes and teeth with
wine and milk, sounds quite different from the comparison
in praise and censure of the tribes. It belongs to a different
context, the praise of beauty, which dominates the Song of
Songs (see below). Conversely praise in the sense of recognition (alongside censure) in the comparisons of the tribes with
animals rests on an objective judgment. This is further proof
of the fact that the comparison receives its function from its
particular context. The comparisons with plants and animals
in Proverbs as well as Song of Songs have functions different
from those in the tribal sayings.

## Comparisons in the Song of Songs

In the Song of Songs comparison has a significance which
determines the whole collection. Gerleman (G. Gerleman,
BK XVIII, ²1981) calls it a 'comparison in pictures', which
is mainly intended 'to illustrate the parts of the human
body'. But are the comparisons in the Song of Songs
intended as 'pictures', as 'illustration'? Do the comparisons
used make the parts of the body any clearer?:

4.1:   'Your eyes are doves . . .'
5.11:   'His head is finest gold; his locks are wavy . . .'
5.14:   'His arms are rounded gold . . .'
1.9:   'I compare you, my love, to a mare of Pharaoh's chariots
         . . .'.

Gerleman feels this intuitively when he goes on to say: 'The wealth of striking imagery and comparisons does not appear primarily to serve the purpose of making a mental image concrete, but rather of increasing the effect on emotions and moods.'

In every case the function of the comparisons has to be explained from their respective contexts. In this case the context is that of the lovesong. Since this is something like an act of homage to the beloved man or woman, the comparisons used serve the purpose of homage. They can be designated as extolling (the beloved is king), as praising or glorifying the beloved. This purpose of paying homage determines all the comparisons. Perhaps a group of these songs could be called 'songs of description'; but they represent no objective description, the latter rather serves the purpose of praise. It is not the body or one of its parts which is compared with an animal or plant, but the beauty of the one with the beauty of the other; that is an entirely different matter. The image: dove, goat, gazelle, hart, horse, grape, apple, bloom, cedar, pillar of alabaster etc., has not been chosen primarily because of its similarity to the object of comparison, but because of its loveliness, beauty, and costliness. These are what they really have in common, what can actually be compared.

This becomes even clearer in the expansions of the comparisons:

4.5:   'Your two breasts are like two fawns,
         twins of a gazelle, that feed among the lilies . . .'
4.1f:   'Your hair is like a flock of goats,
         moving down the slopes of Gilead . . .
Your teeth are like a flock of shorn ewes
that have come up from the washing,
all of which bear twins,
and not one among them is bereaved.'

As in the case of the tribal sayings, these explanations

show that it is not something objective that is being compared. It is beauty which is being compared; but what is expressed in these expansions also belongs to the beauty of the flock; this presupposes the understanding that beauty is primarily an event (cf. C. Westermann, FS W. Zimmerli, 1977, pp. 479–97).

## The Comparative Sayings in Proverbs

In Prov. 10–28 we meet 70 comparative sayings in which a comparison consisting of only two members has become a linguistic unit.
Examples:

> 13.14:   The teaching of the wise – a fountain of life
> 10.15:   A rich man's wealth – his strong city

It is only at a secondary stage of transmission that these sayings were formed into parallelisms. In these comparative sayings what is being compared is invariably a human manner of behaviour, the image (or that with which this manner of behaviour is being compared) is always a phenomenon of extra-human reality as daily seen and experienced.

Among the comparisons a number of groups can be distinguished:

> *The valuable word*: Understanding lips – precious jewellery.
> *The damaging word*: 12.18a: 'There is one whose rash words are like sword thrusts.'
> *The valuable actions, the actions of the wicked*, good and bad in the wrong place: 25.20: 'He who sings to a heavy heart – like vinegar on a wound.'
> Here is also the place of *joking and mockery*: 11.22: 'like a gold ring in a swine's snout.'

That to which human behaviour is being compared is very diverse indeed, but always belongs to day to day reality: the elements, plants and animals, the seasons, the climate, town and home, buildings, rooms, tools and weapons, jewellery, precious articles, crafts, food and luxury items, the human body, and illness.

The functions of the comparisons: the comparisons contain a value judgement. They serve to pass a value judgement on human behaviour, and thus they correspond to what we call ethics. As opposed to an ethic which judges human behaviour in abstract terms here it is the reality in which people live which forms the yardstick for their behaviour. This represents a question to the hearer of the proverb as to whether he accepts the identification involved. If he agrees, he will act accordingly. Such behaviour is motivated by one's own insight, and an exhortation or prohibition from above is not then necessary. The comparison addresses mature adults who have to decide on their own behaviour and are indeed able to do so. This, too, is similar to the parables of Jesus. The reality of daily experience is sufficient to provide criteria for one's own actions. This is based on a correspondence between man as a creature and the rest of creation. This equation is rooted in God's creation. Allied to this is the presupposition that man is created as a social animal. A word is not primarily significant in terms of its content, but in a situation of reciprocal human relationships: 24.26: 'He who gives a right answer kisses the lips', 26.9: 'A proverb in the mouth of fools – a thorn that goes up into the hand of a drunkard.'

One group of sayings consists of observations about people which have become expressed and fixed in a comparison:

27.20:   'Sheol and Abaddon are never satisfied,
             and never satisfied are the eyes of man.'

These remarks about people are an attempt to understand humans arising from astonished observation. The function of these proverbs is insight, the understanding (of man) through a fixing of observations in a comparison. The same happens in a different way in the group of comparative sayings: 'better than . . .'.

## The Significance of Profane Comparisons

(a)   These three completely different collections of texts, the tribal sayings, the Song of Songs, and the comparative sayings, have in common the fact that in each collection the comparison has a necessary special significance. In them the comparison is not a kind of 'epitheton ornans', an added decoration (Aristotle: *ornatus*), rather it is a constitutive element of the speech act in question. What is being said here could not be expressed without the comparison.

(b)   A formal sign of its constitutive significance is that the comparison as such forms a linguistic unit (a 'smallest unit', H. Gunkel). This differentiates these three collections from the comparison in the prophets or the Psalms where the comparison is part of a larger unit. However, a comparison which is part of another larger unit can be expanded in such a way that it again becomes an independent narrative unit: viz. in the parable. We can observe three stages:

> Comparison as speech unit
> Comparison as part of a larger unit
> Comparison as speech unit (parable).

(c)   In none of the three groups is the function of the comparisons illustrative or demonstrative; in the tribal sayings it is praise and censure, in the comparative sayings value judgement, in the lovesongs homage. In every case a process is placed beside another. Even where only an individual phenomenon is compared to a phenomenon in a different realm (a lion to a tribe, a word to a tool), what is being compared is not an existing being but an event. Such a phenomenon is always part of a situation, a sequence of events. A short comparison is never expanded in a description, but always in a happening: the lion is not described, but we are told what he does.

(d)   The image is always a part of reality as seen and experienced every day. It is meant to relate to the subject of comparison; e.g. the value of the living spring is meant to relate to the value of a word at the right time. This equation becomes possible because humans and day to day reality both belong to God's creation. This implies an important positive evaluation of creation.

(e) This comparison addresses the hearer with regard to his common sense, his natural feelings, and his capacity for judgment. He is asked in each individual comparison whether he agrees, whether he sees any point in it. The address is to the adult human being who gains the criteria of his judgment from the daily reality of creation which surrounds him. This is why even humour and jokes, mockery and accuracy of aim have their place in these comparisons.

## Comparisons in the Historical Books

In the narratives and accounts of the historical books comparisons occur only rarely, in all of them together less than in Isa. 1–11, and they are entirely missing in the legal corpora.

### Comparisons in Gen. 1–11 and 12–50

Gen. 1–11, the biblical Primeval History, contains no comparisons apart from metaphors, i.e. comparisons in individual words which are not identified as such, as e.g.:

1.14: 'Let there be lights in the firmament of the heavens . . .'
7.11: '. . . and the windows of the heavens were opened . . .'.

The designation of a well-known and familiar phenomenon is applied to an unfamiliar, but similar phenomenon which has as yet no designation of its own. These metaphors have the function of explanation.

Gen. 12–50, the Patriarchal History. There are a few examples of comparisons with an explanatory function in the Patriarchal stories. The act of comparing is not so far removed here as in the case of the metaphors, but it occurs in the moment when one encounters an unknown or unfamiliar phenomenon; even this is indicated by the comparative particle: 'this is like . . .'. The smoke arising after the destruction of Sodom is explained in 19.28: 'like the smoke of a furnace'.

In addition to these there are comparisons with an intensifying function. These are mostly in a loose relation to another function of the comparison, e.g. the promise of blessing (promise of nourishment) consisting of comparisons which increase size or number: 'like the dust of the earth', etc. 13.16; 15.5; 22.17; 26.4; 32.13; Exod. 32.13. They serve to intensify the blessing. This is also the case in the comparison in Gen. 13.10: Lot looks down on the Jordan valley and it appears to him 'like the garden of the LORD'; this does not mean 'similar to . . .', but 'as beautiful as . . .'. Similarly in the blessing 27.27. The comparison has the function of homage (see above p. 8) when Jacob meets Esau 33.10: 'like seeing the face of God', and the function of characterization in the tribal sayings 16.12: 'a wild ass of a man'. Conversely the sentence 15.1: 'I am your shield' belongs to the context of the motif of trust. For the comparisons in ch. 49 see above p. 6.

## Excursus: Dreams and their Interpretation in the Joseph Story

The dreams in the Joseph story and their interpretation have to be considered here, because both dreams and parables involve interpretation. The author of the Joseph story has made the dream a *Leitmotiv* of his narrative; the three pairs of dreams in Gen. 37; 40; 41 form a structural element of the story. Joseph's interpretation of the dreams appears as a deliberate contrast to that of the Egyptian interpreters. Their interpretation was considered a professional privilege. But while for the Egyptian interpreters the individual features determine the meaning (allegorical interpretation), Joseph's interpretation is based on the dream as a whole, an event which must have its correlate in the life of the dreamer.

The dream motif in the Joseph story teaches us on the one hand that the allegorical interpretation is derived from the interpretation of dreams, and on the other that the author of the Joseph story understands the dreams, in contrast to the allegorical interpretation, along the lines of a parable. When Joseph says: 'Do not interpretations belong to God?', he means: in his dream the dreamer observes a sequence of events which corresponds to a sequence of events in his life. The dreams and the reality of the life of the dreamer belong together in the activity of God the creator. The visions correspond to the dreams insofar that the visionary sees something which has a meaning different from what he actually sees. The allegorical interpretation can belong to the vision as well as to the dream. Thus the allegorical interpretation resurfaces in the latest layers of the OT (Ezek., Zech.) in connection with visions.

## Comparisons in the Books of Exodus and Leviticus

The legal corpora Exod. 21–23; 25–31; 34–40, and Lev. 1–27 contain no comparisons.

In the narrative parts of Exodus the few comparisons mostly have an explanatory function. Exod. 4.6: 'behold, his (Moses) hand was leprous, as white as snow', and v. 7: 'behold, it was restored like the rest of his flesh'. In 16.14 manna is explained as: 'a fine, flake-like thing, fine as hoarfrost on the ground', v. 31: 'it was like coriander seeds, white, and the taste of it was like wafers made with honey' (cf. Numb. 11.7 f.). In the theophany 19.18 'the smoke of it went up like the smoke of a kiln', cf. 24.10: 'and there was under his feet as it were a pavement of sapphire stone, like the very heaven for clearness', and v. 17: 'was like a devouring fire on the top of the mountain'. To these have to be added comparisons in the psalms Exod. 15.1–21 and ch. 32 (Song of Moses) and in psalm language 15.26; 17.15 (on Exod. 13.9, 16 see under Deut.). The 'land flowing with milk and honey', Exod. 3.8 etc., belongs to the promise and description of blessing; but it is questionable whether this can be called a comparison; it is the exaggerating language of the promise of a blessing.

## Comparisons in the Book of Numbers

We meet no comparisons in the laws Numb. 1–9.14; 10.1–10; 15; 18; 19; 25–30 (17 only vv. 1–14); 35–36. In the passages on the wilderness wandering the few comparisons that occur mostly have an explanatory function: 9.15: '. . . and at evening it was . . . like the appearance of a fire until morning'; 11.7 f. on manna cf. Exod. 16.14; 12.10 on leprosy like Exod. 4.6; Numb. 13.34 (EVV v. 33); 'and we seemed to ourselves like grasshoppers' (a contrasting comparison); 22.4: '. . . as the ox licks up the grass of the field' (reinforcing in the address). 12.12 is a comparison which belongs to the lament: 'Let her not be as one dead, . . . when he comes out of his mother's womb . . .'. 33.55 uses the language of the announcement of judgment: 'those . . . shall be as pricks in your eyes and thorns in your sides, . . .'. This is probably deuteronomistic like the common comparison 27.17: 'as sheep which have no shepherd'. On the comparisons in the Balaam pericope 22–24 see on the oracles of the prophets and seers before Amos, pp. 26 f. below.

## Comparisons in Deuteronomy

The deuteronomic law chs 12–26 contains no comparisons, and the introductory and concluding speeches 1–11 and 27–30 respectively only a few. Examples of explanation are: 11.10 which speaks of Egypt: 'like a garden of vegetables'; and 1.44: 'and chased you as bees do', and examples of reinforcement are: 'numerous as the stars of heaven' in 1.10; 10.22; 28.62. Examples of psalm language are 10.21: 'he is your praise'; 1.31: '. . . in the wilderness, where . . . the LORD your God bore you, as a man bears his son', similarly 8.5; examples of parenetic style are: 10.16: 'Circumcize therefore the foreskins of your heart' and 9.3: '. . . a devouring fire is the LORD your God'. While the above comparisons also occur elsewhere, the two following comparisons are typical of Deuteronomy and occur only here, one each in the introductory (6.6–9; 11.18–20) and concluding speeches (30.11–14). Both refer to the law framed by speeches, both want to lay this law on the hearts of its hearers, in a piercing language which goes to the heart:

6.6–9: 'And these words . . . shall be upon your heart;
. . . And you shall bind them as a sign upon your hand,
and they shall be as frontlets between your eyes.
And you shall write them on the doorposts of your
house and on your gates.'

## Similarly 30.11–14:

'For this commandment which I command you this day
is not too hard for you, neither is it far off.
It is not in heaven, that you should say,
"Who will go up for us to heaven, and bring it
to us" . . . Neither is it beyond the sea,
that you should say, "Who will go over the sea for us, and bring it
to us, that we may hear it
and do it?" But the word is very near to you;
it is in your mouth and in your heart,
so that you can do it.'

Neither passage is a comparison in the strict sense, but
both approximate to it. For their understanding it is
important that they belong together as a framework of the
law. Both have a parenetic function: they want to move
the hearers to accept the law with their whole being. Both
have in common with the comparisons the fact that they
emphasize their intent by means of an expansion: what
could be said in one sentence is expanded in story form
(*Fermata*). While 6.6–9 emphasizes that the law should be
firmly connected with one's personal life (heart, body,
house), 30.11–14 stresses that a simple person can live in
accordance with it by means of a constrasting comparison:
not too high, not too far away, but near to heart and
mouth. These two descriptions of the law together form
the most beautiful and fitting expression of what it meant
to ancient Israel.

What this was intended to say could only be expressed
in the form of a comparison (or by something similar to a
comparison). It is important that the one saying speaks
about humans in terms of heart, body, and house, and the
other in terms of nearness in contrast to the two dimensions
of distance. Chs 31–34 mark the conclusion of the Pentateuch. In it we meet comparisons in the 'Song of Moses'
(ch. 32), a psalm (vv. 2, 10, 11, 22, 23, 30, 31, 32 f., 37, 38,

41 f.), and in the 'Blessing of Moses' in the tribal sayings (see above).

## Comparisons in the Books of Joshua and Judges

Comparisons in the Books of Joshua and Judges also have no specific function. Comparisons of various kinds occur only somewhat sporadically. Examples of explanatory comparisons are: the waters of the Jordan stand in one heap, Josh. 3.13–16; 'that laps the water with his tongue, as a dog laps', Judg. 7.5; 'but he snapped the bowstrings, as a string of tow snaps when it touches the fire', Judg. 16.9 (simultaneously an intensifying comparison). All other comparisons are derived from different contexts: Josh. 7.1, 26: the anger of the LORD; 11.4: 'in number like the sand that is upon the seashore'; the following are part of the announcement of judgement: Josh. 23.13 and Judg. 2.3: 'they shall be a snare and a trap for you, a scourge on your sides, and thorns in your eyes' (deuteronomistic = Numb. 33.55). Gideon's naming of the altar 'the LORD is peace' Judg. 6.24 is an example of the praise of God, 14.14 is a riddle. In Judg. 9.8–15 a plant fable serves to veil Jotham's warning against kingship: the trees want to have a king over them, but only the thorn bush is willing. Cf. the plant fable II Kings 14.8–10: Amaziah of Judah provokes Jehoash of Israel, who in turn responds with the mocking plant fable about the thistle and the cedar. It is noteworthy that the Song of Deborah (Judg. 5) contains no comparisons; as opposed to Gen. 49 and Deut. 33, praise and censure of the tribes still appear without comparisons.

## The Comparison in the Book of Ruth

In the Book of Ruth we only meet one comparison, 2.12: '. . . by the LORD, the God of Israel, under whose wings you have come to take refuge!' This comparison belongs to the Confession of Trust and from there has entered everyday language.

## Comparisons in I Samuel

In the 31 chapters of I Sam. we only encounter seven comparisons – apart from the psalm in 2.1–10. 25.37 is an explanatory comparison: 'and his heart died within him, and he became as a stone'. The comparison, 'he loved him as his own soul', occurs twice in 18.1–3; similarly 29.9: 'as blameless in my sight as an angel of God', cf. II Sam. 1.26: 'your love to me was wonderful, passing the love of women'. The reason that such a strong comparison is used is the fact that friendship between men only began to be spoken of from the beginning of the monarchy. The comparisons in the language of the Psalms are similar. I Sam. 1.15 has the style of the Lament in the Psalms: 'I have been pouring out my soul before the LORD'. 25.29 corresponds to the Double Wish at the end of the Individual Lament:

'The life of my lord shall be bound in the bundle of the living in the care of the LORD your God; and the lives of your enemies he shall sling out as from the hollow of a sling!'

The two comparisons in David's words addressed to Saul, 24.15 and 26.20, shall be dealt with in the context of words addressed to kings in II Sam. The comparisons in I Sam. 2.20: 'for the loan which you have made to the LORD', and 28.9: 'Why are you laying a snare for my life . . .? are better described as metaphors.

## Comparisons in II Samuel

Comparisons occur in psalm passages, e.g. the Song of David, II Sam. 22 = Ps. 18, and prophetic sayings: the promise of Nathan ch. 7 (cf. 5.2) and the indictment veiled in a parable 12.1–7.

A third type of comparison appears in a new context which we have not yet encountered. It is based on the origin of the monarchy, but it is not at all obvious that it first occurs in this particular historical context. To this type belongs primarily the speech of a wise man/woman addressed to the king, in which counsel is given or a request made of him: 14.1–24 the wise woman of Tekoa; 17.7–13 the counsel of Hushai.

In 17.1–3 we have the comparison (v. 3):

'and I will bring all the people back to you
as a bride comes home to her husband'.

This comparison is intended to reinforce and support the counsel given by Ahithophel: 'this is as beautiful as when . . .'. A similar reinforcing comparison can be found in the counsel of Hushai 17.12: 'and we shall light upon him as the dew falls on the ground!'

The same is intended by two animal comparisons in 17.8,10: to reinforce the warning not to delay the attack on David. David and his band will resist 'like a bear robbed of her cubs in the field', so that even the most valiant man 'whose heart is like that of a lion' will not be able to prevail. The rhetorical reinforcement achieved by these comparisons is plain for all to see. In the third passage, II Sam. 14.1–24, it is a wise woman who comes to the king as a supplicant in the pay of Joab with a fictional story about the reprieve of a culprit, in order to move the king to pardon Absalom. She pays homage to (or flatters) the king by means of a comparison: 'But my lord has wisdom like the wisdom of the angel of God!', vv. 17,20; cf. Gen. 33.10. She supports her request for a reprieve by describing the loss of the mother in two comparisons, v. 7: '. . . thus they would quench my coal which is left!' She sets the special situation in which a mother is to lose her only son against the background of the Lament of Transitoriness, v. 14: 'We must all die, we are like water spilt on the ground, which cannot be gathered up again . . .'. The art of speech in the counsel of a sage is often as well thought through as in these two comparisons, which are voiced together and mutually support one another.

These speeches of the sages, directed to the king, are particularly important for the history of the comparisons in the OT, for they reveal a high point in the history of the latter. This demonstrates their function very clearly: in the Succession Narrative as well as in the Story of the Rise of David the comparisons as such have virtually no function; i.e. they are not used to illustrate or adorn the narrative. But they have an important function in the address, viz. in achieving an effect on the person addressed (as in a different way also in prophecy and in the Psalms). The counsel of the wise men was the most suitable place for this in the early monarchy.

Closely related to this is another group, Songs at the Royal Court: David's death lament over Saul and Jonathan II Sam. 1.19–27, the Song of David ch. 22 = Ps. 18, David's last words 23.1–6, and David's victory song 5.20.

In this transitional period during the early monarchy one function of the comparison becomes particularly significant: exaltation and humiliation. It is the time in the history of Israel when the upper and lower levels of society drift apart, the time in which a person can rise and fall. This is demonstrated by the narratives and by the speeches, and the comparisons emphasize it.

Concerning exaltation, at this time the praise of the mighty ruler, the praise of the hero becomes important, and the comparisons also serve this purpose. Cf. the praise of the just king II Sam. 23.3f: 'When one rules justly over men . . . he dawns on them like the morning light, like the sun shining forth . . . like rain that makes the grass to sprout from the earth'; the praise of the hero in the death lament II Sam. 1.19: 'Thy glory, O Israel, is slain upon thy high places . . .'; 1.23: 'they were swifter than eagles, they were stronger than lions'; 1.27: 'the weapons of war perished' (cf. 'chariot of Israel and its horsemen!'); 2.18: 'swift of foot as a wild gazelle'. Two of these sentences are animal comparisons in the line of the tribal sayings, but with a striking difference: whereas there the praise voiced in the animal comparison related to a tribe, here it refers to an individual, the king, the hero. The praise of the king is also expressed in the act of homage: II Sam. 14.17,20: 'But my lord has wisdom like the wisdom of the angel of God' (similarly Jacob's address to Esau in Gen. 33.10, which deliberately uses court language; cf. my *Genesis 12–36*, p. 524f.).

This exaltation is contrasted with an act of self-deprecation in front of the king, again in comparisons, I Sam.
24.15 (EVV v. 14): 'After whom has the king of Israel
come out? After whom do you pursue? After a dead dog?
After a flea!'; 26.20: 'the king of Israel has come out . . .
like one who hunts a partridge in the mountains'; II Sam.
9.8: 'What is your servant, that you should look upon a
dead dog such as I?' See on this II Sam. 3.8; II Kings 8.13.
All these comparisons give a clear indication of the intention to influence the person addressed. It is remarkable
how far these comparisons succeed in enlivening the actions
concerned.

## Comparisons in the Books of Kings

In the historical narrative of the two Books of Kings
comparisons recede completely into the background. They
are virtually confined to two areas which both have the
character of address: prophetic oracles or political speeches.
These prophetic oracles will be dealt with among the
comparisons in the oracles before Amos (see below p. 25).
In the main they are addressed to kings. They dominate
the tradition, whereas in contrast to I and II Sam. the
counsel of the wise man to the king completely recedes
into the background. This leads accordingly to a change in
the political and military speeches. In I Kings 12 we encounter yet again two contradictory counsels to the king in a
critical situation. The counsel of the old men in 12.7 is
only briefly reproduced, containing no comparison; this is
however the case with the counsel of the young men in
vv. 10–11 which Rehoboam follows in v. 14:

'My little finger is thicker than my father's loins . . .
My father chastised you with whips,
But I will chastise you with scorpions.'

The narrator means to say by this that the young king is
no longer prepared to listen to sensible counsel; instead of
this he makes an uncouth and foolish boasting speech.
Wise counsel declines while the country is on the road to

catastrophe after the division of the kingdoms. The plant fable with which Jehoash, the king of Israel, rejects Amaziah, the king of Judah, in II Kings 14.8–10 also points solely to his own strength. In his masterful speech the Assyrian Rabshakeh ridicules the mighty kingdom of Egypt in the hearing of the fighters on the walls of Jerusalem, II Kings 18.21:

> 'Behold, you are relying on Egypt, that broken reed of a staff,
> which will pierce the hand of any man who leans on it.'

In II Kings 19.3 a comparison occurs in the context of the lament:

> 'This day is a day of distress, of rebuke, and of disgrace;
> children have come to the birth,
> and there is no strength to bring them forth.'

With regard to the counsel to the king and the political and military speeches one could conclude: this is an independent group of comparisons in the OT alongside the two main groups, the Psalms and the prophetic oracles, which must have had a much greater significance in Israel than the relatively few examples suggest. Because they are firmly rooted in the context of narratives, in contrast to Psalms and prophetic oracles, they have not been collected and separately transmitted like the latter. We are only aware of the few examples which occur in the historical books. The rich display of possibilities in these few examples suggests an abundant development of the profane form of the political and military speeches and songs. They have in common with the Psalms and prophetic oracles that they are addresses, and the comparisons in them receive their function from the situation of such address. The effect of the address on the persons addressed is increased in various ways by the comparisons. In such speeches, particularly in the counsels of a wise adviser to the king, are preserved the beginnings of an art of speech, a kind of rhetoric, which flourished during the early monarchy, as it developed under quite different circumstances in Greece and Rome.

When the simple address develops into more elaborate speech in the early monarchy we have to be mindful of an important difference. The address to a king or an army chief is now something different from what it used to be; it has now become an address in front of an audience, the royal court or an assembly of high-ranking persons, viz. officers. The audience has a significance in its own right for these speeches: not only the persons addressed but also the audience passes judgment on them, the address becomes a speech which is adjudged to be good or bad. Thus the address becomes the speech, and an art of speech develops, the speech becomes a work of art. We encounter this development in Israel in the first beginnings of the early monarchy. This difference is important for understanding the comparisons. In addition to their functional role they also gain an aesthetic one, due to the intended effect not only on the persons addressed, but also on the audience. However, in the examples which have been preserved from the early monarchy, the whole emphasis is still on the functional role. But because of this role we have to realize that the understanding which has grown out of Aristotle's Rhetoric (the metaphor) must needs be different from one based on the Psalms, prophetic oracles, and addresses to the kings in the OT.

In conclusion: it has become apparent that we have to distinguish in the historical books between comparisons which form an integral part of narratives or reports, and such comparisons as belong to an independent unit which has been inserted into the text. The latter are far more numerous; the number of comparisons in reports and narratives is conversely very small, they have no specific function in them.

There are in the main three groups of added units in which the majority of the comparisons occur: Psalms (psalm motifs), prophetic oracles and political and military speeches and songs, which are concentrated in I Sam. to II Kings. Comparisons which form part of the report or narrative have in the main two functions: explanatory comparisons: Gen. 19.28; Exod. 16.14,31; 4.6; Numb.

11.7f; Exod. 19.18; 24.10,17; Numb. 9.15; 12.10; Deut. 11.10; Josh. 3.13,16; Judg. 7.5; I Sam. 25.37. Metaphors too, are often explanatory, e.g. Gen. 1.4; 7.11.

Comparisons which strengthen or emphasize: Gen. 13.10; 22.17; Numb. 13.34 (EVV v. 33); 22.4; Deut. 1.44; Judg. 16.9. A large number are of this strengthening type ('as sand on the seashore') Gen. 13.16; 15.5; 22.17; 26.4; 32.13 (EVV v. 12); Exod. 32.13; Deut. 1.10; 28.62; Josh. 11.4; I Kings 4.20.

Comparisons in independent units: comparisons in psalms and psalm motifs: Gen. 15.1; 49.17; Exod. 15.1–21; 15.26; 17.15; Numb. 12.12; Deut. 10.21; 1.31; 8.5 (?); 32; Judg. 6.24; Ruth 2.12; I Sam. 2.1–10; 1.15; 25.29; II Sam. 22; II Kings 19.3, cf. the victory song II Sam. 5.20 (these passages will be dealt with under the Psalms).

Comparisons in prophetic oracles (and in the oracle of a seer): Numb. 22–24; 27.17 (?); 33.55; Deut. 9.3; Josh. 7.1,26; 23.13; Judg. 2.3; II Sam. 7; 12.1–7 cf. 5.2 and in many prophetic oracles in I and II Kings (they will be dealt with under the prophetic oracles before Amos).

While comparisons in psalms (and psalm motifs) and prophetic oracles occur in all the historical books, the following kinds of units containing comparisons belong either to the Pentateuch or to the historical books from I Sam. to II Kings, with a few exceptions. The Pentateuch contains two: the Tribal Sayings in Gen. 49 and Deut. 33, and the praise of the law in Deut. 6.6–9; 30.11–14. Whereas the function of the comparisons in the Tribal Sayings is praise and censure of the tribes, in a political context, the function of the comparisons in Deut. 6 and 30 is parenesis, in a theological context. These two passages, although relatively independent units, form an integral part of the deuteronomic parenesis. In I Sam. to II Kings it is above all in the political and military speeches that comparisons occur; a warning against the monarchy in the form of a plant fable Judg. 9.8–14 (prior to the origin of the monarchy). In the counsel of a wise man to a king: II Sam. 14.1–24; 17.1–3; 17.7–13; 14.7, 14, 17, 20 (cf. Gen. 33.10); I Kings 12.10–11, 14. In songs at the royal court: death lament II Sam. 1.19–27; 5.20 David's victory song. The Song of David II Sam. 22 = Ps. 18; 23.1–6 David's last words (cf. Ps. 1). Elevation and self-deprecation in comparisons, homage to the king: II Sam. 14.17, 20 (cf. Gen. 33.10); praise of the king, of the hero: II Sam. 1.19, 23; 1.27; 2.18. Self-deprecation: I Sam. 24.15; 26.20; II Sam. 9.8; cf. in insults II Sam. 3.8; 16.7. In the speech of an army chief: I Kings 18.21; II Kings 14.8–10 in the form of a plant fable.

# Comparisons in Prophecy

## Comparisons in the Prophetic Oracles before Amos

The prophetic oracles before Amos transmitted in the historical books rarely contain comparisons. The relevant passages are: I Sam. (1–3); 7; 8; 10.17–21; 12; 13.7–15; 15; II Sam. 7; 12; 24; I Kings 13.1–14.28; 16.1–4; 17–20; 22; II Kings 1–9; 13.14–21; 19–21. Whenever words of Samuel are mentioned in I Sam. they are parts of the narrative and contain no comparisons. Neither the promise of Nathan in II Sam. 7.8–16 nor the oracle of Gad to David 24.11–15 contain any comparisons, but Nathan's announcement of judgment to David II Sam. 12.1–13 has the form of a parable. In I Kings the oracles of the men of God 12.21–24 and 13 have no comparisons. Ahija's oracle of judgment against Jeroboam contains as part of the announcement of judgment an intensifying comparison, which corresponds to those in the writing prophets: I Kings 14.10: '. . . as a man burns up dung until it is all gone'. There are no comparisons in the oracles of Elijah and Elisha in I Kings 17–19; 20.35–43 and 21.17–19, and the oracle of Micaiah ben Yimlah in 22 is a vision. The words of Elijah and Elisha in II Kings 1–9; 13.14–21 contain no comparisons. The Isaiah oracles II Kings 19–21 will be dealt with under that prophet.

As a result we see that the prophetic oracles reported

before Amos are predominantly without comparisons.
When Nathan dresses up his indictment of David as the
parable of the poor man's ewe lamb in II Sam. 12.1–7 and
Micaiah ben Yimlah his announcement of defeat as a
vision in I Kings 22, this arises in both cases out of the
situation, as in Jotham's fable in Judg. 9. This is particularly
apparent in such oracles of judgment as have the same
structure as those in the prophetic books, viz. I Kings
21.17–19 and II Kings 1.2–4. The reason for this is the
shorter gap between announcement and fulfilment and the
fact that the indictment refers to a definite and obvious
issue. It is plain in this case that the comparisons in the OT
are determined by their respective functions.

The parable of Nathan in II Sam. 12.1–13 is an independent narrative like the parables in the synoptic Gospels in
that it provokes a response from the person addressed in
the parable. V.1a introduces the narrative 1b–4; David
pronounces judgment, v. 5, and Nathan tells him that he
(David) is the target, v. 7a. Only then does there follow in
vv. 7b–12 the indictment and announcement in the style of
a prophetic oracle of judgment. David's reaction is a
confession of guilt, v. 13a. As regards content, the narrative
vv. 1b–4 is very close to the parables. I Kings 20.39–43
also serves the purpose of a prophetic indictment. The
fictional case vv. 39–40 is meant to convince the king of
his guilt. The king pronounces judgment v. 40b, and the
prophet reveals his identity. Here, too, there follows indictment and announcement of judgment v. 42, and its effect
on the king v. 43. In both cases the parable has a veiling
function because of the difference in power between king
and prophet. There are some comparisons in Balaam's
oracles Numb. 22–24. The first saying is Numb. 23.7–10.
23.10 reads:

> 'Who can count the dust of Jacob, or number the fourth part of
> Israel?
> Let me die the death of the righteous,
> and let my end be like his!'

The preceding passage makes it clear that v. 10 is meant as

a word of blessing: Yahweh turns the intended curse into blessing. In v. 10a the 'dust' which is parallel to the 'fourth part of Israel' is intended as an abbreviated comparison. V. 10a is a blessing which corresponds to the promise of multiplication. V. 10b contains a comparison, too. The seer by wishing for himself the death of a (righteous) Israelite wishes for a 'blessed end', a death in peace, 'old and full of years'. Thus a blessing is pronounced indirectly over Israel.

The second saying is Numb. 23.18b–24. 23.22 reads:

'God brings them out of Egypt;
they have as it were the horns of the wild ox.'

V. 24:

'Behold, a people! As a lioness it rises up
and as a lion it lifts itself;
it does not lie down till it devours the prey,
and drinks the blood of the slain' (= 24.8b, 9).

In v. 21 God's presence indicates that he grants to his people victory over their enemies (multiplication and victory can also be found in a blessing in Gen. 24.60). This is emphasized by two comparisons: the power given to them is like the horns of a wild ox; and Israel when attacking her enemies is compared to a lion devouring its prey. This recalls the Judah saying in Gen. 49; it can be assumed that both belong to a common tradition (the comparison recurs in 24.8f).

The third saying is Numb. 24.3b–9: in the middle of this saying vv. 5–7 describe the blessed land of Israel:

'How fair are your tents, O Jacob, your encampments, O Israel!
Like valleys that stretch afar, like gardens beside a river,
like aloes that the LORD has planted, like cedar trees beside the
    waters.
Water shall flow from his buckets,
and his seed shall be in many waters'.

This is a typical description of blessing, particularly poetic and beautiful, in which there is only an echo of the comparison. This shows that the description of beauty arises in the discourse about blessing, especially in the promise of blessing. Because by describing the beautiful land of Israel the outcome of that blessing is promised to Israel, the description of blessing can have the function of the promise of blessing.

The fourth saying is Numb. 24.15–19. Numb. 24.17 reads:

> 'A star shall come forth out of Jacob,
> and a sceptre shall rise out of Israel . . .'

The monarchy is promised in the comparison with star and sceptre, but at the same time in a vision, v. 17a:

> 'I see him, but not now;
> I behold him, but not nigh'.

The sequence of sayings vv. 20–24 concerns Israel's neighbours. Numb. 24.21 reads:

> 'Enduring is your dwelling place,
> and your nest is set in the rock . . .'.

This comparison, which frequently occurs, approximates to metaphorical usage. An explanatory comparison lies behind it.

The saying of a seer is distinguished from a prophetic oracle by its present tense: the seer sees what will happen some day. This is true of the earliest sayings of seers right up to Apocalyptic. Here one could justifiably speak of an 'image'; in 24.5–7 such an image is described. However, in the early sayings of the seers the image needs no interpretation because the point of the image is clear from the context. It is only as a result of a later development that a distinction is made between image and interpretation ('what do you see?').

## Comparisons in the Prophets Amos, Hosea, Micah

*Comparisons in Amos.* The appropriate passages are: Amos 1.2; 1.4 (cf. 1.7, 10, 12, 14; 2.2, 5); 2.9; 2.13; 3.3–8; 3.12; 4.1; 4.11; 5.1–3, 16–17; 5.6, 7, 11; 5.18–20, 24; 6.12; 7.4; 8.1; 8.11 (?); 9.1. The comparisons belong predominantly to the two parts of the prophetic oracle of judgment: to the announcement and to the indictment which is the basis of the former (cf. C. Westermann, *Basic Forms of Prophetic Speech*, 1967). All the comparisons are assigned directly or indirectly to prophetic speech forms.

Comparisons belong to the announcement: Amos 1.2; 1.4 (cf. vv. 7, 10, 12, 14; 2.2, 5); judgment in the image of fire can also be found in 4.11; 5.6; 7.4; and as earthquake: 'as a cart . . . presses down', 2.13; as death lament 5.1–3, 16–17; as darkness 5.18 and as the end (= the basket of summer fruit) 8.1. In the case of the announcement we also have to distinguish the two parts in the comparisons: intervention of God – result of that intervention. The former, one should note, is predominantly compared with natural catastrophes, particularly fire, earthquake, drought, darkness (cf. the visions). More emphasis lies on the result of the intervention of God in the comparisons, what the consequences are for the persons addressed: that nobody can escape from it, that it signifies the end, that the destruction is total and only a tiny remnant survives (3.12 the death lament). This emphasis shows the function of these comparisons, to make the announcement more pressing. Comparisons belonging to the indictment: Amos 4.1; 5.7, 11, 12 (cf. v. 24; 6.12). These comparisons concentrate entirely on the social accusation; this shows the special significance which the latter has for Amos. By calling the rich women of Samaria 'cows of Bashan' Amos accentuates the self-satisfied sense of security which is only concerned with one's own wellbeing. In 5.7 and 6.12 the comparisons intensify the indictment (justice turned to wormwood/poison) that law and justice, on which the common welfare depends (5.24), have been perverted. The accusation of oppressing the poor is described in 5.11 as 'trampling' upon them.

Comparing the Amorites to tall and strong trees in 2.9 assists the understanding of God's acts of salvation in the historical review; it comes close to the praise of God's mighty acts (many scholars regard 2.9–11 as an addition).

5.24: 'But let justice roll down like waters,
and righteousness like an everflowing stream.'

This comparison actually belongs to the description of blessing. Here it is used to indict the perversion of law into its opposite, in 5.7 and 6.12 as a positive reverse image: where righteousness prevails it is the cause of blessing. The comparison is thus indirectly assigned to the indictment. 3.3–8 refers to the call of the prophet. Amos compares the necessity with which he must needs carry out God's commission with a series of processes from day to day reality which demonstrate the necessary connection between cause and effect. The comparisons are intended to reinforce this necessity. The comparison with the roaring lion would suffice for this, but Amos wants to go on to say: such is the case everywhere in life. 3.3–8 has in common with the parables the fact that the sequence of comparisons forms an independent unit. The question form shows that the comparison takes place in a dialogue; it presupposes the denial of the authorization of the word of Amos, a denial of Amos's right to announce judgment, to which Amos responds just as in the parables Isa. 5.1–7 and 28.23–29.

Thus we have a clear picture as regards the comparisons in Amos. All the comparisons which we meet are assigned to prophetic speech forms (in one case indirectly 5.24), namely to the announcement of judgment as well as the indictment in its two respective parts (cf. 3.3–8 the prophet's call). Hence we can be sure that the function of the comparisons in each case is determined by their connection with the various elements of prophetic speech.

One has to distinguish from the comparisons the descriptions of what was seen in the *visions* 7.1–3, 4–6, 7–9; 8.1–3; 9.1–4. What is seen in a vision is different from what is being compared in a comparison. What is being seen (e.g. the basket of summer fruit) is meant to signify something other than what the eye of the visionary (the one who has the vision) sees. Therefore an interpretation has been added to the image, which is never necessary in the case of the comparisons. In this the vision is similar to the dream ('night vision'), of which the same is true, as is shown by the dreams in the Joseph Story. The fact that in many cases in the NT the interpretation is part of the parable means that two originally independent processes, which therefore have originally nothing to do with one another, have been intermingled. On the one hand we have dream and vision, which need an interpretation insofar as they mean something other than what was seen by the dreamer or visionary, on the other we have the parable, insofar as it represents an extended comparison (R. Bultmann *et al.*), which speaks for itself and needs no interpretation.

Visions and dreams have to be investigated separately in the OT, because they form a line of tradition in their own right, independent of comparisons and parables. It was only at a secondary stage that both were combined with each other.

*Comparisons in Hosea.* Looking at all the comparisons in Hosea together, we note that in spite of their extraordinary abundance they can be attributed to only a few contexts and functions. The vast majority of comparisons occur in the context of the announcement of judgment (18 examples) and of the indictment (20), i.e. in the speech form characteristic of the message of this particular prophet.

Comparisons in the context of the oracle of salvation very rarely occur (4), three of which (1.10; 11.10f; 14.5–7, 8) are probably later additions, and only one in a Confession of Trust (psalm language) in 6.1, 3.

By contrast, many comparisons occur in a motif typical of Hosea: the review of the relevant pre-history which leads to an indictment of, and announcement of judgment in, the present (8–10 examples). Thus these passages, too, are connected with indictment and announcement of judgment.

On the whole this yields a uniform and convincing picture: the comparisons further Hosea's commission; they nearly all belong to the direct or indirect context of the announcement of judgment and of the indictment on which it is based.

(a) The comparison in the context of the announcement of judgment: the comparison marks the phrases of the announcement of judgment which are characteristic of Hosea, as in

> 5.12: 'I am like a moth . . . and like dry rot . . .'.
> 5.14: 'For I will be like a lion to Ephraim,
> and like a young lion to the house of Judah.
> I, even I, will rend and go away,
> I will carry off, and none shall rescue'.

That God has to intervene in judgment against his own people is hardly anywhere else so passionately expressed (one might compare the Judah saying Gen. 49.9 where Judah is likened to a young lion). Hosea 13.7f. is similar:

> '. . . like a lion,
> like a leopard I will lurk beside the way.
> I will fall upon them like a bear
> robbed of her cubs,
> I will tear open their breast',

cf. 5.10b; 'upon them I will pour out my wrath like water'. Further, of the two parts of the oracle of judgment, Hosea emphasizes the intervention of God more frequently and more strongly by means of comparisons: 1.5; 2.3; 2.6b (4.18); 5.10; 5.12–14; 7.12; (8.1); 13.7–8; 13.14–15; the following describe the result of this intervention: 4.3; 4.5; 5.5; 9.11, 16a; 13.3. The intensity of the personal, one might say almost 'human', element in God's decision to destroy is shown in 13.14:

> 'Shall I ransom them from the power of Sheol?
> Shall I redeem them from Death?
> O Death, where are your plagues?
> O Sheol, where is your destruction?'

The first of these sentences clearly reflects the people's cry to be saved in a Communal Lament, which is opposed by God's decision to destroy. The function of the comparisons in all these places is most clearly recognizable here: it is plainly and evidently the intensification of the announcement which the prophet is forced to make, because God

has to destroy his own people. It is this terrible element –
necessary in its awfulness – which the comparisons emphasize and intensify. That these comparisons are 'images'
is absolutely out of the question. To claim that they
illuminate or illustrate something would be to misinterpret
their function entirely. Perhaps the most striking passages
which show this are: 5.12–14; 13.7–8; 13.14–15; 5.10b. In
all of them what is being compared is not one object with
another, but one process with another. In 5.14 it is represented by means of a sequence of verbs, approximating to
a parable. When God's judgment of his people is compared with the plundering of a lion, the terrible reality of
this divine judgment then becomes direct and concrete for
the hearers, because it relates to a terrible reality in their
own experience. Precisely what is inconceivable to Hosea's
audience, that God should turn with destructive power
against his own people, is given by the comparisons a
degree of reality which they must confront.

(b) The comparison in the context of the indictment: the
predominant indictment in Hosea is the charge of unfaithfulness. In chs 1–3 this accusation is given a parabolic
treatment in a comparison with marital infidelity. Israel
has deserted Yahweh like a woman deserting her husband
and pursuing other men:

> 'for the land commits great harlotry
> by forsaking the LORD' (1.2),

cf. 4.10f.; 2.6; 3.1. Consequently the prevailing accusation
is one of immorality: 4.12, 15, 18; 5.3, 4; 6.10; 7.4; 9.1;
12.7. The meaning and purpose of this comparison is clear:
Hosea understands the relationship between Israel and her
God as above all personal, as a relation between two
persons (in which Israel is considered a 'corporate per-
sonality'). He considers marriage particularly appropriate
to represent this relationship. This comparison is aimed at
a particular aspect of marriage: the history of Yahweh and
Israel is like the history of a marriage. Marriage originates
through choice, and this choice is conditional on a mutual
decision (the marriage covenant). This is the reason why

marriage can be broken. But the breach of a marriage is not necessarily the last word, the possibility of healing the breach remains open. The comparison serves to intensify and sharpen the accusation. In this case the comparison has taken on a role of its own and has been expanded into a symbolic action: in the comparison with marriage, as in the NT parables, one sequence of processes has been juxtaposed with another. The indictment of 'immorality' is intensified by the fact that the marriage parable shows up Israel's apostasy as an act in the context of a story. This is confirmed by a group of texts in Hosea in which her present apostasy from Yahweh is seen in connection with or in contrast to her previous history: 4.16; 6.5; 7.9; 8.8 (?); 9.10; 10.1; 10.11–13; 11.1–4; 13.5–8; 13.12, 13 (?), 14–15 (?). These texts, too, employ comparisons all the way through, but they are different ones. 13.5–8 may serve as an example: God has 'chosen Israel in the wilderness' as a grazing animal and given it pasture in the desert. When they had plenty of pasture, 'their heart was lifted up' and they forgot God. Then there follows in vv. 7–8 the announcement of judgment comparing God with wild animals which fall upon the grazing beast. This passage hints at the course of history from the exodus from Egypt until the announced destruction; thus history serves as proof for the present indictment. It is the same accusation as in the parable of Israel's unfaithfulness.

In addition Hosea uses a great variety of comparisons in connection with the indictment: stubborn heifer, 4.16; Israel is defiled, 5.3 (cf. 5.5); like a dove without sense, calling to Egypt, going to Assyria, 7.11 (5.13; 12.2 EVV v. 1); like treacherous bow, 7.16; judgment like poisonous weeds, 10.4; ploughed iniquity and reaped injustice, 10.13; cf. 8.7. The same goes for the indictment of the priests, 5.1; 6.9, the princes, 5.10, and the prophets ('a fowler's snare'), 9.8.

The range of comparisons in Hosea: only when one looks at all the comparisons in the 14 chapters of the Book of Hosea together does one realize how deeply rooted the prophetic word is in the day to day life shared by the prophet and his hearers. We hear about husband and wife (courtship, engagement, and wedding), the harlot and her fee, the people and the land of Israel, the fertile soil, desert, steppe, and wilderness, about the sea and the land with its routes and paths, about the produce of the land, of its vegetation and of plants of all kinds, about the elements (fire, water, air, and earth), and about the weather in all its varied moods. We hear about all kinds of animals: lions, snakes and eagles, doves, moths and worms. Manifold human actions are mentioned, thoughts and feelings, work and play, feasts and loneliness, the tools and products of work. We hear about enmity and crime, sickness and health, wounds and their healing, war and peace, youth and old age, oven and unturned cake, and early figs on the young fig tree. And this is by no means all!

By continually using images from daily life, these numerous comparisons give a high degree of reality to what happens here between God and man. What God says in the words of the prophet and what is announced in these oracles is as real as the comparisons used.

*Comparisons in Micah.* Comparisons in the 8th century prophet Micah are essentially confined to chs 1–3 (although even here there are additions), since 'chs 4–7 scarcely contain a passage which is linguistically . . . related to Micah's oracles' (H. W. Wolff, *Micha*, BK XIV/4, p. XXII).

(a) Comparisons in the announcement of judgment. Judgment is compared with a yoke laid on the people, 2.3:

> 'from which you cannot remove your necks;
> and you shall not walk haughtily'.

One could also mention 1.14: 'Therefore you shall give parting gifts to Moresheth-gath'. This phrase 'points to the carrying-off into exile' (Wolff, *ad loc.*), but is more of an allusion than a comparison. Hence there is really only one comparison in Micah's announcement of judgment. But indirectly related to it are comparisons which describe the lament about the (coming) judgment, 1.8: 'lamentation like the jackals, and mourning like the ostriches'; and the comparison with animal noises is intended to intensify the lament. The reason for the lament is that 'her wound is incurable'; this is, however, more of a metaphor than a comparison. The description of the lament continues in 1.16: 'Make yourselves bald and cut off your hair, . . . make yourselves as bald as the eagle, for . . .'.

(b) Comparisons in the indictment. In Micah 3.1–12 the accusation against the heads and leaders is twice combined with comparisons; in vv. 2b–3 it is a very blunt social indictment:

> 'who eat the flesh of my people,
> and flay their skin from off them,
> and break their bones in pieces,
> and chop them up like meat in a kettle,
> like flesh in a cauldron.'

(V. 2b, 'who tear the skin from off my people, and their flesh from off their bones', is probably an addition.)

These words reflect the bitterness of someone who has himself experienced such treatment of the lowly by the mighty. Wolff observes: 'No other prophet spoke in such an uncouth manner . . ., such a chain of rough action, in which humans are treated like cattle for slaughter, remains the unique preserve of the peasant prophet from Moresheth.' With regard to the function of the comparisons in the prophets, this Micah oracle strikingly demonstrates the inadequacy of the term 'image' for them. What we have here is a passionate intensification of the indictment, as, in a similar context, 3.10: 'who build Zion with blood and Jerusalem with wrong'.

'Micah alludes to the brisk building activity in Jerusalem which under Hezekiah had reached unusual proportions' (Wolff). The indictment achieves its effect by contracting several processes into one sentence: the 'material' with which Zion is being built is the unjust and brutal treatment of the workers, who are apparently carrying out the building as corvée labour. Strictly speaking, this contraction is not a comparison, but it implies one: the equation

of the building material with the unjust and brutal treatment of the workers.

7.1 is also similar to a comparison in the context of
indictment. According to Wolff, this passage (7.1–7) belongs to the early post-exilic period; Jer. 57.1–2; 55.4–8
represent similar complaints about general wickedness.
Micah 7.1:

> 'Woe is me! For I have become as when the summer fruit has been
>     gathered,
> as when the vintage has been gleaned;
> there is no cluster to eat,
> no first-ripe fig which my soul desires!'

Vv. 2 and 4 interpret this comparison:

> 'The godly man has perished from the earth . . .
> each hunts his brother with a net.
> The best of them is like a brier,
> the most upright of them like a thorn hedge.'

This oracle does not really sound like a prophetic indictment, but more like a lament about the general wickedness of the time in which the temple and the political
order no longer exist. One accusation includes the statement:

> 'For from the hire of a harlot she gathered them,
> and to the hire of a harlot they shall return' (1.7).

It is particularly characteristic of Hosea's indictment to
compare the apostasy from Yahweh to other gods with
harlotry. Here it is probably an addition. In Micah there
are two remaining comparisons, 3.2b–3 and 3.10, both
part of the social accusation, both typical of Micah.
(c) Comparisons in oracles of salvation. In the Book of
Micah we meet a number of comparisons in oracles of
salvation, all of which derive from a later time and most
of which have parallels in other prophetic books, e.g. the
promise of return, and Yahweh as shepherd, 2.12: 'I will
surely gather . . . I will set them together like sheep in a
fold, like a flock in pasture . . .'; 4.6: 'I will assemble the
lame and gather those who have been driven away . . .';
7.14: 'Shepherd thy people with thy staff, the flock of thy

inheritance, who dwell alone in a forest in the midst of a garden land; let them feed in Bashan and Gilead as in the days of old' (here as a request). In the messianic promise, 5.1, 3, 5b, it is the coming prince of peace who will shepherd Israel, 5.3 (EVV v. 4): 'He shall stand and feed his flock in the strength of the LORD', v. 4a (EVV v. 5a): 'and this shall be peace'. An addition vv. 4b–5b (EVV 5b– 6a) announces in sharp contrast to this 'seven shepherds and eight princes of men; they shall rule the land of Assyria with the sword . . .'. The promise 2.12 is followed in v. 13 by another which illustrates the same thing by means of a different comparison. V. 13 promises a sortie from a fortified city whose leader is Yahweh the king of Israel. The language of this promise presupposes Deutero-Isaiah, it is a post-exilic addition. In it, too, liberation is promised.

A promise of the return of the monarchy, also from the post-exilic period, refers to Jerusalem as 'tower of the flock', 4.8: 'And you, O tower of the flock, hill of the daughter of Zion . . .'. This is probably not a comparison, but each refers to Jerusalem according to a particular characteristic.

4.9–10 is a promise of liberation from Babylon in which rescue follows the previous distress, vv. 9–10a. Here the cry of distress during the siege of Jerusalem is compared with the crying of a woman in travail, 4.9, 10:

> '. . . that pangs have seized you like a woman in travail?
> Writhe and groan, O daughter of Zion, like a woman in travail
> . . .'.

4.11–13 announces that Israel will take revenge on her enemies; it is a post-exilic text. In v. 12 the charge is hurled at the opponents:

> 'they do not understand his plan,
> that he has gathered them as sheaves to the threshing floor.'

In connection with the cue 'threshing floor' there follows in v. 13 the invitation:

for I will make your horn iron and your hoofs bronze;
you shall beat in pieces many peoples . . .'.

Vv. 12 and 13 indicate that in this case the comparisons no longer have an organic function derived from the context, but rather are employed in a mechanical way as comparisons familiar from tradition. The result is that the crass contrast of the comparison with the harvest in vv. 12 and 13 is no longer felt, nor the fact that in v. 13 two comparisons clash.

Another late promise for the 'remnant of Jacob' (Micah 5.6–7; EVV 7–8) holds out new blessing and new strength (or power) for Israel in comparisons in the form of the description of blessing:

'Then the remnant of Jacob shall be in the midst of many peoples
like dew from the LORD, like showers upon the grass . . .
like a lion among the beasts of the forest,
like a young lion among the flocks of sheep,
which, when it goes through, treads down and tears in pieces,
and there is none to deliver.'

It is the old promise of blessing consisting of fertility and strength which lives on here in the traditional comparisons, the secondary usage being betrayed by the 'like dew . . . like rain', which are really gifts of blessing transformed here into comparisons on account of v. 8.

7.7–19, a modified and expanded psalm, concludes the Book of Micah. The comparisons in it belong to the context of Psalm motifs: to the Confession of Trust, 7.8b: 'When I sit in darkness, the LORD will be a light to me . . .'; to the Certainty of Hearing, v. 19: 'He will again have compassion upon us, he will tread our iniquities under foot. Thou wilt cast all our sins into the depths of the sea.' To the Double Wish, 7.10, 14: '. . . now she will be trodden down like the mire of the streets', v. 14: 'Shepherd thy people with thy staff, the flock of thy inheritance . . .'.

## Comparisons in Isaiah

As a preliminary consideration, it should be noted that ox

and ass round the crib at the birth of Jesus have penetrated so deeply into the Christian tradition that they are a familiar part of representations of the crib throughout the world. By becoming a picture in this way they have lost their original significance. In the first oracles of the Book of Isaiah the ox and the ass are not pictorial. They are part of a comparison and derive their meaning solely from this comparison. Isa. 1.2–3 is a divine lament over the disobedience of his people. The lament compares Israel's apostasy with children running away from their parental home (the same in 1.4), contrasting it with the way domestic animals remain in their stable, where they have cover and food. It is a comparison of two processes: Yahweh's experience with Israel is placed side by side with a process taken from the experience of the audience – this is what happens, however unnatural it is! It is only in the context of these parallel processes that what is being said here about the ox and the ass can become clear; this is no longer possible when ox and ass have become fixed in and as a picture.

The function of the comparison in this lament is clear: it is meant to highlight the unbelievable apostasy of Israel. This comparison does not illustrate the lament but rather intensifies it, and closely resembles the parables of Jesus insofar that a process between God and man takes on a striking degree of reality by means of a process between man and man or man and beast respectively. What God has done towards Israel is as real as what a father does towards his child, a farmer towards his animals.

The vast majority of comparisons in Isa. 1–39 (excluding 24–27) occur in the context of the announcement of judgment and the reason for it in the indictment. Because of the number of oracles against the nations in Isaiah it is useful to distinguish between comparisons in them and those in the Israel oracles.

Comparisons in the indictment. The indictment of apostasy corresponds to the lament in Isa. 1.2–3. Israel has become a harlot, 1.21. But in Isaiah, as far as these comparisons indicate, this indictment is not as dominant as in Hosea. In a number of indictments the comparisons simply indicate that Israel has sinned, without any more detailed description, 1.15 f.:

'your hands are full of blood';

their sin is as red as scarlet and crimson, 1.18–20; there are a number of accusations that precious things have been spoilt: silver has become dross, wine mixed with water, 1.22. Instead of proper grapes Israel has only yielded wild grapes, 5.2; Israel has become like the people of Sodom, 3.9.

The comparisons in the context of the social indictment show the passion with which Isaiah has uttered them, 3.14 f.: 'It is you who have devoured the vineyard . . . What do you mean by crushing my people, by grinding the face of the poor?'; in 10.1–2: they decree iniquitous decrees, they plunder the orphans, the widows become their spoil. The parable of the vineyard, 5.1–7, culminates in an indictment of the corruption of the legal system, 5.7; 'bloodshed and lawbreaking'.

There are examples of an indictment of those who despise the word of God spoken by the prophet, such as 5.18 f.: 'Woe to those . . . who draw sin as with cart ropes, who say: "Let him make haste, let him speed his work that we may see it!"' The rejection of God's word in the Syro-Ephraimite war (cf. H. Wildberger's interpretation in his commentary, BK X, *ad loc.*) is expressed by the prophet in the comparison 8.6f.: 'Because this people have refused the waters of Shiloah that flow gently . . .'. This comparison has been chosen to correspond with the one in the announcement: 'therefore, behold, the LORD is bringing up against them the waters of the River, mighty and many'. In Isaiah the comparison frequently embraces both indictment and announcement of judgment. In all these cases the comparison has the function of stressing that divine judgment inevitably follows hard on Israel's guilt.

The indictment of the hybris of the people, of their arrogance, is especially characteristic of the prophecy of

Isaiah. This is already shown by ch. 2, although it contains no comparisons. However, they do occur in chs 28 and 29. The oracle against Ephraim, 28.1–4, is marked by it:

'Woe to the proud crown of the drunkards of Ephraim,
and to the fading flower of its glorious beauty,
which is on the head of the rich valley of those overcome with
    wine!'

Here, too, the announcement in v. 3 corresponds verbatim to the indictment; the comparison embraces both. The indictment of hybris is raised against the rulers of Judah in 28.14–22: 'We have made a covenant with death, and with Sheol we have an agreement' (Meaning: we have concluded political treaties which will protect us from death and Sheol). It is hybris when Israel revolts against her creator (29.15 f.):

'Shall the potter be regarded as the clay; . . .
or the thing formed say of him who formed it,
"He has no understanding"?'

Hence it is no coincidence that in the accusations against the nations that of hybris is emphasized by comparisons as well. Corresponding to the comparison 29.15 f. (clay – potter), in the indictment of Asshur 10.15 the hybris of a superpower is depicted:

'Shall the axe vaunt itself over him who hews it,
or the saw . . . against him who wields it?
As if a rod should wield him who lifts it.'

In the preceding v. 14 the spoiling of the nations is compared with the robbing of birds' nests; the comparison in v.14b is developed in the direction of a parable:

'. . . and there was none that moved a wing,
or opened the mouth, or chirped.'

Asshur is also accused of hybris in 14.13:

'I will ascend to heaven,
above the stars of God I will set my throne on high.'

Here, too, the comparison is hyperbolical.

(a) The function of comparisons in the indictments. All comparisons serve to intensify the accusation. They are all meant to help the addressees to understand the seriousness of their crime. The comparisons force them to understand the reality of their deeds, to comprehend what they have done ('those . . . who draw sin as with cart ropes'). As the indictment is concerned with actions, so, too, the comparisons are compared with actions or processes; hence they cannot be merely pictorial: become a harlot – silver turned to dross – sour grapes produces instead of good ones – my vineyard grazed quite bare – my people trampled down – the poor ground down. It is precisely these accusations, which could even be described as hyperbole (you trample down my people – we have made a covenant with death – I will ascend to heaven), which clearly express the passionate character of the comparisons and the way they urgently press on the hearer.

(b) The function of the comparisons in the announcement of judgment. Corresponding to the structure of the announcement of judgment in the prophetic oracle, these comparisons are to be classified according to the Intervention of God and the Result of that Intervention.

Comparisons in connection with the intervention of God, e.g. from the world of flora: God will destroy the vineyard, Isa. 5.5–6, fell the lofty wood, 10.33:

> '(the LORD) will lop the boughs with terrifying power;
> the great in height will be hewn down,
> and the lofty will be brought low.'

8.7 describes the end of Israel as a natural catastrophe, viz. a flood: a 'destroying tempest' with 'overflowing waters', 28.2. The following passages represent destruction by hostile armies: 'the LORD will whistle for the fly which is at the sources of the streams of Egypt, and for the bee which is in the land of Assyria', 7.18; a razor which will shave Israel's entire body and 'which is hired beyond the river', 7.20; 'smite with a scab' and 'lay bare', 3.17; cf. 22.8; God will take away from the people leadership (and food!), 3.3–4.

Excursus on 'Stay and Staff'

Isa. 3.1 (cf. Wildberger, BK X/1, *ad loc.*):

> 'For, behold, the LORD, the LORD of hosts, is taking away
> from Jerusalem and Judah stay and staff,
> (the whole stay of bread and the whole stay of water);
> the mighty man and the soldier, the judge and the prophet . . .'.

This passage is instructive as regards the use of a comparison. The noun (in three forms) can literally mean staff or stay: a staff on which the sick (Exod. 21.19) or the old (Zech. 8.4) lean. It can be a sign of rank (Numb. 21.18; Judg. 6.21; II Kings 4.29, 31). In addition it can be used in a metaphorical sense. (a) In the oracle of judgment it is applied to the leadership of the state: Yahweh takes away from Jerusalem and Judah stay and staff, 3.1; (b) it is also used of a foreign power on which Judah relies, as in the speech of the Rabshakeh according to whom Judah is relying on Egypt, which is unable to help, II Kings 18.21 = Isa. 36.6. This comparison is taken over and modified in Ezek. 29.6 f.: Egypt is accused of being an unreliable support for Israel. In this secondary usage the comparison loses its precision and becomes clumsy. Nevertheless this passage shows that such a comparison can become engraved on and transmitted in folk memory. (c) Yahweh himself can be a stay: in the Confession of Trust, Ps. 23.4, 'thy rod and thy staff comfort me'. In narrative praise, II Sam. 22.18; Ps. 18.19 (EVV v. 18): 'but the LORD was my stay' is a late passage turned into a promise which refers back to Isa. 36.6. (d) Isa. 10.20: 'In that day (the remnant of Israel . . .) will no more lean upon him that smote them, but will lean upon the LORD, the Holy One of Israel'; cf. also Ecclus 3.31: 'at the moment of his falling he will find support'. This passage employs the verb rather than the noun. This verb (used only in the *niphal*) is employed both for leaning on a stick as well as on Yahweh. This represents metaphorical usage, and not an actual comparison. This example shows the easy transition from metaphorical usage to an explicit comparison.

The use of the word 'stay' demonstrates the many possibilities of comparison by means of the same term. Stay and staff can apply to a foreign power, to the leadership in Judah/Jerusalem, and to God. In the last case one can speak about God as staff (stay) in various contexts. The comparison means the same in its political and theological applications, i.e. it is not a specifically theological comparison (= relating to God) at all. This applies to most comparisons involving God.

In Isa. 3.1 'stay and staff' refers to the leaders of Judah and Jerusalem who are subsequently listed in vv. 2–3. Hence v. 1b: 'the whole stay of bread and the whole stay of water', is to be regarded with most commentators as an addition. The comparison with 'stay and staff' is not so fixed that it could not also apply to eating and drinking. This example shows that such a comparison is never restricted to only one possibility of interpretation. But it also shows the converse: the added comparison is not as precise as the original one. The intention behind the addition was probably to strengthen the announcement of the deprivation, but its effect is rather the opposite.

In II Kings 18.21 = Isa. 36.6 the comparison with a stay is expanded by the element 'unreliable, harmful stay': '. . . Egypt, that broken reed of staff . . .'. This expansion makes it clear that the comparison (in all cases) is not between two existing states (so Aristotle in his doctrine of metaphor) but between two processes.

In a series of comparisons the emphasis is laid on the fact it is God himself who intervenes to destroy his people: according to Isa. 8.14, he will become 'a stone of offence, and a rock of stumbling to both houses of Israel, a trap and a snare to the inhabitants of Jerusalem'; it is an oracle of judgment leading to the destruction of Israel. Or again: 'The LORD has sent word against Jacob, and it will light upon Israel' (9.7; EVV v. 8); his word becomes a tool of destruction. He himself destroys Israel by 'cut(ting) off from Israel head and tail, palm branch and reed in *one* day', 9.14; 'and its breaking is like that of a potter's vessel', 30.14. Destruction by a strange people with a strange tongue is his work: 'Nay, by men of strange lips and with an alien tongue the LORD will speak to his people', 28.11.

In the two announcements, Isa. 9.7 and 28.11, the action of God in judging Israel is an action by means of his word. The two half-verses of 9.7 supplement each other in a parallelism: God sends a word – it comes down, and in both cases against Israel – upon Israel. His word is compared to a missile; but there is a subtle difference of meaning between vv. 7a and 7b: 7a refers to the announcement of judgment spoken by the prophets against Israel, 7b refers to the actual judgment suffered by Israel which is announced in this word. This is probably the shortest and most concentrated comparison in the whole of prophecy, which expresses the oracle of judgment, its fulfilment, and that with which both are compared, in a single two-member sentence. Similarly in Isa. 28.11 the prophetic announcement ('the LORD will speak to this people') and its fulfilment in the conquest by an alien people ('with an alien tongue') are compressed into a single sentence. What is being compared here is the arrival of judgment in form of an enemy army with the announcement of this judgment through the prophetic oracle. This contains an allusion to the fact that the hearers who are rejecting the prophetic word are now feeling the effects of it on their own lives.

Both oracles in a subtle way see the word of God and what it achieves as one. The word goes forth and, as God's word, has some effect. We can trace a clear line here from Isaiah through Jeremiah to Deutero-Isaiah.

The result of God's intervention: this is compared with processes in creation. Israel will become 'like an oak whose leaf withers, and like a garden without water', Isa. 1.30; 'instead of perfume there will be rottenness; and instead of a girdle, a rope', 3.24; a demolished vineyard, 5.1–7; 'their root will be as rottenness, and their blossom go up like dust', 5.24; 'Surely for this word which they speak there is no dawn' (8.20), but only 'darkness' (8.22) and 'anguish' (9.1). A forest with majestic trees will be cut down, fall, 10.34; it will be like an early fig, which once seen is immediately devoured, 28.4b. In the following verses Israel will be consumed by a conflagration, 1.31; 5.24; 9.14; 9.18 (EVV v. 19): 'Through the wrath of the LORD of hosts the land is burned, and the people are like fuel for the fire'. Israel will be swallowed up by Sheol, 5.14; thrown to the ground, 28.2; trampled under foot, 28.3; beaten down by the overwhelming scourge, 28.18; only a remnant will remain, 30.17.

God's intervention causes the collapse, 30.13–14, which is compared with the collapse of a wall:

> 'therefore this iniquity shall be to you
> like a break in a high wall, bulging out, and about to collapse,
> whose crash comes suddenly, in an instant;
> and its breaking is like that of a potter's vessel
> which is smashed so ruthlessly
> that among its fragments not a sherd is found
> with which to take fire from the hearth,
> or to dip up water out of the cistern.'

In the case of this comparison, which includes the reason for the collapse (break in the wall – your iniquity), the collapse of the wall (v. 13) is followed apparently abruptly by the breaking of the potter's vessel (v. 14). This hardly contributes to clarity but rather represents a sequence of events: the collapse and its consequences, only small sherds remain. What we have here, therefore, is not two different images juxtaposed but the sequence of two comparisons strengthening the sequence of the collapse and its effect on the people (like the other comparisons involving a remnant).

Comparisons in the announcement of judgment against the nations. While in the indictments of the nations we only find a few comparisons and these few agree with indictments of Israel, in the case of the announcement of judgment against nations we find very many. This difference is probably due to the fact that the indictment of the nations does not directly concern those addressed by the prophetic oracle, whereas the announcement does concern them very much indeed.

The intervention of God. This is compared to processes

in the realm of creation: 'The glory of his forest and of his fruitful land the LORD will destroy', 10.18a; God is compared to a reaper who gathers standing grain and who harvests the ears, 17.5. He 'will send wasting sickness among his (Assyria's) stout warriors', 10.16, 'I will make men more rare than fine gold, and mankind than the gold of Ophir', 13.12. He will come over them like storms in the south, 'Like the thundering of the sea, . . . like the roaring of mighty waters!', 17.12. A warlike intervention by Yahweh is hinted at in comparisons: 'And the LORD of hosts will wield against them a scourge', 10.26, and 'The Light of Israel will become a fire, and his Holy One a flame', 10.17a; 'the day of the LORD is near, as destruction from the Almighty it will come!', 13.6. The destruction of the enemy is mentioned in 14.25: 'I will break the Assyrian in my land, and upon my mountains trample him underfoot', and in v. 23 'and I will sweep it with the broom of destruction'. He has taken away its power: 'The LORD has broken the staff of the wicked, the sceptre of rulers', 14.5.

The result of God's intervention against the nations. There are comparisons from the realm of nature like 18.4–5: 'he will cut off the shoots with pruning hooks, and the spreading branches he will hew away'. Destruction reaches them like the deadly bite of the serpent, 14.29: 'for from the serpent's root will come forth an adder, and its fruit will be a flying serpent'. The king of Babylon is thrown down like a dead body trodden under foot, 14.19, 'the fields of Heshbon languish, and the vine of Sibmah', 16.8. – In their flight they become 'like chaff . . . before the wind and whirling dust before the storm', 17.13; 'like fluttering birds, like scattered nestlings, so are the daughters of Moab', 16.2; 'and every man will flee' . . . 'like a hunted gazelle, or like sheep with none to gather them', 13.14. – Judgment is compared to a conflagration in 10.16b: '. . . and under his glory a burning will be kindled, like the burning of fire': and in 10.17b 'and it will burn and devour his thorns and briers in one day'. – The following mention sickness and bodily pain: 'and it will be as when a sick man wastes away', 10.18b; 'they will be in anguish like a woman in travail', 13.8; 'pangs have seized me, like the pangs of a woman in travail', 21.3; 'Wail, O ships of Tarshish!', 23.1. – Judgment causes a plunge into the depths:

> 'How are you fallen from heaven,
> O day Star, son of Dawn!
> How are you cut down to the ground,
> you who laid the nations low!' (14.12)
> 'But you are brought down to Sheol,
> to the depth of the Pit.' (v. 15)

In 13.15 the destruction of Babylon is likened to that of Sodom and Gomorrah.

## Two Parables in Isaiah: 5.1–7 and 28.23–29

These two texts can justifiably be described as parables, because, like the Gospel parables, they are independent units with narrative character, comparisons expanded into narratives.

5.1–7: The Song of the Vineyard. Its structure:

> V. 1a: Announcing the song. (This is not the announcement of a wisdom teacher to his pupils, but the invitation of someone who wants to tell a story = sing a song to his audience.)
> Vv. 1b–2: The story of the friend's vineyard.
> Vv. 3–4: Invitation to the audience to pass judgment.
> Vv. 5–6: The narrator reveals his own judgment.
> V. 7: The meaning of the story ( = the indictment of the audience).

In Isa. 5.1–7 two structures have been combined with each other: (a) the structure of a short story (a story can also be sung). Vv. 1–2: He did everything for his vineyard – but it produced wild grapes. This structure recurs in the form of a question in v. 4. However, vv. 5–6 also belong to this structure, for the announcement tells us what is going to happen to the vineyard subsequently. (b) This narrative structure has been combined with that of a prophetic oracle of judgment: vv. 1–2a review of God's previous acts of salvation (with v. 4), indictment v. 2b (interpreted in v. 7b), the announcement of judgment vv. 5–6, whereby the parable passes over into the interpretation. Vv. 3–4 clearly shows the dressing-up of a prophetic oracle of judgment as a (parable) narrative: it is meant to provoke the audience to pass their own judgment on the announcement of judgment based on the indictment, by juxtaposing with it a process which is parallel and familiar to them. This is exactly like Nathan's parable in II Sam. 12. But this juxtaposed process can only become a proper narrative by the addition of a contrasting motif. Only thus does it become a 'drama' in three acts, by introducing an element of tension into the process. In this way it becomes a parable narrative in the true sense of the word.

Isa. 28.23–29: This is a very different kind of parable from Isa. 5.1–7; it reminds us of the parables of growth in the Gospels. Its structure is as follows:

| | |
|---|---|
| V. 23: | Invitation to listen. |
| Vv. 24–26: | First question: does the farmer always plough? |
| V. 24: | Does he who ploughs plough continually? |
| V. 25: | No, rather he does all sorts of different things. |
| V. 26: | God has taught him thus. |
| Vv. 27–28: | Second question: does the farmer in the harvest treat all his produce in the same way? |
| V. 27: | Dill and cummin receive their special treatment. |
| V. 28: | The same goes for bread grain. |
| V. 29a: | This, too, has come from God. |
| V. 29b: | (Praise of God) Wonderful is his counsel (plan), great his success. |

This text is not easy to understand. Most expositors agree that Isaiah is replying to an objection here, the objection which he himself cites in the oracle of woe, 5.19: 'Let him make haste, let him speed his work that we may see it; let the purpose of the Holy One of Israel draw near, and let it come, that we may know it!' 28.23–29 is then the reply in a disputation, dressed up as a parable, as is the case in many of Jesus's parables. While this is no story in three acts like Isa. 5.1–7, here, too, it is the case that in vv. 24–26 and 27–29 not only have two examples been joined on to each other, but what is more in both parts the entire process from seed to harvest has been alluded to (cf. Mk 4.26–29). This process from seed to harvest Isaiah sets over

against the acts of God in history, which lead from plan
(*'ēsāh*) to fulfilment (*tūshiyāh*), v. 29.

To this objection (5.19) Isaiah retorts: God does not
always do the same (vv. 24–26), he does not treat all in the
same way (vv. 27–29), the story as well as history contains
pluriform growths and humanity must act accordingly.
Isaiah does not set this in the context of a divine oracle as
in 5.10, but on the same level as his audience in the form
of an argument with which they can agree or disagree.
This parable is particularly important for our understanding of Isaiah's prophecy, because only in this one passage
does he address himself to the issue of God's acts in history
as a whole. Isaiah replies to the objection: God's actions in
history do not consist only of what I have to announce
just now, the judgment which follows the transgressions of
Israel. They are manifold and multiform and take their
time. History requires growth and ripening (as opposed to
the objection in 5.1: 'who draws sin as with cart ropes').
Cf. on this also the other comparison for God's waiting in
Isa. 18.4. That Isaiah's reply in this disputation ends in
praise of God demonstrates far better than a host of words
the fact that Isaiah sees his commission to announce judgment over Israel in a far wider context than simply that of
God's judgment on his people. The whole activity of God,
he retorts to his opponents, we cannot comprehend; but
we know that his plan exists and that he will wonderfully
bring it to fruition.

Both parables have in common the fact that the audience
are invited to make their own independent judgment by
means of the juxtaposed process. In Isa. 28.23–29 Isaiah
speaks expressly not as God's messenger but as his audience's equal who courts their understanding, their agreement. This has important implications for the parables of
Jesus. They, too, appeal to thoughtful judgment and hope
to gain a free agreement, based on conviction.

These comparisons have the particular potential of containing two or three parts of the prophetic oracle, viz. that
a comparison can consist of indictment and announcement
of judgment or God's intervention and its results or histor-

ical review and indictment. This is not only the case in the
parable Isa. 5.1–7, but also in several other comparisons.
The comparison includes both indictment and announcement of judgment in Isa. 28.1, 3: 'Woe to the proud
crown of the drunkards of Ephraim . . . The proud crown
of the drunkards of Ephraim will be trodden under foot';
in 8.5–8: '. . . the waters of Shiloah that flow gently – the
waters of the River (Euphrates)', cf. 9.17–18; 28.14 ff.;
30.13 f. – The comparison contains historical review and
indictment, Isa. 1.2–3: 'Sons I have reared and brought up,
but they have rebelled against me', cf. 1.22. Both passages
are close to the lament whose motif of contrast appears
here. – The comparison involves God's intervention and
its results, Isa. 17.5 f.: 'the reaper gathers standing grain
. . ., and as when one gleans'; cf. 7.20; 8.14, 15; 18.4–6. In
30.13 f. the indictment is added as well: break in a high
wall – bulging out – collapse. This particular potential of
the comparisons of containing several parts of the prophetic
oracle of judgment confirms the fact that the comparisons
in the prophetic oracles do not illustrate an 'object' by
means of an 'image', but rather they place a process (what
happens in a prophetic oracle between God and his people)
alongside a process from a well-known and familiar realm.
The intention of this is that the comparing process should
ring in harmony with the compared.

Comparisons in Isaiah's oracles of salvation. A preliminary survey of all the oracles of salvation in Isa. 1–39
shows that they only contain a few comparisons which do
not readily fall into clear groups. The comparisons have
no intrinsic significance for these oracles of salvation.
These oracles are dominated by the description of blessing,
i.e. the description of a state of salvation which is going to
be present continually (for all time) in the coming age of
salvation. In some passages it is preceded by the final
destruction of the enemies of Israel, partly described in
apocalyptic language. This is most evident in chs 34 and
35, where the judgment of the world, represented as the
final destruction of Edom (ch. 34), is followed by the age
of salvation which is now final (ch. 35), in the style of

Deutero-Isaiah's message of salvation. The post-exilic character of chs 34 and 35 is generally recognized. Hence it can be assumed that oracles of salvation with a similar form are also late. These are 29.5–8 (destruction of the enemies) with 29.17–24 (description of blessing), 30.27–33 (destruction of the enemies and description of blessing), similarly 31.4–9 and 32.1–5. We find only the description of blessing in 4.2–6; 11.11–16 (gathering and reunification); 30.19–26; 32.15–20; 33.17–24. A few texts combine the description of blessing with the promise of a king of salvation, 4.2–6 (?); (9.1–6?); 11.1–9, 10; 1.15b. There are furthermore some individual sentences which probably belong to the description of blessing, such as 28.5.

In these texts comparisons seldom occur and crop up in completely different contexts. In 4.4–6, v. 4 speaks of forgiveness as purification: 'when the LORD shall have washed away the filth of the daughters of Zion . . .', similarly 30.26: 'in the day when the LORD binds up the hurt of his people, and heals the wounds inflicted by his blow'. In 4.5b–6 Yahweh's protection for the remnant is promised in comparisons which correspond to the expression of trust: 'for over all the glory there will be a canopy and a pavilion. It will be for a shade by day from the heat, and for a refuge and a shelter from the storm and rain', similarly 28.5: 'In that day the LORD of hosts will be a crown of glory, and a diadem of beauty, to the remnant of his people' (in the style of Trito-Isaiah), similarly 31.5.

Comparisons occur in the case of God's intervention against the enemies of Israel. 31.4: 'As a lion . . ., so the LORD of hosts will come down to fight upon Mount Zion'; 11.4: 'he shall smite the earth with the rod of his mouth, and with the breath of his lips he shall slay the wicked'; 29.5: 'But the multitude of your foes shall be like small dust, and the multitude of the ruthless like passing chaff . . .'; 29.8: 'As when a hungry man dreams he is eating and awakes with his hunger not satisfied, or as when a thirsty man . . .'.

Comparisons in the description of blessing. Isa. 11.5:

'Righteousness shall be the girdle of his waist, and faith-fulness the girdle of his loins', v. 9: '. . . as the waters cover the sea'. 30.29 contains an extended comparison:

'You shall have a song
as in the night when a holy feast is kept;
and gladness of heart,
as when one sets out to the sound of the flute
to go to the mountain of the LORD, to the Rock of Israel',

representing the age of salvation as a feast; cf. 9.2. – 35.1 ff. resembles the language of Deutero-Isaiah: 'like the crocus it shall blossom abundantly'; the king of the age of salvation is the shoot from the stump (of Jesse), 11.1–5; 11.10. He is 'an ensign to the peoples', 11.10, 12.

In summary: the manifold comparisons in various con-texts in the descriptions of blessing do not appear to have a specific function. Also few comparisons occur in those oracles of salvation which can be attributed to the prophet Isaiah. God's judgment serves the purpose of purifying the people, 1.25: 'I will turn my hand against you and will smelt away your dross as with lye and remove all your alloy'; cf. 4.4. In the oracle of salvation, 7.1–10, addressed to the king, the enemy who is threatening Jerusalem is 'done down', v. 4: 'and do not let your heart be faint because of these two smouldering stumps of firebrands!' The people of God transformed by the judgment is to receive a new foundation, 28.16 f.: 'Behold, I am laying in Zion for a foundation a stone, . . ., a precious cornerstone, . . . And I will make justice the line, and righteousness the plummet . . .'. The announcement of judgment, 10.22, quotes the promise of multiplication: 'For though your people Israel be as the sand of the sea . . .'.

### Comparisons in Jeremiah

The distribution of the comparisons to the various sections of the Book of Jeremiah shows that they are concentrated in chs 1–25; 30–35; 46–51, i.e. the Baruch narrative as such (19.1–20.6; 26–29; 36–45) contains no comparisons. The few that are found in it belong to prophetic quotations; nor are any present in the historical appendix ch. 52. This confirms our earlier result that in reports and narratives comparisons occur rarely or not at all. The comparisons lose much of their importance in the deuteronomistic sections of the Book of Jeremiah which are rather characterized by the stereotyped repetition of the same comparisons.

As with the other prophets, the comparisons in the Book of Jeremiah are also subordinated to the prophetic oracle of judgment and its constituent parts: to the announcement of judgment, the indictment, and some to the review of God's previous acts. A few comparisons occur in the context of the call narrative, and further in oracles concerned with Jeremiah as a tester. In this connection the oracles against the nations have to be treated separately. In them the comparisons in the announcement of judgment far outstrip those in the indictment. To these we have to add the comparisons in the context of the lament as a group particularly characteristic of Jeremiah, and further the symbolic actions which are more frequent in Jeremiah than in his predecessors.

Comparisons in the announcement of judgment. God's judgment of his people is compared to the devouring, destroying fire, and it is often the wrath of God which kindles this fire, 4.4: 'lest my wrath go forth like fire, and burn with none to quench it!' In the dispute with the prophets of salvation the oracle of judgment which announces the destruction is identified in the following comparison with this destruction, 23.29: 'Is not my word like fire, and like a hammer which breaks the rock in pieces?' The comparison with fire frequently occurs, 4.8, 26; 11.16; 15.14b; 21.12b, 14 f.; 23.29; 25.37. God's judgment is compared to tempest, storm, and flood:

4.11, 13:  'A hot wind from the bare heights in the desert
toward the daughter of my people, not to winnow or cleanse, . . .
Behold, he comes like clouds,
his chariots like the whirlwind . . .'.
18.17:  'Like the east wind I will scatter them before the enemy',
cf. 10.22; 23.19; 30.23.

Sometimes judgment is compared to wild animals. 'A lion has gone up from his thicket . . .', 4.7; 'Panthers come from a distant land, they roar against the cities of Judah' (author's translation), 4.16; 'Therefore a lion from the forest shall slay them, a wolf . . ., a leopard . . .', 5.6; 'For behold, I am sending among you serpents . . .', 8.17, cf. 2.15; and also birds of prey, 12.9. When God's judgment is compared to destructive elements and wild animals, these are given a positive significance as the tools of that judgment. If God is recognized as judge even of his own people, the same then applies to the tools of his judgment.

Various comparisons for God's intervention. Comparisons with poisonous food, 9.15: 'Behold, I will feed this people with wormwood, and give them poisonous water to drink' = 23.15, on this see above p. 52, comparisons with drunkenness, 13.12–14. The following point to exile and imprisonment:

> 'Behold, I am sending for many fishers . . ., and they shall catch them; . . . I will send for many hunters, and they shall hunt them from every mountain and every hill, and out of the clefts of the rocks', (16.16).

'Gather up your bundle from the ground, . . . Behold, I am slinging out the inhabitants of the land . . .', 10.17 f. 'Behold, I will lay before this people stumbling blocks against which they shall stumble; father and sons together . . .', 6.21, cf. 45.4. The announcement of the descending conqueror in 5.16 describes his equipment: 'Their quiver is like an open tomb'. It is not as if the open tomb is intended as an image for the quiver here, but rather the comparison is a kind of contraction. It points to a sequence of actions: to begin with, the deadly arrow is taken out of the quiver, there follows the fatal shot and finally the opening of the grave.

Whereas the comparisons mentioned so far (the greater majority of this group) all belong to the first part of the announcement of judgment, the intervention of God (1st person), others belong to the second part, the result of God's intervention (3rd person): the destruction of fields and gardens by enemies, 5.10: 'Go up through her vine-rows and destroy, . . . strip away her branches . . .'; v. 16 f.: 'Their quiver is like an open tomb . . . They shall eat up your harvest . . ., vines and figtrees . . .', also 17.6; 11.16. The following describe the result as wound or illness:

'Is there no balm in Gilead? Is there no physician there?
Why then has the health of the daughter of my people
not been restored?' (8.22)

Its consequence is the death of the people which is the subject of the death lament: 'O daughter of my people, gird on sackcloth, and roll in ashes; make mourning as . . .', 6.26; 'O that my head were waters, and my eyes a fountain of tears . . .', 9.1; 'Take up weeping and wailing for the mountains, and a lamentation for the pastures of the wilderness', v. 10; 'Call for the mourning women . . ., let them make haste and raise a wailing over us . . .', v. 17; 'Hear, O women, . . . teach to your daughters a lament, . . . For death has come up into our windows, . . .', vv. 20–21;

'How long will the land mourn,
and the grass of every field wither?
For the wickedness of those who dwell on it
the beasts and the birds are swept away . . .' (12.4).

'Let my eyes run down with tears night and day,
. . . for the virgin daughter of my people
is smitten with a great wound, with a very grievous blow' (14.17).

The death lament as a reaction to the result of God's intervention as judge of his people is (as in Amos 5.1–3, 16) a comparison insofar as the rite of the death lament in the case of the death of an individual – usually limited to the family and the dwelling place – is applied to the death of the entire people. A magnificent and daring conception which probably occurs for the first time in human history in Israel's prophets. This concept only becomes possible as an announcement, because only as such can the future event be announced in such a concentrated way as the fate of the entire people in the form of an individual

death. Because of this peculiarity the comparison is also
expanded here into a dirge, as a kind of *fermata*, Jer. 9.16,
17, 20, 21, which, thus understood, comes close to a parable.

Comparisons in the oracles of judgment concerning
kings.

> 'Say to the king and the queen mother;
> "Take a lowly seat,
> for your beautiful crown has come down from your head"' (13.18).

'With the burial of an ass he shall be buried, dragged and
cast forth beyond the gates of Jerusalem', 22.19; 'Though
Coniah . . . were the signet on my right hand, yet I would
tear you off', v. 24.

Typical of Jeremiah's usage is a form of comparison
which combines two motifs: the historical review and the
announcement of judgment, as in 45.4: 'Behold, what I
have built I am breaking down, and what I have planted I
am plucking up', cf. 1.10; 11.16: 'A green olive tree . . .
but with the roar of a great tempest he will set fire to it,
and its branches will be consumed'. Perhaps 12.13 is
another example: 'They have sown wheat and reaped
thorns'. 2.26 suggests a combination of the announcement
of judgment with the indictment: 'As the thief is shamed
when caught, so the house of Israel shall be shamed'. This
combination of two motifs also occurs in the indictment
(see below).

The comparison in the indictment. 2.20 contains the
indictment of apostasy: 'For long ago you broke your
yoke and burst your bonds'. The breaking of the yoke
signifies the breaking of the promise to serve God, as
in 5.5b. Apostasy can be compared with adultery or
harlotry, as in 2.1–5: 'If a man divorces his wife . . ., You
have played the harlot with many lovers'; vv. 6–10: Israel
and Judah have both committed adultery, cf. 4.30–31. This
is one of the few comparisons from the deuteronomistic
layer of the Book of Jeremiah. In it the frequent and
stereotyped indictment has become almost exclusively one
of apostasy. In 2.23b–25 apostasy is compared to a female

camel in heat; in 2.22 with dirt and defilement: 'Though
you can wash yourself with lye . . ., the stain of your guilt
is still before me . . .', v. 23: 'How can you say, "I am
not defiled" . . .'; 4.14: 'O Jerusalem, wash your heart
from wickedness!'

In the indictment Israel is confronted in comparisons
with the incomprehensibility of her apostasy from God, it
is stubbornness or folly, 5.3: 'They have made their faces
harder than rock; they have refused to repent', cf. 13.23;
4.22: 'For my people are foolish . . ., they are stupid
children, they have no understanding', so also 5.23. This
unnatural behaviour is shown in the following comparisons:

> 'When men fall, do they not rise again?
> If one turns away, does he not return?
> Why then has this people turned away
> in perpetual backsliding?' (8.4 f.)
> 'Even the stork in the heavens knows her times;
> and the turtledove, swallow, and crane
> keep the time of their coming;
> but my people know not the ordinance of the LORD' (v. 7)
> 'Does the snow of Lebanon leave the crags of Sirion?
> Do the mountain waters run dry, the cold flowing streams?
> But my people have forgotten me!' (18.14 f. cf. 13.23)

These comparisons, 8.4; 8.7; 18.14 f., also 2.13, are cast in
deliberately pointed language. Because the prophet Jeremiah considers the apostasy of the people from their God so
incredible and unnatural, he confronts his people with it in
comparisons which are meant to illustrate and emphasize
the incredible and unnatural character of this apostasy.
This was something which Isaiah had already done (Isa.
1.2: 'The ox knows its owner . . .'); but now, just before
the end, this argument becomes even more pressing. The
comparisons are meant to say to the people: nothing
special, nothing extraordinary is demanded of you. Had
Israel acted like a humble animal and according to everyday experience (cf. also 2.10–11), then she would have
remained faithful to her God or have returned to him after
her lapse. This is expressed in a way only possible in
comparisons. Religion at that time in the history of Israel,

unlike today, was a necessary constituent of the life of the people, not something individuals could decide for themselves. Hence it should be as natural as the route of migrating birds for Israel to remain faithful to her God. It corresponds to the fact of creation. In these comparisons the migrating birds and the snowy mountains are given a language which accompanies the prophet's indictment of his people. They have something to say which the people could have heard, but did not. Israel's relationship with her God corresponds to the behaviour of the creatures. God has created them all, the migratory birds, the mountains, and his people Israel.

Comparisons in the indictment of behaviour towards one's fellow men. 'They set a trap; they catch men', 5.26; 'Like a basket full of birds, their houses are full of treachery', v. 27; 'As a well keeps its water fresh, so she keeps fresh her wickedness', 6.7; 'Every one turns to his own course, like a horse plunging headlong into battle', 8.6; 'They bend their tongue like a bow; falsehood . . . has grown strong in the land', 9.3; 'Their tongue is a deadly arrow', v. 8; 'They were well-fed lusty stallions, each neighing for his neighbour's wife', 5.8, cf. 7.11.

Comparisons in the indictment of the prophets. 'They healed the wound of my people lightly, saying, "Peace, peace" . . .', 8.11; 'What has straw in common with wheat?', 23.28. The following are directed against the entire leadership: 'Woe to the shepherds who destroy and scatter the sheep of my pasture', 23.1; 'You have scattered my flock, and have driven them away, and you have not attended to them. Behold . . .', v. 2; 'Then I will gather the remnant of my flock out of all the countries . . . and I will bring them back to their fold', v. 3, an almost identical comparison to which appears in Ezek. 34. 8.8 is also an indictment of the leadership: 'the false pen of the scribes has made it (the law) into a lie'.

Comparisons combining several motifs. This group includes the comparison of the leadership with the wicked shepherd in 23.1–3. The prose form of these verses indicates that we are dealing with a later revision. To what extent this is based on a woe oracle of Jeremiah we are no longer able to recognize. As in Ezek. 34, an oracle of judgment on the current leaders of the people has here been combined with an oracle of salvation which promises restitution by Yahweh, the good shepherd. Cf. my remarks on Ezek. 34 below on p. 79 f.

Jer. 2.13 (18) is a comparison which combines the historical review (contrast motif) with the indictment:

'for my people have committed two evils:
they have forsaken me, the fountain of living waters,
and hewed out cisterns for themselves, broken cisterns,
that can hold no water!'

This comparison summarizes what had been set out earlier in vv. 4–7, viz. from the point of view: what did it mean to you, what benefit did you derive from it? The answer given by this comparison points once more to the incomprehensible and senseless nature of apostasy, as many other comparisons do. The special feature of this passage lies in the fact that the contrast between God's acts of salvation towards his people and their response to them is expressed in a contrasting comparison, which clearly says to everyone: what a foolish thing to have done! The tendency to further development is shown by the resumption of the comparison in v. 18: 'What do you gain by going to Egypt, to drink the waters of the Nile? . . . to Assyria, to drink the waters of the Euphrates?' The statement of 2.13a is repeated in 17.13b. The same contrast forms a different comparison in 2.21: 'Yet I have planted you a choice vine, wholly of pure seed. How then have you turned degenerate and become a wild vine?' Closely resembling it is the comparison in 8.13: 'When I would gather them, there are no grapes on the vine, nor figs on the fig tree', cf. Isa. 5.1–7. In addition, the two comparisons pointing to the folly of the apostasy, 8.7 and 18.14, implicitly combine the same two motifs. Another combination of motifs is contained in the comparison in Jeremiah's temple speech, 7.11:

'Has this house, which is called by my name,
become a den of robbers in your eyes?'

The meaning of the comparison is this: as a robber secures his spoil in his den, so the Israelites intend to secure their debauched and rapacious life in the temple cult. This profound comparison combines the accusation of crimes against one's neighbour – which are enumerated in v. 9 – with the accusation of desecrating worship. This comparison, which forms the climax of Jeremiah's temple speech, can illustrate particularly clearly the function of comparisons in prophetic preaching. The outrageous nature of this contrast, the temple – a robbers' den, would be bound to impress every hearer. It is the strongest possible intensification of the accusation of desecrating worship while simultaneously implying the reason for this desecration. It was inevitable that this would be passed on by word of mouth.

Comparisons in the historical review. The contrast motif, which can be found in nearly all pre-exilic prophets of judgment, in most cases confronts the people with their present apostasy as compared to God's previous acts of salvation. We have already mentioned these passages in connection with the indictment where the same comparison links both: 2.13 fountain – cistern; 2.21 choice vine – wild vine; 11.16 green olive tree – consumed one. Further passages are: 2.2–3; v. 2: 'I remember the devotion of your youth, your love as a bride . . .', these expressions refer to the wilderness wandering: 'how you followed me in the wilderness, in a land not sown'; the corollary of this is Israel's preservation by God, compared to something consecrated which may not be touched, v. 3: 'Israel was holy to the LORD, the first fruits of his harvest . . .'. In the sequence of vv. 2 and 3 the comparisons point to a larger context which is immediately clear to the audience – precisely because it is only hinted at in the comparisons: the consequences of God's saving acts in Israel's early history was that she remained faithful to her God and followed his word. The comparisons by evoking the past make the contrast with the present all the more apparent.

Again and again the comparisons emphasize the unnatural and unbelievable character of apostasy, 2.32: 'Can a maiden forget her ornaments, or a bride her attire? Yet my people . . .', cf. 13.1–11. The comparison alludes to the precious and valuable nature of God as experienced by his people in his works, as voiced in the psalms of praise.

The same can be expressed negatively:

'O generation, heed the word of the LORD.
Have I been a wilderness to Israel,
or a land of thick darkness? Why then . . .' (2.31).

6.17 points to a part of the divine action in the past which was important for Israel: 'I set watchmen over you saying, "Give heed to the sound of the trumpet"'. 5.22, however, does not point back to God's acts in past history, but to his acts in creation, wholly in the style of creation psalms. This is probably a later saying which already presupposes Deutero-Isaiah.

Combinations of several motifs in comparisons are more frequent from Jeremiah onwards, even more so in Ezekiel. The prophetic oracle of judgment is originally intended for the precise moment of an announcement or indictment. The comparisons are a means by which the form of the prophetic word is extended by the juxtaposition of larger contexts. In Jer. 2.2–3 the expansion of the motif 'God's previous acts of salvation' by Israel's obedience in her early history is indicative of the tendency of the prophets around the time of the exile – particularly strong in Ezekiel – to review, also in comparisons, the entire history of Israel from the perspective of the present.

Comparisons in the context of Jeremiah's call. In 1.10 the prophet Jeremiah is commissioned to intervene in history by means of his announcement, to build and to destroy:

'See, I have set you this day over nations and over kingdoms,
to pluck up and to break down, . . .,
to build and to plant'.

These verbs are really metaphors; all of them have metaphorical significance in German also (and in English). These verbs are given the weight of a comparison because through them the prophet is granted a share in God's acts in history (thus they are used in 45.4); for the announcement and its execution belong together. The prophet's commission is followed by his equipment for the task, 1.18: 'Behold, I make you this day a fortified city, an iron pillar, and bronze walls'. In this verse Jeremiah is promised the strength to resist and persevere in the face of the bitter hostilities which he is to meet. This promise is repeated at the point at which the hostilities become most severe, 15.20. Two oracles, in which the close connection of the prophetic word with God's activity is intensified by means of comparison, refer back to Jeremiah's call:

'Behold, I am making my words in your mouth a fire,
and this people wood' (5.14).
'Therefore I am full of the wrath of the LORD;
I am weary of holding it in. "Pour it out . . ."' (6.11).

In these two particularly powerful comparisons several motifs have been combined: in 5.14 the motif of Jeremiah's call and commission with that of the announcement of judgment, and in 6.11 the former with that of God's intervention. The prophet's task and manner of life can hardly be more powerfully and effectively expressed than in these comparisons.

In Jer. 1.11–15 the two visions of the almond rod and the seething pot have been added to the call of Jeremiah. The two visions represent the two parts of the announcement of judgment: God is watching over his word (intervention) – a catastrophe befalls the land (result of the intervention). The vision belongs originally to the seer, and from there has entered prophecy. This process shows that the vision needs an interpretation, whereas comparison and parable do not. Originally the interpretation belongs only to dream and vision; only through the combination of both was the interpretation applied to comparison and parable.

Only in the prophet Jeremiah is the call connected with a special commission: he is appointed a tester. This implies the question whether really all are to be rejected, and hence whether judgment should be passed on all of them.

In 5.1–6 the prophet calls for this to be investigated (without a comparison: 'Run to and fro through the streets of Jerusalem, . . . if you can find a man, one who does justice and seeks truth . . .'). In 6.9 such a request is made of the prophet including the use of a comparison: 'Glean thoroughly as a vine the remnant of Israel; like a grape-gatherer pass your hand over its branches'. In a further comparison he is commissioned as a tester, 6.27–29 (30):

> 'I have made you an assayer and tester among my people,
> that you may know and assay their ways.
> They are all stubbornly rebellious . . .
> The bellows blow fiercely, and the lead is consumed by fire;
> in vain the refining goes on, . . . Refuse silver they are called.'

Cf. also 9.7: 'Behold I will refine them and test them . . .'. In this context the comparison receives a special significance through the fact that no clear term for Jeremiah's commission exists; it can only be described verbally (as in 5.1–6 without a comparison) or be named in a comparison. The noun 'tester' in the sentence 'I have made you a tester' has probably been specially formed from the verb for this purpose; it only occurs in this one place. In 6.27–29 (30) the comparison has been extended in a parable-like direction; this gives it a kind of *fermata* underlining its significance.

The symbolic actions in Jeremiah. These are simply comparisons transformed into actions. They are intended to express something which through the action is meant to become more intense and impressive. Thus is it not only a matter of a word which can be repeated, but rather of a story which can be told. The message of the symbolic actions of Jeremiah is without exception subjected to his prophetic preaching, in most cases to the announcement of judgment. 13.1–11: Jeremiah is told to acquire a linen waistcloth and to put it on, vv. 1–2, and then to hide it in a cleft of the rock, 3–5, and to check after a while whether it is spoilt, 6, 7. This is how he is supposed to symbolize the judgment upon Israel, indicating the former close connection between God and his people: 'For as the waistcloth clings to the loins of a man . . .'. – In chs 18 and 19 Jeremiah is told to buy a clay pot and to smash it in front of the elders as witnesses outside the Potsherd Gate. – 18.1–10: he is to go into the potter's house and himself become a witness of the process by which the potter destroys a misshapen vessel and creates a new one: this is an announcement of judgment which implies the indictment. – In the vision of the two fig baskets in ch. 24, one side, the basket with the bad figs, is an announcement of judgment (with an implied indictment) against those who remained in Judah after 597. – In ch. 27 Jeremiah is told to wear a yoke in front of the ambassadors of the neighbouring states who have come to Jerusalem. Judah and her neighbours are to be bent under the yoke of the king of Babylon. The following are announcements of judgment against foreign nations: 43.8–13 (against Egypt) and 51.59–64. While the former has been combined with the instruction to bury stones at the gate of Pharaoh's palace, the latter includes the commission of Jeremiah to Seriah to sink Jeremiah's oracles of judgment against Babylon in the Euphrates. The introduction to the oracles against the nations, 25.15–31, also has the form of symbolic action. Jeremiah is given by the Lord the cup of the wine of wrath and is told: 'Make all the nations to whom I send you drink it', 25.15. This commission leads to an announcement of judgment. But while chs 27; 43.8–13; 51.59–64 presuppose certain circumscribed situations in Jeremiah's ministry, 25.15–31 is a summary of all Jeremiah's oracles of judgment against the nations, later shaped as a symbolic action.

Some symbolic actions, which announce judgment against Israel, are continued in a way unique to Jeremiah: in 20.1–6 Jeremiah, after having repeated the announcement of judgment following his symbolic action in ch. 19 in the forecourt of the temple (vv. 14–15), is beaten by Pashhur, the chief officer of the temple, and placed in the pillory. – In ch. 28, after Jeremiah with the yoke on his neck has announced the submission to the king of Babylon, Hananiah, the prophet of salvation, snatches it from his shoulders and breaks it. As Jeremiah at this point has no word from the Lord, he has to go home pursued by the mockery of the people. – The burning of the scroll in ch. 36 is not a proper symbolic action, but this report is connected with the genre of symbolic actions insofar as even this event leads to the proclamation of the announcement of judgment against Judah and Jerusalem, and here, too, the prophet's life is put at risk. He is lucky to escape arrest, as in the case of the temple speech.

What is new, as compared to the symbolic actions in prophecy before him, is that Jeremiah is personally involved in them and that they lead to the prophet's own suffering. In the case of this prophet, immediately prior to the fall of Jerusalem, the announcement of judgment against the whole people includes the suffering of the messenger (lament).

Symbolic actions in connection with oracles of salvation. Ch. 24, the vision of the two baskets of figs, is structured in terms of vision and interpretation of that vision, as in 1.11–15. The vision requires an interpretation. To the difference between the two baskets corresponds the different fates of the two sections of the people after 597. Judgment is announced to those who have remained in Judah and Jerusalem, salvation to those exiled to Babylon (cf. ch. 29). This is only a symbolic action insofar as the prophet Jeremiah is shown through the vision that from now on the announcements of judgment and salvation apply to different groups; see Jeremiah's letter in ch. 29. – The purchase of the field in ch. 32 is a symbolic action which is of decisive significance for the ministry of Jeremiah. God's commission to Jeremiah to buy a field in Anathoth, an area which is now occupied by the enemy besieging Jerusalem, means: 'Houses and fields and vineyards shall again be bought in this land', 32.15. This is a promise of blessing which does not alter the announcement of judgment in any way. It only says: even after the fall of Jerusalem God will continue to deal with his people, but in a different way from before.

Symbolic actions in the context of the indictment, e.g.

the Rechabites in ch. 35. This symbolic action, like the one in ch. 24, also alludes to a division among the people, in this case a division between obedience and disobedience. However, the main emphasis is placed on the fact that Jeremiah confronts his audience with the Rechabites' faithfulness in contrast to Israel's unfaithfulness.

Comparisons in the announcements of judgment against the nations. In the oracles against the nations the enemies who execute judgment upon the people in question are never mentioned by name. They are always described in a roundabout way in comparisons which express the destruction, but do not allow us to recognize a particular enemy. They never point to anything specific about one particular opponent, but are always only comparisons for the destruction as such. The enemy is the 'sword', 46.10, 'sword of the LORD', 47.6; the woodcutter, 46.22; 'How the hammer of the whole earth is cut down and broken', 50.23; the harvester, 51.33; 'tilters who tilt him', 48.12; 'If grape-gatherers came to you', 49.9; 'upon your summer fruits and your vintage the destroyer has fallen', 48.32; 'and I will send to Babylon winnowers', 51.2; the layer of a snare, 50.24.

In 47.2 and 49.35 judgment is described as a tempest. The following describe the enemies as wild beasts or stinging insects: 'A beautiful heifer is Egypt, but a gadfly from the north has come upon her', 46.20; 'She makes a sound like a serpent gliding away', 46.22; 'Behold, one shall fly swiftly like an eagle, and spread his wings against Moab', 48.40; 'like a lion coming up from the jungle of the Jordan', 49.19; 50.44; 51.38.

All comparisons mentioned so far belong to the first part of the announcement of judgment, the intervention of God, the second part, results of the intervention, is completely missing, with the possible exception of 46.11: 'Go up to Gilead, and take balm, O virgin daughter of Egypt! In vain you have used many medicines; there is no healing for you'; similarly 51.8 f. (applied to Israel in 8.22). The whole of ch. 48 is concerned with the results of the judgment insofar as in the announcement of judgment we are able to recognize a different genre, viz. a song of lament over Moab – as in Ezekiel's oracles against the nations. This lament alludes to the special character of Moab as a wine region: 'I weep for you, O vine of Sibmah! . . . upon your summer fruit and your vintage the destroyer has fallen', 48.31, 32. In the Book of Ezekiel the oracle against the nations is combined with the lament to an even greater degree. One could almost reconstruct an independent genre 'Lament over a city / country'.

The indictment in comparisons in the oracles against the nations. We find in the case of the announcements of judgment that we encounter comparisons almost exclusively in the first part, God's intervention. And there are also hardly any comparisons in the context of the indictment. Only Jer. 46.7 is worth mentioning, where the rising of the Nile is compared to the 'rising' of Egypt so as to cover a country and to destroy its inhabitants. Moab is accused of having made Israel an object of derision, therefore he is to be made drunk and also become an object of derision, 48.26, 27. Of Babylon it is said that she is 'making the whole earth drunk', 51.7.

The oracles against the nations in chs 50 and 51 are not by Jeremiah, they have originated during the exile and are intended as oracles of salvation for Israel. Yahweh's judgment over Egypt is announced so that Israel can be liberated and return to her own land. An investigation of the comparisons in the oracles against the nations in Jer. 46–51 leads us to suggest that while the oracles of judgment against the nations show their derivation from the oracles of judgment against Israel by their very firm structure, they nevertheless differ greatly from them. This is particularly evident in the connection with the lament over a country (Moab) in ch. 48.

Comparisons in oracles of salvation. Only the symbolic action in ch. 32 can confidently be ascribed to Jeremiah; the few comparisons in oracles of salvation all belong to later additions. In 31.10b Yahweh is referred to as Israel's shepherd, and in v. 9 as his father. He represents the promise of new blessing in 31.27: 'I will sow the house of Israel and the house

of Judah with the seed of man and the seed of beast'. And in
v. 29 the validity of the old saying, 'the fathers have eaten sour
grapes . . .' (cf. Ezekiel), is abolished. In 33.22 the comparison
from the patriarchal promises returns: multiplication countless as the stars of the heavens and as the sand of the seashore;
and in 42.10 the promise of building and planting (cf. 1.10).
Finally, the comparison of the pious individual with the tree
planted by the water in 17.7 f. corresponds almost word-for-
word to Ps. 1, and like it belongs to theological Wisdom.

## Comparisons in Jeremiah's Laments

The lament runs right through the entire ministry of
Jeremiah. God himself suffers from what he has to do to
his people (ch. 45). In addition to the previously mentioned
death lament over the people there are two further
passages: 'O that my head were waters, and my eyes a
fountain of tears', 9.1, and 'How long will the land mourn
. . .?', 12.4. Jeremiah's laments correspond to the Individual
Lament in the Psalter with its three elements, I-laments:
'Woe is me because of my hurt! My wound is grievous',
10.19; 'I sat alone, because thy hand was upon me, for
thou hadst filled me with indignation', 15.17; and 'But I
was like a gentle lamb led to the slaughter', 11.19.

The God-lament: 'Wilt thou be to me like a deceitful
brook, like waters that fail?', 15.18; with regard to per-
secutors: 'Thou plantest them, and they take root; they
grow and bring forth fruit', 12.2; and

'Why should thou be like a stranger in the land,
like a wayfarer who turns aside to tarry for the night?
Why shouldst thou be like a man confused,
like a mighty man who cannot save?' (14.8 f.).

Foe-lament: Enemies conspire against him: 'Let us destroy
the tree with its fruit, let us cut him off from the land of
the living', 11.19; and Jeremiah's lament: 'Yet they have
dug a pit for my life', 18.20, 22. God's initial reply to
Jeremiah's lament is that things will be even worse for
him:

'If you have raced with men on foot,
and they have wearied you,
how will you compete with horses?' (12.5).

But Jeremiah is assured of help: 'But the LORD is with
me as a dread warrior', 20.11. In his laments, too, Jeremiah
uses the standard prayer language of his people of which
the comparisons are an integral part. (For further details cf.
p. 112 on the Laments in the Psalms). It is important for
the connection of these laments with Jeremiah's preaching
that the two large areas in which OT comparisons occur
come together in the ministry and suffering of one and the
same prophet.

To summarize the comparisons in Jeremiah: a collection
of the most frequent or important comparisons in the
preaching of Jeremiah would not indicate their real significance. It is rather the complete process, the total event of
this prophecy, which is given a sharp and clear profile by
the comparisons. It is the elementary character of the
judgment which Jeremiah has to announce as coming
upon Israel (flood, lion, panther) caused by the unbelievable apostasy of the people from their God (the living
spring – the leaking fountain; have I become a desert for
Israel?). Here the comparisons pile up, here their language
is at its most passionate. Everything else issues from or is
dependent on this. Announcing judgment in this situation
of an incredible hardening of the people's heart is given
great significance: it is the word of God which intervenes
in history, is active in it. There is furthermore the difficult task of the one who has to announce it and who
suffers from this task, who seeks to understand the inconceivable and therefore looks for connections, who himself
has to examine whether it is really inevitable. He it
is who with his whole person is drawn into what he has
to announce, and in spite of everything perseveres in the
conviction that he is acting on God's behalf.

## Comparisons in Nahum, Habakkuk, Zephaniah

*Comparisons in Nahum.* See on this J. Jeremias, *Kultpro-phetie und Gerichtsandkündigung in der späten Königszeit Israels* (WMANT 35), pp. 11–54. Among the oracles concerning Israel 2.3 (EVV v. 2) is usually interpreted as an oracle of salvation for Israel: 'For the LORD is restoring the majesty (alternative reading: vine) of Jacob as the majesty (vine) of Israel, for plunderers have stripped them and ruined their branches'. Thus understood it is an exilic–post-exilic oracle of salvation which clearly takes up the comparison 'vine – branches' from earlier oracles of judgment (Isa. 5.1–7) and turns it into an oracle of salvation. 3.1–7 is an oracle of woe over Asshur: 'Woe to the bloody city . . .', v. 7: 'Wasted is Nineveh . . .'; Jeremias deletes v. 7 as an addition (together with v. 6) and understands 3.1–5 as an oracle of judgment over Judah. His main reason is the fact that the indictment of fornication in v. 4 corresponds to the indict-ment of Israel typical of judgment prophecy from Hosea onwards (Jeremias, p. 34, notes 2 and 4). But this is contradicted by the wording of the accusation in v. 4:

'And all for the countless harlotries of the harlot,
graceful and of deadly charms,
who betrays nations with her harlotries,
and people with her charms.'

The relative clause fits the superpower Nineveh, but not Judah. 'Harlotry' in this context can quite properly mean 'idolatry' in a wider sense, as e.g. in Isa. 23.27 f. with reference to Tyre. Deleting v. 7 is also rather daring and there are no good reasons for it. These few sketchy remarks on Jeremias's thesis are able to show that under certain circumstances the comparisons can have consider-able significance for the dating of an oracle.

The Asshur oracles in Nahum 2.4–14; 3.12–19 are a dramatic description of the conquest of Nineveh. The comparisons in use are explanatory, as in v. 5 (EVV v. 4): 'they gleam like torches', and v. 8 (EVV v. 7): 'her maidens lamenting, moaning like doves,' and in one case original: 'Nineveh is like a pool whose waters run away', v. 9 (EVV

v. 8). The whole description reaches its climax in a comparison in vv. 12–13 (EVV 11–12) which establishes the completeness of the destruction:

> 'Where is the lion's den, the cave of the young lions,
> where the lion brought his prey, where his cubs were, with none to disturb?
> The lion tore enough for his whelps and strangled prey for his lionesses;
> he filled his caves with prey and his dens with torn flesh.'

The initial question: 'Where is the lions' den?' points to the unspoken answer: it is no longer there!, and at the same time, however, to the earlier power and self-assurance of the lion and to the way in which he used to be spoken of. This is originally praise of power and of the mighty, like the comparison with the lion in the tribal saying concerning Judah, Gen. 49.9, but also like the comparison in Jer. 2 with the enemy who rises against Judah. This is now all over, says the comparison; the lion has been killed (this is the meaning of the probably independent announcement of judgement in v. 14; EVV v. 13). Both in vv. 12–13 and in a different way in v. 14 a traditional comparison lives on by receiving a different meaning, a different function, as e.g. in Nahum 2.3. In 3.8–19 – vv. 8–11 belong to the Asshur oracle (contra Jeremias) – Asshur's inability to resist the conqueror is expressed in two comparisons, in v. 12 and 15b, 17b. V. 12: 'All your fortresses are like fig trees with first-ripe figs – if shaken they fall into the mouth of the eater.' Whereas the above refers to the strength of the city, vv. 15b, 17b are concerned with the number of her defenders: 'Multiply yourself like the locust, multiply like the grasshopper! . . . settling on the fences in a day of cold – when the sun rises, they fly away; no-one knows where they are.' The correspondence between these two comparisons shows clearly how well thought out their use is. They are related to each other as regards their meaning: the strength of the fortified city and the number of her inhabitants cannot prevent her conquest. Further, more common comparisons are used in the description: in v. 18 the leadership is compared to shepherds who have been asleep so that the flock (the people) has scattered on the mountains, while v. 19 compares their defeat to a fatal wound. Cf. Jer. 30.12: 'Your hurt is incurable, and your wound is grievous.'

*Comparisons in Habakkuk.*   The woe oracles in Habakkuk 2.5–20 show yet again the entire power and art of the comparisons which derive directly from the function of the prophetic word, in this case from a superpower's ravenous lust for conquest:

> '. . . the arrogant man shall not abide.
> His greed is wide as Sheol;
> like death he has never enough' (2.5).

In the following vv. 6b–7 the indictment expresses a social aim:

> '"Woe to him who heaps up what is not his own –
> for how long? – and loads himself with pledges!"
> Will not your debtors suddenly arise . . .?'

The comparison means to say: stolen goods never become the property of the conqueror; they are rather pledges which will have to be redeemed one day. Those who have been robbed remain the creditors of the conqueror who one day will demand settlement of the debt. A profound comparison which declares political conquests to be theft! The comparison in the third oracle of woe points in the same direction: 'Woe to him who gets evil gain for his house, to set his nest on high . . .', 2.9–10. In the fourth oracle of woe (2.11, 12, 13, 17) text and sequence are in doubt, but the comparisons are clearly recognizable:

> 'Woe to him who builds a town with blood,
> and founds a city on iniquity! (v. 12)
> For the stone will cry out from the wall,
> and the beam from the woodwork respond. (v. 11)
> (. . . that the peoples labour only for fire,
> and nations weary themselves for naught?) (v. 13)
> The violence done to Lebanon will overwhelm you;
> the destruction of the beasts will terrify you.' (v. 17)

A brutal ruler here stands accused, because he builds the

city and its fortifications by corvée labour with the use of brute force against humans, animals, and plants. Here, too, a social accusation is applied to the power politics of a brutal ruler. What is peculiar to this comparison is the contraction: blood and violence become building materials! This language reflects a passionate intervention on behalf of the abused and tortured labourers: 'For the stone will cry out from the wall . . .'. The power of a comparison is seldom shown as clearly as here; the building which is meant to represent power and splendour is, for the speaker of this oracle, in the first place a witness to the brutal rape of the workers who built it. The stones will remind us of this! Jesus has taken up this comparison and given it a slightly different direction: 'When these are silent, the very stones will cry out!'

In the description of the conqueror's assault it is again the comparisons which lend weight and depth to this description, 1.9, 14, 15 f., 11b:

'. . . They gather captives like sand. (v. 9)
For thou makest men like the fish of the sea,
like crawling things that have no ruler. (v. 14)
He brings them all up with a hook,
he drags them out with his net,
he gathers them in his seine;
so he rejoices and exults.
Therefore he sacrifices to his net
and burns incense to his seine;
for by them he lives in luxury,
and his food is rich. (v. 15 f.)
. . . whose own might is their god!' (v. 11b)

For the brutal ruler excessive power becomes his god, he elevates it to the realm of the divine, and the same applies to the means by which he executes his power. Power is, like a god, capable of yielding blessing, it therefore also deserves sacrifices like a god. The comparison is in the process of becoming a parable. Both in his judgment on the conquests of a superpower as also in the power and targeting of his language in the comparisons Habakkuk is quite close to Isaiah.

Compared to Isaiah as well as Jeremiah Habakkuk's

prophecy, as represented in the comparisons, achieves a unique significance. The prophet who forms these comparisons does not speak as one directly affected. He views the conqueror, whom he describes so impressively, from a certain distance, a critical distance. The effect of this is that in his indictments he does not directly visualize Israel's enemy but objectively has in mind the superpower and its rule. In the Bible, and beyond it in the whole corpus of Near Eastern literature, there is no sharper, clearer and more fitting characterization of a superpower which conquers and annexes other nations. This is done in marked contrast both to any glorification of political power and greatness for its own sake and to every kind of hero worship. 2.5: '. . . the arrogant man shall not abide. His greed is wide as Sheol; like death he has never enough.'

> 1.15: 'He brings them all up with a hook.
> he drags them out with his net, he gathers them in his seine;
> so he rejoices and exults.
> Therefore he sacrifices to his net and burns incense to his seine.
> V. 11b: . . . whose own might is their god!'

It is the distancing involved in this wording which makes possible an objective view of the historical phenomenon of a superpower which knows no bounds to its conquests. The prophet sees in this a transgression of the limits imposed on man as a creature: power becomes his god. This insight is based on the prophetic tradition, Isaiah in particular, but also on intensive personal reflection, and it has found expression in the comparisons. This shows the possibilities of comparisons.

*Comparisons in Zephaniah.* Zephaniah is structured like the major prophetic books: 1.2–2.3 and 3.1–8 oracles of judgment over Judah; 2.4–15 oracles against the nations; 3.11–20 oracles of salvation for Judah. Comparisons in the oracles of judgment over Judah, 1.1–2.3; 3.1–8. The heat or the fire of God's wrath is frequently proclaimed, 1.18; 2.1; 3.8; the day of Yahweh's judgment is described as sacrifice, 1.7. The result of God's intervention: distress comes over humans 'so they shall walk like the blind',

1.17. They become 'like the drifting chaff', 2.1. God's intervention is preceded by a test, 1.12: 'At that time I will search Jerusalem with lamps', as in Jeremiah.

In the context of the indictment we find an original and expressive comparison, 1.12b: '. . . and I will punish the men who are thickening upon their lees'. It contains a historical perspective: once there was fresh, pure wine, but all that is left are stale, dry lees. The people of Jerusalem have become torpid on these worthless remains. Their actions, speech, and thought have become torpid. This leads to an indictment of the leadership in 3.3: 'Her officials within her are roaring lions; her judges are evening wolves . . .'. They have sinned in robbing those who have been entrusted to them. With the exception of 1.12 these comparisons frequently occur.

Oracles against the nations in Zeph. 2.4–15: among them there occurs a historical comparison in 2.9: 'Moab shall become like Sodom, and the Ammonites like Gomorrah.' Oracles of salvation over Judah in Zeph. 3.11–20: the oracle of judgment against the wicked shepherds in 3.3–4 has been supplemented (as often) in 3.13 by an oracle of salvation: 'For they shall pasture and lie down, and none shall make them afraid.'

We can recognize additions at several points. Some comparisons in the announcement of judgment differ from the others by the extravagance of the manner or extent of the destruction, 1.17: 'Their blood shall be poured out like dust, and their flesh like dung', and 1.18: 'In the fire of his jealous wrath all the earth shall be consumed', similarly 3.8b. This reveals a transition to apocalyptic. The exaggerating comparisons often lose their sharpness: that blood shall be poured out like dust is an inappropriate comparison.

## Comparisons in Ezekiel

A first glance at the comparisons in Ezekiel gives a contradictory impression. One is inclined to ask whether they really all reflect the language of one person, and if so, how these considerable differences are to be explained. At any

rate the distance between Ezekiel and the comparisons in
the prophets prior to him is self-evident. Some texts give
the impression of an exuberant, almost explosive use of
comparisons, which breaks the previous mould of the
genre and which as such does not occur previously. In
some of these texts the transition from prophecy to apocalyptic is apparent.

In line with the style of Ezekiel's prophecy, simple
comparisons recede in the face of larger constructions. As
in the previous prophets the comparisons are related to the
respective speech forms.

Comparisons in the announcement of judgment: 7.10 f.:
'Violence has grown up into a rod of wickedness; none
of them shall remain . . .' (text corrupt); 12.13 catching
with a net (repeated almost verbatim in 17.20 and 32.3);
13.11, 13 judgment as a tempest; 21.1–5 destruction by
fire: 'against the wood in the South' (author's translation);
22.17–22 purification in the fiery furnace, cf. 15.1–8; 21.6–
12, 13–22, 23–27 judgment represented by the sword.

Comparisons in the indictment: these are concentrated
in the indictment of the leadership. (a) Against the prophets, 13.4: 'Your prophets have been like foxes among
ruins', i.e. they settle on the ruin of Israel (W. Eichrodt).
13.5: they 'have not gone up into the breaches, or built up
a wall for the house of Israel'; 13.10: '. . . when the people
build a wall, these prophets daub it with whitewash', cf.
vv. 12, 14; 22.28. (b) Against the princes – against the
nobles, 22.25: they are 'like a roaring lion tearing the
prey', cf. v. 27: 'like wolves tearing the prey, shedding
blood'. Typical of Ezekiel is the combination of several
motifs in a *single* comparison, as e.g. in 15.1–8. The basic
comparison between divine judgment and destruction by
fire is expanded in this case by the antithesis between
ordinary brushwood and the wood of the noble vine:
both, when they are dried up, are only of use for the fire:
'how does the wood of the vine surpass any wood?', 15.2.
This implies the accusation that Israel, the noble vine, has
become worthless, cf. Jer. 2.21. This combination is also
hinted at in 6.1–10 where the announcement of judgment

is addressed 'toward the mountains of Israel': this implies the indictment of idolatry in high places.

The use of metaphors is also typical of Ezekiel. In 36.25 the metaphor of cleansing ('to sprinkle with water', 'to cleanse') is used for forgiveness. Transformation and renewal is also described in metaphors: to put a new heart and a new spirit within them (cf. Jeremiah), heart of stone – heart of flesh (v. 26). The promise of the repopulation of Jerusalem in v. 30 is strengthened by the comparison with the large number of sacrificial lambs which are brought to Jerusalem for the great festivals. The promise in the call vision in 3.9 also has a similar intensifying function: 'Like adamant harder than flint have I made your forehead'.

A parable in the oracle of judgment against the leadership (ch. 34). In contrast to the oracles of judgment against the leadership in ch. 13.1–23, which correspond to those of the earlier prophets, ch. 34 is a genuine parable thought through right down to the smallest detail. This parable elaborates on the relationships between shepherd and flock. The actions of the shepherd and the fate of the flock correspond entirely to the everyday experience of the prophet's audience. The parable is based on a tradition of clearly defined duties of the shepherd which can be found in Gen. 31.38–41 as well as in the Codex Hammurabi. It is the most detailed pastoral parable in the Bible. Ch. 34 is a genuine parable insofar as in it one process in one area, which is well-known and familiar to the audience from their day to day experience, is juxtaposed with another process from another area, which it is to address. With the help of the former the audience is meant to come to a conclusion which also then applies to the latter. Both processes, the events between shepherd and flock (the image used for the comparison) and what happens between the rulers (kings) of Israel and the people of Israel (what is being compared), have the same aim: the scattering of the flock (= the scattering of Israel in exile). The parable is intended as support for the judgment on the shepherds in v. 10. As such, the parable in Ezek. 34 functions in the context of a prophetic speech form, the announcement of judgment against the leaders of Israel. The structure of Ezek. 34.1–31:

> 1–2a:  Introduction, commission.
> 2b–10:  Woe to the bad shepherds.
>> 2b–6:  Indictment.
>>> 2b–4:  They have not fed the sheep properly.
>>> 5–6:  My sheep were scattered.
>> 7–10:  Announcement of judgment against the bad shepherds.
>>> 7–8:  Repetition of the indictment.
>>> 9–10:  I will put an end to their shepherding.
> 11–16: I myself will shepherd my sheep.
>> 11:  I myself will search for my sheep = v. 16.
>> 12:  As a shepherd I will rescue them and bring them back, gather them from the nations.
>> 13, 14:  I will feed them on the mountains of Israel.
>> 16:  the lost, the strayed, the crippled.
> 17–22: Expansion:  I will judge between the strong and the weak.
> 23–24: Expansion:  I will set up David as shepherd over them.
> 25–30: Expansion:  I will make a covenant of peace with them.
>> 27, 30:  And they shall know that I, the LORD their God, am with them.
> 31: Supplementary conclusion: you are the sheep of my pasture.

The structure of this chapter, which is dominated from beginning to end by the comparison with shepherd and flock, is easily recognizable. The comparison comprises vv. 1–16; what follows are additions (by whom can remain an open question) recognizable by the fact that in v. 31 they are linked by means of a supplementary bracket with vv. 1–16. The comparison vv. 1–16 is divided into an oracle of judgment vv. 2b–10 and an oracle of salvation vv. 11–16, held together by the comparison: the bad shepherds – the good shepherd. The difference between both parts is that, while vv. 2b–10 have the structure of a prophetic oracle of judgment (vv. 2b–6 indictment, vv.7–10 an- nouncement, which, corresponding to Ezekiel's style, re- peats the indictment at the beginning of the announcement in vv. 7–8), the oracle of salvation in vv. 11–16 displays no recognizable structure, but simply enumerates what the shepherd plans to do with the flock. This structure reveals the following: in vv. 2b–10 a pro- phetic oracle of judgment has been dressed up as a com- parison between shepherd and flock, which is based on the indictment against the leadership in Israel. The same can be found in the Song of the Vineyard in Isa. 5.1–7. But unlike Isa. 5.1–7, in Ezek. 34 an oracle of salvation, which continues the parable, follows the oracle of judgment. This is necessitated by the special commission due to the situation in which the prophet Ezekiel finds himself; after the judgment he becomes the messenger of rescue and return (the same in ch. 37). The oracle of salvation in vv. 11–16 could just as well form an independent unit; it is, however, the prophet's intention in 34.1–16 with its two parts to present the two sections of his commission as a connected narrative in two acts. This is made possible by the comparison which has been expanded into a two-part parable.

The parallelism of image and subject matter cannot be found in the expansions in vv. 17–30. Whether they are by Ezekiel or are secondary, they show that the sense of this parallelism has disappeared.

The comparison which dominates vv. 1–16 often occurs in later texts. We can confidently assume that Ezek. 34 represents the original form which was frequently copied.

Allegories for the history of Israel. Typical of Ezekiel's prophecy is the expansion of the indictment against Israel to cover her entire history. This is a continuation of the contrast motif of earlier prophecy in which Israel's present apostasy is confronted by God's previous acts of salvation towards her. In the face of the immediately imminent end of the people's history (ch. 7), the prophet views this history which as a whole is now reaching its end. For him the comparison expanded into an allegory serves to represent this whole:

16.1–63:   the two sisters
17.1–24:   the great eagle and the trees
19.1–14:   lament over the fate of the royal family
(20.1–31:  'let them know the abomination of their fathers!')
23.1–49:   the two sisters.

In 20.1–31 the prophet receives the commission: 'let them know the abominations of their fathers!' (as in 16.1); the following development is a summary of the history of Israel as a history of apostasy. In it Ezekiel uses no comparisons. Such an accusatory summary of the history of Israel is framed as an allegory in chs 16 and 23. In both cases the story of two sisters is told, the difference being that in ch. 16, in accordance with the contrast motif of pre-exilic prophecy, the time of apostasy (vv. 15–34 the whore) follows a positive section (vv. 3–14 the foundling; cf. Hos. 9.10), whereas in ch. 23 the two sisters practise wantonness right from the start. This means that the history of Israel is presented in a one-sided fashion as a history of apostasy.

The two chapters 17 and 19 deal with the history of the monarchy; both are allegories, the character of the allegory being more pronounced in ch. 17 than in ch. 19. The allegory dealing with two Judaean kings (ch. 17) has the structure of an oracle of judgment: judgment falls on a king who has broken his word. Ch. 19 is a lament concerning the fate of the royal dynasty (the lioness). Ch. 17 proves to be an allegory from the fact that in vv. 11–21 the interpretation of the 'propounded riddle' (v. 2) follows: 'Do you not know what these things mean?' (v. 12). Moreover, the juxtaposition of eagle and trees can only be understood allegorically.

The symbolic actions. In Ezekiel symbolic actions proliferate. This may be due to the proximity of the judgment, but it is also in accordance with the character of his prophecy. The majority have the function of intensifying the announcement of judgment, as when the prophet represents the siege and capture of Jerusalem in a symbolic action in 4.1–3; cf. 4.4–8, 9–17; 5.1–4; 6.11–14; 12.1–7, 17–20; 24.1–14, 15–24. In some of these symbolic actions he has to suffer, as in 3.22–27; 4.4–8, 9–17; 12.1–7, 17–20; 24.15–24. In 4.4–8 he bears the guilt of Israel. But in all symbolic actions the prophet's existence has become part of his message, as in Jeremiah.

The two symbolic actions 2.8–10; 3.1–3 (the eating of the scroll) and 3.4–21 = ch. 33 (the watchman) belong to the context of the prophet's commission. In the commission to eat the scroll with the message of judgment, the intensification over against Jer. 1 has been increased to almost grotesque proportions, which is typical of Ezekiel.

Comparisons in the oracles against the nations Ezek. 25–32; 35. The oracles against Israel's smaller neighbours include no comparisons: 25; 26; 28; 35, and the same is true of the oracle against Egypt in ch. 30. But comparisons completely dominate chs 27 (Tyre); 29 (Egypt); 31 (Egypt) and 32 (Egypt). In ch. 27 Tyre is compared to a stately ship, Egypt in 29 and 32 to a crocodile, and in 31 to a noble tree. In 27; 31; and 32 the modified structure of a death lament can be recognized, partly combined in various ways with the structure of a prophetic oracle of judgment. Ch. 27 is a lament over the fall of Tyre (vv. 25b–26), sung by the sea peoples (vv. 28–36). The size and beauty of the city is represented by the comparison with a stately ship, an originally independent song; the comparison has the same function as the praise of a tribe in the tribal sayings Gen. 49, perhaps as a further development of the latter. The style of this song shows no connection with the language of the prophet Ezekiel and the whole chapter has no connection with his prophecy (Tyre is not accused and her fall is not a judgment of God). There has been appended to the song in prose a list of the commercial goods of the city (vv. 12–25) in quite a different style and of quite different origin. The comparison vv. 4–10 therefore has no original connection with prophecy, but rather resembles the comparisons in the tribal sayings.

All these oracles against the superpowers, with their extended comparisons, give the impression of being secondary literary compositions combining elements of diverse origin. In them borrowed motifs crop up all the time. That the comparisons have a history in the OT is nowhere as apparent as in Ezekiel's oracles against the nations. These expanded comparisons no longer have the spontaneous and original character of those of the pre-exilic prophets; unlike them they no longer follow necessarily from the context of the prophetic speech form (the oracles against Israel's small neighbours do not employ any comparisons). The connection has become looser, the comparisons belong in part originally to different contexts. In this case one really does get the impression that some of these comparisons are purely decorative (Aristotle's 'ornatus').

The visions. In contrast to previous prophecy the visions form an essential part of the Book of Ezekiel. That fact already demonstrates the transition here to apocalyptic. The visions have only peripheral contact with the comparisons. But they are clearly connected with each other in the three parts chs 1–3; 8–11; 37; 40–48. Chs 1–3 culminate in the prophet's commission to announce judgment in 2.8–10 and 3.1–3. Then there follows a series of symbolic actions concerning this announcement of judgment. Chs 8–11 partly repeat chs 1–3, partly develop them further; in them the emphasis is on the indictment. This leads to accusations spanning the whole history of Israel. In chs 33–37 there follows the message of salvation with the vision of the resurrection of the dead bones at the end of ch. 37. The book concludes in chs 40–48 with the vision of the new temple; but all the previous visions have also been profoundly influenced by the cult. The two passages at the end of chs 1–3 and 33–37 respectively (i.e. 2.8–10; 3.1–3 and ch. 37) could be described as symbolic actions (as by G. Fohrer, 1953, and W. Zimmerli, Ezekiel, Introduction, p. 28). But they differ from prophetic symbolic actions inasmuch as they do not occur in front of witnesses and should therefore rather be included among the visions. Both texts have in common the fact that in 2.8–10 and 3.1–3 the prophet receives the commission to announce judgment, and in ch. 37 the commission to announce the rescue of the people from death; the first is compared with the eating of the scroll, the other with the word addressed to the dead bones. This time the transition to apocalyptic is evident in the transcendent character of the symbolic actions.

The new function of comparisons in the description of the vision, which occurs only here in the OT, also belongs to the transition to apocalyptic. It is the explanatory function of comparisons (see above p. 12) which occurs in reports, applied in both cases to explain what is unknown from what is known (e.g. the manna), but in this case with the deliberate intention of highlighting what is seen in the vision in all its transcendence. These comparisons run through the descriptions of the visions almost line for line: 'like the gleaming of a chrysolite', 'like the sound of many waters'; in ch. 1 alone vv. 4, 7, 13, 14, 16, 22, 24 (three times), 26, 27, 28 (twice). It is worth noting in this regard that in these visions at the point of transition to apocalyptic, at the time of the exile, we meet for the first time in the OT comparisons which to a considerable extent describe something existing, to which they relate. Previously the act of comparing referred predominantly to an event. When, however, comparisons become of essential significance for describing an existing thing, then this latter represents something transcendent, beheld in a vision. This explains the fact that the Greek understanding, derived from Aristotle, of the comparison as a metaphor, which is basically related to being, is radically different from the OT understanding of the comparison, which refers primarily to an event.

To sum up: in the comparisons in the Book of Ezekiel we find, in accordance with our first impression, a transition, which could also be called a break (see above p. 78), corresponding to the transition from prophecy to apocalyptic. Ezekiel still has comparisons of the same sort and with the same function as the prophets before him, but at the same time there is apparent a kind of disintegration, on the one hand in the transition to allegory, and on the other in the exuberant growth of the comparisons and at the same time a loosening of the strict parallelism between the subjects of comparison and their images. This is particularly evident in the comparisons in the oracles against the nations and in those in the description of visions. In ch. 27 (Tyre – stately ship) the comparison does not correspond to the process which is mentioned in vv. 26b, 27, but rather the previous splendour of the city is compared to the splendour of a ship (motif of the death lament). In the vision the comparison serves predominantly to describe something transcendent. In both cases the comparison has a decorative function. At the same time the connection between the comparison's subject and its image is loosened, particularly in the historical allegories. The Book of Ezekiel represents a clear turning-point in the function and significance of comparisons. When Ezekiel is told to speak in riddles (17.1 f.) and the people reply: 'Does he not always speak to us in riddles?', this shows a decline in prophetic immediacy.

### Comparisons in Deutero-Isaiah (Isa. 40–55)

In Deutero-Isaiah we meet very few standard comparisons taken over from tradition. The overwhelming majority of them have been coined afresh in the context of the prophet's message. These comparisons are such an integral part of the prophet's message that they cannot be extricated from it. Often it is scarcely possible to decide with certainty whether we are dealing with a comparison or with direct speech. The prophet's language has such a powerful poetic colouring that the line between reality and comparison becomes blurred. When Deutero-Isaiah speaks of the way through the wilderness he means the way back to Canaan from Babylonian captivity. But this is so full of allusions that it becomes more than, and something different from, just the march of a group liberated from captivity. On the one hand it is simultaneously the 'classic way through the wilderness', the exodus from Egypt (43.16–21), on the other it can also be the 'way' in the metaphorical sense of making possible the liberation, as in the prologue 40.1–11.

Another metaphorical usage, which can hardly be understood as a comparison in the usual sense and which in the OT occurs only in Deutero-Isaiah, is present where different meanings of the same verb confront one another: burdening and burdening 43.22–28, carrying and carrying 46.1–4. In this case the comparison contains such a concentrated reflection that it is only possible in this one place, viz. the message of Deutero-Isaiah. Because of the decidedly poetical language of the prophet his comparisons have a strongly rhetorical character. They are consciously and deliberately aimed at affecting the audience. One

example of this is the extended poem 40.12–31 where the
fact of Yahweh's unmeasurable nature is made concrete in
rhetorical questions which illustrate it: 'Who has measured
the waters in the hollow of his hand?' Here as in many
other places the comparison (in this case a contrasting one)
passes over into hyperbole which is, of course, a typical
rhetorical device. In Deutero-Isaiah it is often impossible
to draw firm distinctions between hyperbole and comparison. If one attempts to classify the comparisons in
Deutero-Isaiah in groups, this is best done in accordance
with the speech forms used; a different classification is
hardly possible. Since Deutero-Isaiah's message is one of
salvation, one would expect the largest group of comparisons in this context. Not only is this the case, however,
but furthermore the majority of groups of comparisons are
allocated to the message of liberation in a clearly recognizable context:

1. The captives receive the message of liberation. It is
based on the message of forgiveness.

2. Liberation includes preparing the way, Cyrus' permis-
sion to return, and the return itself.

3. The disputations (God – Israel) and the trial speeches
(God – the nations) are indirectly connected with the
message of liberation.

4. The promise of liberation is augmented by the promise of blessing for the time after the return.

5. The praise of God, which transforms the lament, is
the response to the saving message.

6. The comparisons in the Servant Songs form a special
group.

This leaves very few passages unallotted.

The message of liberation is presented as the report of a
watchman on a high mountain 40.9 f., of a messenger
who comes across the mountains 52.7, 9 (marking beginning and end of chs 40–52). It is a joyful message: 'How
beautiful . . . are the feet of him who brings good tidings',
52.7, it makes the 'waste places of Jerusalem . . . break
forth together into singing', 52.9. The unspecific meaning
of 'messenger' in the prologue is characteristic of

Deutero-Isaiah: the messenger – the watchman on the high mountain – Zion, herald of good tidings. This represents only a hint that the prophet who speaks here is a different kind of messenger from his predecessors; bringing a message of joy is rather different from bringing one of judgment. With him the messenger's language becomes completely irrelevant; everything is geared to getting the joyful message accepted. Hence Zion becomes the herald of joy. Hence, too, the reaction of the addressees is part of Deutero-Isaiah's preaching. For the liberation is achieved by God's coming and intervention, which is sought in the laments of the oppressed and which in early narratives is described as God's epiphany. This epiphany is also reflected in some Psalms, e.g. 18, and is echoed in the comparisons:

> 'God comes with might, and his arm rules for him' (40.10)
> 'The LORD goes forth like a mighty man' (42.13).

He cries out like a woman in travail 42.14–17, after a long silence. The comparison with the cry of a woman in travail is used here in contrast to that of a lamenting woman: this cry marks the beginning of new life! The message of liberation is based on forgiveness:

> 'her time of service is ended,
> that her iniquity is pardoned' (40.2).

In the disputations God confronts the accusation that he has deserted his people with the assertion that Israel's guilt necessitates judgment, but that he has now forgiven his people:

> 'I, I am he who blots out your transgressions' (43.25).
> 'For you will forget the shame of your youth,
> and the reproach of your widowhood
> (the indictment: you have deserted me!)
> you will remember no more' (54.4b).

Cf. the allusion in 54.9: 'like the days of Noah . . .'. It is part of the prophet's message of forgiveness that Israel has to understand the fall of Jerusalem and the exile as God's judgment. It was 'time of service', 'iniquity' from which Israel is now liberated, 40.2, this was due to Yahweh's wrath: 'So he poured upon him the heat of his anger', 42.25; 'Jerusalem, . . . who have drunk to the dregs the bowl of staggering', 51.17–23; 'for your iniquities you were sold . . . put away', 50.1–3; 52.3; the deserted woman 54.4–6. It is significant that in the review of God's judgment now completed the comparisons more than once resemble those of the prophets of judgment.

The whole emphasis of Deutero-Isaiah's message of salvation lies on the return; here we also find most of the comparisons and those specific to him. The prologue 40.1–11 has as its goal the announcement of the return, vv. 9–11. Yahweh comes with the 'reward', the 'recompense' of his saving act:

> 'He will feed his flock like a shepherd,
> he will gather the lambs in his arms,
> he will carry them in his bosom,
> and gently lead those that are with young.'

When the returning one is not Israel, but Yahweh himself who brings his people with him as a 'reward', as 're-compense', the poet means to express by this the fact that the return is wholly and completely Yahweh's liberating and redeeming act. Thus God's intervention has two aspects: one of them is the mighty act v. 10, the other God's gracious condescension, as the comparison with the shepherd shows in this case. This is just like Ps. 80.2 where his people beg for the help of the gracious shepherd. Therefore the prologue deliberately emphasizes the fact that the shepherd graciously turns to each individual. Similarly 42.16: 'And I will lead the blind in a way that they know not'; 52.12: 'for the LORD will go before you, and the God of Israel will be your rear guard', as a marching army needs a vanguard and a rearguard. The comparison with the shepherd as used here (the return of the exiles depicted as the coming of the shepherd who brings his flock) is unique in the OT. Part of the shepherd's activity is also the gathering of those dispersed, 43.5–6. But the way must first be prepared, 40.3–5:

> 'In the wilderness prepare the way of the LORD,
> make straight in the desert a highway for our God.
> Every valley shall be lifted up,
> and every mountain and hill be made low;
> the uneven ground shall become level,
> and the rough places a plain.
> And the glory of the LORD shall be revealed . . .'.

Preparing the way in the desert and removing obstacles means that Yahweh through his intervention in history (Cyrus) makes the return of the people possible. All passages in Deutero-Isaiah which deal with Cyrus relate to this preparing the way, in the first place the Cyrus oracle 44.24–45.7. The comparison in 40.3–4 is taken up again here and related to Cyrus, 45.1–2:

> 'Thus says the LORD to his anointed, to Cyrus . . .
> to open doors before him
> that gates may not be closed:
> I will go before you and level the mountains,
> I will break in pieces the doors of bronze
> and cut asunder the bars of iron . . '.

This comparison links ch. 45 with ch. 40 and confirms the interpretation offered there. The meaning of the other comparison, the opening and breaking of the gates, is equally unspecific. On the one hand it implies that Cyrus in his victorious triumph overcomes all obstacles; but the literal sense also comes through, viz. that the gates of cities and fortresses open up before him. As in the prologue 40.1–11, God's activity in history, here in the form of the Persian king Cyrus, is seen at one with his dominion over creation, 44.27–28:

> 'who says to the deep, "Be dry,
> I will dry up your rivers";
> who says of Cyrus, "He is my shepherd,
> and he shall fulfil all my purpose".'

This reveals a different peculiarity of Deutero-Isaiah's message also shared by the comparisons: it is akin to the

Psalms and includes psalm motifs. The Cyrus oracle is dominated by the praise of God, 45.5–7; in the Psalms the praise of God's majesty is unfolded: he is the creator – he is the Lord of history. Calling Cyrus in this way 'my shepherd' implies: he is my appointed leader who as such brings about the return of the people of God. In a different passage he is called the 'bird of prey from the east', 46.11:

'calling a bird of prey from the east,
the man of my counsel from a far country.'

A further group of passages deals with the return of the people on the way through the wilderness. In all of them protection for the people on the way is promised, protection from dangers, 43.1–7:

'When you pass through the waters I will be with you;
and through the rivers, they shall not overwhelm you;
when you walk through fire you shall not be burned,
and the flame shall not consume you.'

This includes provisions, the preservation from hunger and thirst, 41.17–20: 'I will open rivers on the bare heights . . . fountains . . . I will put in the wilderness the cedar, . . . olives . . .'; 43.16–21: 'I will make a way in the wilderness and rivers in the desert . . . to give drink to my chosen people . . .'; 48.21: 'They thirsted not when he led them through the deserts; he made water flow for them from the rock; he cleft the rock and the water gushed out'; 49.7–12: 'They shall feed along the ways, on all bare heights shall be their pasture; they shall not hunger or thirst . . . for he who has pity on them will lead them, and by springs of water will guide them.' All these passages are also comparisons in a different sense: they point to the exodus from Egypt; this will happen to you, too! The old exodus and the new! As in the Book of Exodus, here too the way through the wilderness follows the act of liberation.

Indirectly linked to the message of liberation are the disputations (God – Israel) and the judgment speeches (God – the nations). In both the comparisons have a

somewhat reduced significance, being essentially argu-
mentation. The main purpose of the disputations is to
make Israel understand that judgment had to overtake her;
the people are addressed as blind and deaf (42.18 f.; 43.8–
15), who will nevertheless have to be God's witnesses. In
face of the lament that God has deserted her, 50.1–3 asks:
'Where is your mother's bill of divorce . . .?' cf. 49.14–26:
'Can a woman forget her sucking child?' Countering the
doubts that God is active through Cyrus, 45.9–13: 'Woe
to him who strives with his maker, an earthen vessel . . .';
he refuses the objection that Israel did sacrifice to God for
such a long time in 43.22–28: You did not really serve me
with your sacrifices, and you made me serve with your
sins. 46.1–4, a judgment speech (God – the nations) is, like
43.22–28, based on a different use of the same word. This
passage is an imitation of a message of victory. The
carrying off of the idols on beasts of burden is contrasted
with Yahweh's carrying of Israel through the catastrophe
and into the future. A truly profound comparison! The
mighty gods of a powerful empire are in the case of defeat
not even able to rescue their own images, let alone their
people! It is left to animals to carry off the images.
Yahweh by contrast has carried his people through the
gravest catastrophe in her history and: 'even to your old
age . . . I will carry you'.

The two chapters 54 and 55 are no longer, like the
beginning, determined by the promise of saving, but by
the future blessing. This is also evident in the language of
the comparisons: the promise of multiplication forms the
background to 54.1–10:

> 54.1: 'Sing, O barren one, who did not bear;
> break forth into singing . . ., you who have not been in travail!
> For the children of the desolate one will be more
> than the children of her that is married'.
> V. 2: 'Enlarge the place of your tent,
> and let the curtains of your habitations be stretched out;
> hold not back, lengthen your cords and strengthen your stakes'.
> V. 3: 'For you will spread abroad to the right and to the left,
> and your descendants will possess the nations
> and will people the desolate cities.'
> V. 4: '. . . for you will forget the shame of your youth,

and the reproach of your widowhood you will remember no
more'.
V. 6: 'For the LORD has called you like a wife forsaken . . .'.

The compassion which God now shows to his people
remains forever,

> 54.9–10: 'For this is like the days of Noah to me:
> as I swore that the waters of Noah should no more . . .,
> so have I sworn that I will not be angry with you . . .
> For the mountains may depart and the hills be removed,
> but my steadfast love shall not depart from you,
> and my covenant of peace . . .'.

The everlasting covenant (promise to David) is also proclaimed in 55.1–5, which opens with the call to the
(hungry and) thirsty: 'Ho, every one who thirsts, come to
the waters . . .!', and which promises the supply of food
and drink in plenty. 55.6–11 gives the assurance that the
promise will come true, by means of a comparison taken
from creation which is close to a parable, 55.8 f.: 'For my
thoughts are not your thoughts . . ., for as the heavens are
higher than the earth . . .', v. 10 f.: 'For as the rain and the
snow come down from heaven, and return not thither
but water the earth, making it bring forth and sprout,
. . . so shall my word be that goes forth from my mouth,
it shall not return to me empty, but it shall accomplish
that which I purpose, and prosper in the thing for which
I sent it'.

As in the whole OT saving and blessing belongs to the
gracious acts of God, so in Deutero-Isaiah God's liberating
deed includes blessing, which makes growth and continual
dwelling on the land possible. This is made plain in the
final section (chs 54–55) which is quite distinct from what
goes before, which is determined by God's saving action.
The fact that all comparisons in this part (54–55) derive from
the sphere of God's creation is sure and unequivocal proof
that the comparisons grow out of their respective contexts,
belong to them, and receive their function from them. The
comparison in 55.10–11; 'For as the rain . . . so shall my
word' receives its special weight from the fact that it forms a
conclusion and, at the same time, a counterpart to the

beginning, 40.8: 'but the word of our God will stand for ever'. This weight has the effect of expanding the comparison into a short story. Thus the comparison comes close to being a parable, similar, as regards content, to Jesus' parables of the sower (Mk 4.3–9) and the self-growing seed (Mk 4.26–29). This is thus a classic example of the way leading from the comparison in the OT to the parables in the NT.

As the two passages about the word of God which frame the whole of Deutero-Isaiah's message are determined by the counterpoint of lament and praise, so is his whole message. His message of salvation is addressed to the situation of suffering which followed the fall of Jerusalem, and to the lament in which the suffering found expression. This is clear from the lament about the evanescence of all things in the prologue 40.6–7, the lament of the people 40.27 to which vv. 28–31 reply and in contrast to which in 40.12–26 the praise of God's majesty is unfolded as an address to the tired and despondent. The whole of Deutero-Isaiah's message is determined by a call to praise in the short songs of praise at the respective conclusions of the larger parts, a call to joy which echoes through the whole and which is extended to all creatures.

The many comparisons in 40.12–31 all serve the purpose of reviving and reawakening the praise of God, which is familiar to the exiles here addressed from the services of the past, but which has fallen silent among them. They are contrasting comparisons:

40.12: 'Who has measured the waters in the hollow of his hand . . ., and weighed the mountains in scales . . .',

or hyperboles:

40.15: 'Behold, the nations are like a drop from a bucket . . . behold, he takes up the isles like fine dust . . .'.

V. 16: 'Lebanon would not suffice for fuel, nor are its beasts enough for a burnt offering'.

V. 22: 'It is he who sits above the circle of the earth, and its inhabitants are like grasshoppers . . .';

V. 23: 'who brings princes to naught . . .'.

V. 24: 'Scarcely are they planted . . .,
when he blows upon them and they wither . . .'.

In the Psalms of Praise God's majesty manifests itself
through creation and history. The praise of God's majesty
in Isa. 40 has the same structure whereby the many
comparisons have the function of intensifying and thus, in
the disputation, of reawakening the praise of God which
had been silenced. This whole fugue of praise of the
majesty of God tends towards the praise of his mercy in
vv. 27–31, which supplements the former and is also
expanded by a contrasting comparison:

'He gives power to the faint . . .,
even youth shall faint and be weary, . . .
but they who wait for the LORD shall renew their strength,
they shall mount up with wings like eagles . . .'.

This 'renewal of the strength' of the tired and despondent
is the subject of the whole poem vv. 12–31. Thus the
prophet, who is a poet, fulfils the commission which he
has from God: 'Comfort my people!' But merely to
remind them of the Psalms of Praise previously sung by
quoting them verbatim would not be of any real comfort.
Through the many comparisons the old words become
new and living; through them he adapts the Psalms to the
changed situation. Only in this way do they regain their
old power of expression. 40.12–31 is an example of the fact
that a complete and extensive text only comes to life by
means of the comparisons. The same is also true in another
way of the Imperative Call to Praise, changed into a call to
rejoice, which permeates the whole section. This call anticipates the reaction, the response of those liberated, and
combines it with the announcement,

52.9: 'Break forth together into singing, you waste places of
Jerusalem,
for the LORD has comforted his people,
he has redeemed Jerusalem.'

When this Call to Praise addresses the 'waste places of
Jerusalem', this is not an actual comparison, but rather the
daring personification of a destroyed city, applying in fact
to the remnant of the people. They can be summoned to

rejoice already because: 'the return of the LORD to Zion'
(v.8) is certain.

Poetic power and depth are evident in the way that
Deutero-Isaiah takes up the wider dimension of the Call
to Praise in the Psalms: all creatures are summoned to
praise,

> 55.12: 'The mountains and the hills before you shall break forth
> into singing,
> and all the trees of the field shall clap their hands'.

The reason for this is given in 52.10: '. . . and all the ends
of the earth shall see the salvation of our God.' These calls
to rejoice which permeate Deutero-Isaiah's message give it
from beginning to end its basic tone of joyous expectation.
This is made possible by the combination of announcements of salvation and psalms which only occurs here in
the entire OT.

Comparisons in the context of the ministry of the
Servant of the Lord. The use of comparisons is typical
of the songs of the suffering servant, as the servant is
spoken of in a merely allusive and sometimes deliberately
veiling way. The comparisons have at least in part a
deliberately disguising function. It is said of the person
of the servant:

> 53.2 f. 'For he grew up . . . like a young plant,
> and like a root out of dry ground; . . .
> a man of sorrows, and acquainted with grief;
>
> and as one from whom men hide their faces . . .'

His ministry is one through the word:

> 49.2: 'He made my mouth like a sharp sword,
> in the shadow of his hand he hid me;
> he made me a polished arrow,
> in his quiver he hid me away'.

> 50:4: 'The LORD God has given me the tongue of those who are
> taught,
> that I may know how to sustain with a word him that is weary.
> Morning by morning he awakens . . . my ear to hear as those who
> are taught.'

His word is not meant to destroy, but to heal and alleviate, 42.3: 'A bruised reed he will not break, and a dimly burning wick he will not quench'. He himself will be preserved in executing his ministry, v. 4: 'He will not burn dimly or be bruised' (alternative reading, similarly 50.7). But in his ministry he is to suffer as a representative, 50.7: 'therefore I have set my face like a flint'; 53.4: 'he has borne our griefs . . .', v. 5: 'But he was wounded for our transgressions, he was bruised for our iniquities', v. 7: 'He was oppressed, and he was afflicted, yet he opened not his mouth; like a lamb that is led to the slaughter, and like a sheep that before its shearers is dumb, so he opened not his mouth.' Of those for whom he suffered it is said 53.6: 'All we like sheep have gone astray; we have turned every one to his own way', and of those who cause him to suffer and kill him 50.9: 'all of them will wear out like a garment'. His ministry is not confined to Israel 42.6: 'I have given you . . . as a light to the nations' (=49.6). He will gain recognition after his death 53.12: 'Therefore I will divide him a portion with the great, and he shall divide the spoil with the strong.'

There is no need to comment on the individual comparisons. As in Deutero-Isaiah's message, the comparisons reflect in general outline what the songs say about the Servant of the Lord.

The few comparisons in Isa. 40–55 which do not fit the main drift of Deutero-Isaiah's message are either untypical of him or secondary additions,

> 42.15: 'I will lay waste mountains and hills,
> and dry up all their herbage;
> I will turn the rivers into islands,
> and dry up the pools'.

Although this does not appear to fit the context (return through the desert 42.14–17), what we have here are, as in the Psalm of Praise (e.g. Ps. 107), simply the two sides of the transforming acts of God 41.15: 'Behold I will make of you a threshing sledge, new, sharp, and having teeth; you shall thresh the mountains and crush them, and you shall make the hills like chaff.' This cannot mean that God makes Israel an instrument for the destruction of her enemies, 'mountains and hills' are rather to be understood as in the prologue, i.e. as obstacles for the journey home. According to 41.15, Israel will overcome these obstacles. The comparisons in 48.4, 'Because I know that you are obstinate, and your neck is an iron sinew and your forehead brass', belong to divine speech, a secondary expansion of 48.1–11 (for the detailed argument cf. my commentary *ad loc.*) – 47.1–15 contains the personification of Babylon; this chapter belongs to the oracles against the nations and is similar to those of Ezekiel.

In attempting to summarize the function of the comparisons in Deutero-Isaiah we can say that all of them, although in different ways, serve to illustrate the cry at the beginning of the book: 'Comfort my people!' They all intensify the comforting message, make it alive and relevant, and help it to be accepted. In addition to this is possible to define more precisely the particular functions of the comparisons in their respective contexts. Nevertheless, their one common function is rooted in the structure of the elements of the prophet's message of joy, as shown above (p. 87).

# Comparisons in Post-exilic Prophecy

## Comparisons in Trito-Isaiah

The following is based on the assumption that Trito-Isaiah is a post-exilic prophet of salvation, a successor of Deutero-Isaiah whose message he presupposes, but modifies in a changed situation. (See C. Westermann, *Isaiah 40–66*, OTL, 1969; W. Zimmerli, 'Zur Sprache Tritojesajas' . . . (1950). Only chs 60–62; 57.14–26; 65.16b–25; 66.6–16 are to be attributed to Trito-Isaiah.

Comparisons in the context of the message of salvation.

In 61.1–3 the prophet describes himself as messenger of salvation who has to announce the turning-point of the people's suffering: 'to bind up the brokenhearted', 'to grant to those who mourn in Zion – to give them a garland instead of ashes, the oil of gladness instead of mourning, the mantle of praise instead of a faint spirit; that they may be called oaks of righteousness, the planting of the LORD, that he may be glorified.' This message is unfolded in 60–62. The coming of salvation is compared to the coming of the light:

'Arise, shine;
for your light has come,
and the glory of the LORD has risen upon you.'

Similarly 62.1–2. The call to return and to prepare the way in 62.10–12 and 57.14 is formulated in close imitation of 40.1–11; the same is true of the call to rejoice in 65.18 and 66.10–11 and of the statement that the end of the time of suffering has arrived (61.10; 62.4 f.). But since Trito-Isaiah does not have a definite historical event to announce, but only the indefinite coming of an age of salvation, his comparisons are more general, not clearly circumscribed, and often have a wide range of meanings. The coming of Yahweh is several times announced in the mode of an epiphany: 59.15b–20; 62.10–12; 66.6, 15, 16, but the stage where the epiphany reaches earth is missing. The invitation to prepare the way in 57.14–21; 62.10 (Mk 1.3) in comparison with 40.1–11 lacks the connection with the real way of the return. The preparation of the way is meant to be understood in a 'spiritual sense' (W. Zimmerli, P. Volz, commentaries *ad loc.*).

Accordingly, Trito-Isaiah's message of salvation has hardly any concern with the past; it consists almost entirely of the promise of blessing. Whereas in Deutero-Isaiah the act of God is the reason for the call to rejoice, in Trito-Isaiah it is the participation in the blessings of the age of salvation, 66.10–11. Correspondingly, nearly all comparisons are derived from the sphere of creation. Salvation has risen upon Israel like a light, 60.1–3 (similarly 62.1;

60.19–20; 58.8–10; 59.9–11). Salvation is depicted as growth and prospering, as expansion, also as abundance, riches, and splendour. Israel is 'a people whom the LORD has blessed', 61.9; 65.23; 'oaks of righteousness', 61.3; 'the planting of the LORD that he may be glorified', 61.3; 61.11:

> 'For as the earth brings forth its shoots,
> and as a garden causes what is sown in it to spring up,
> so the LORD God will cause righteousness and praise
> to spring forth before all the nations'.

The people are promised multiplication (60.22) and long life (65.21). Israel is no longer deserted, but God has turned to her again like the bridegroom to the bride, 61.10; 62.4–5. The paltry and valueless is replaced by the precious and splendid, 60.17; 61.3; 66.11. The treasure of the nations are brought to Israel on ships 'that fly like a cloud', 60.8 f. (cf. 60.13; 61.5 f.; 66.12).

In Deutero-Isaiah the oracles of salvation are aimed at a definite event, in Trito-Isaiah they are predominantly descriptions of a continuous state; the same is true of the comparisons. They are frequently piled up (as e.g. in 61.1–3) and thereby lose their power and precision. The comparisons alone make it absolutely certain that chs 56–66 cannot be attributed to the same author as chs 40–55.

Comparisons in other contexts. The oracles of salvation in 60–62 have been framed by two communal laments in 59 and 63–64, whereas in Deutero-Isaiah elements of the communal lament have been integrated into the saving message. The comparisons occurring in this section belong to the context of the communal lament. It is worth noting that here, too, comparisons occur in large numbers: in 59.15b–20 Yahweh's intervention is described as an epiphany and Yahweh as a warrior:

> 'He put on righteousness as a breastplate,
> and a helmet of salvation upon his head;
> he put on garments of vengeance for clothing,
> and wrapped himself in fury as a mantle' (v. 17),

taken up in Eph. 6.14–17. This is no genuine comparison,

but rather a decoration bordering on allegory. Ch. 59 is shown to be a late text as well by the fact that the enemies of the people of God have been replaced by the wicked, as in the late Ps. 83. – 57.20 f. and 65.11–12 are descriptions of the wicked too. This is apparent in the comparisons:

'But the wicked are like the tossing sea;
for it cannot rest,
and its waters toss up mire and dirt.
There is no peace, says my God, for the wicked!' (57.20 f.).

'They hatch adders' eggs, they weave the spider's web . . .', 59.5 f.; 'These are smoke in my nostrils, a fire that burns all the day', 65.5. These comparisons belong to the context of the description of the wicked, as found in the expansion of the Foe-lament and in the speeches of Job's friends.

While the promises in Trito-Isaiah are unconditional and addressed to the people as a whole, in a later layer can be found conditional promises addressed to individuals who fulfil these conditions: 58.8–12, 13–14; 65.8–16a. The right kind of fasting is the subject of the exhortation 58.1–12: the one who fasts correctly is promised:

'Then shall your light break forth like the dawn . . .,
and you shall be like a watered garden, like a spring of water,
whose waters fail not' (vv. 8–11).

A comprehensive investigation of the comparisons in the OT would require a summary of the comparisons in all oracles of salvation. This has been omitted here because, in my opinion, it would presuppose a comprehensive investigation of salvation speech in the whole of the OT (not only in the prophets). At this point the results of previous scholarship are very uncertain. In my view research would have to start from the distinction between the promises of saving and of blessing, because these have different roots and a different history of transmission. It would have to begin with Deutero-Isaiah's message of salvation, because it can be dated with certainty, but also because in it the promises of saving and of blessing can be clearly distinguished. Further, the fact that Trito-Isaiah's oracles of salvation follow those of Deutero-Isaiah provides us, to start with, with a definite criterion for the history of salvation speech.

## Comparisons in Joel

Joel 1.1–5 is a call to communal lament because of an invasion of locusts which threatens to destroy everything (vv. 4, 6–7, 9–12, 16–18, 20). V. 6a compares this invasion with the attack of a powerful people whose 'teeth are lions' teeth', according to v. 6b. Vv. 13–14 summon to a fast, vv. 15 and 19 are beginning of the lament. It is only in ch. 2 that the announcement of God's judgment commences. In 2.1–3a the 'Day of the LORD' is announced, the approach of a mighty army (vv. 2b, 3a, 10–11). This approach is compared in vv. 3b–9 with the onset of a swarm of locusts, an extremely lively, poetically beautiful description. A development of the same motif occurs in 1.6. This description, however, is only very loosely connected with the frame of vv. 1–3a, 10–11, and has originally nothing to do with it. This is obvious from the 'awkward transition' (H. W. Wolff) between vv. 9 and 10, as also between 3a and 3b. The style of this description vv. 3b–9 is also different from that of the frame vv. 1–3a, 10–11. It represents a small independent poem similar to the description of the splendid ship of Tyre in Ezekiel. This poem has grown out of the observation of animals; v. 7b has an exact parallel in Prov. 30.27: 'The locusts have no king, yet all of them march in rank'.

The remaining comparisons in the Book of Joel. To the call for the people to lament is attached in 1.8 the comparison: 'like a virgin girded with sackcloth (who laments) for the bridegroom of her youth', a frequent personification of the people and their suffering. In the valley of Jehoshaphat Israel executes judgment on the nations:

'Put in the sickle, for the harvest is ripe.
Go in, tread, for the wine press is full.
The vats overflow, for their wickedness is great' (4.13; EVV 3.13).

The same comparison occurs in Micah 4.11–13 in the same context. 4.16b (EVV 3.16b): 'But the LORD is a refuge to his people, a stronghold to the people of Israel', is a motif of trust like Isa. 25.4; cf. Ps. 31.3; Isa. 17.10; Nahum 1.4.

## Comparisons in Obadiah

The Book of Obadiah is a small collection of oracles against the nations (principally against Edom). This is the context of the comparisons. Typically retribution is announced on Edom for her actions against Judah: 'your deeds shall return on your own head', v. 15; 'for as you have drunk . . ., all the nations round about shall drink', v. 16. God will execute his judgment on Edom through Israel:

> 'The house of Jacob shall be a fire,
> and the house of Joseph a flame,
> and the house of Esau a stubble;
> they shall burn them and consume them . . .' (v.18).

All the comparisons in vv. 4, 5–6, 15, 16, 18 also occur outside the Book of Obadiah; particularly obvious is the agreement of v. 4: 'Though you soar aloft like the eagle, though your nest is set among the stars', with Hab. 2.9. Drinking from the cup of wrath (or staggering) is a frequent image, e.g. Lam. 4.21, as is the comparison in v. 18.

## Comparisons in the Book of Jonah

The narrative contains no comparisons. This is in marked contrast to the psalm in ch. 2 which in vv. 4, 6, and 7 contains a host of comparisons for the agony of death.

## Comparisons in Zechariah

In the eight night visions 1.7–6.8 the prophetic word is replaced by that of the seer. Each one is divided into vision and interpretation, e.g. 1.8, 9. The interpretation is given by an *angelus interpres*; what God has announced in the vision is in code and must be decoded, as opposed to the comparison which is self-explanatory and needs no interpretation. As Zechariah's 'prophecy' in chs 1–8 is characterized by the visions in 1.7–6.8, this change marks the end of prophecy as it had continued right into the exile. Apart from the night visions chs 1–8 contain only a few comparisons, in part merely hinted at and peripheral. The high priest Joshua, rehabilitated by Zechariah, is called 'a brand plucked from the fire', 3.2. In 3.3–5 his filthy garments are taken off and festal clothes put on; this is something like a symbolic action. The king of the age of salvation is called 'the Branch', 3.8; 6.12. The obstacles to Zerubbabel's rebuilding of the temple are called 'the great mountain' in 4.7. The city is promised God's protection: 'For I will be to her a wall of fire round about' (2.5), and with regard to the earlier announcement of judgment: 'and I scattered them with a whirlwind among the nations', 7.14.

### Zech. 9–14. Deutero- (and Trito-) Zechariah

In an oracle of promise 9.11–17 Judah is assured, as retribution for her suffering, of bloody vengeance on her enemies. This includes several comparisons:

'For I have bent Judah as my bow:
I have made Ephraim its arrow.
. . . and wield you like a warrior's sword' (9.13).

God himself will intervene in battle, as in the Yahweh wars of the early period: 'and his arrows go forth like a lightning', v. 14, he 'will protect them' with his shield, v. 15a. The destruction of the enemy is painted in a harsh picture: 'they (subject uncertain) shall drink their blood like wine, and be full like a bowl', v. 15b. 'They are the flock of his people' as the result of God's victory. The sense of the following sentence is uncertain: 'for like the jewels of a crown they shall shine on his land'. 10.3–12 is a similar promise. 10.3a is the fragment of an oracle of judgment against the leadership, who here as so often are called shepherds (alternative reading: he-goats). 11.17 is also an oracle of woe over the wicked shepherd. As in Ezek. 34, God himself will take charge of his flock. In what follows the image is strangely changed: 'and he will make them like his proud steed in battle', 10.3b. The people are promised victory over their enemies, again in a very striking comparison: '. . . trampling the foe in the mud of the streets', v. 5.

11.1–3 is the announcement of the demise of a super-power in a comparison which imitates the lament about the demise of a community. The strong trees and the mighty lion represent the greatness and pride of the super-power; they are summoned to lament (to wail) over this demise, because its splendour has been destroyed. The section 11.4–16 ('Become shepherd of the flock doomed to slaughter') has a strongly allegorical character, and its interpretation is controversial.

Chs 12–14 show in different ways the transition from prophecy to apocalyptic, most strikingly ch. 14. Here, too, we meet comparisons, but they are all either taken over from older prophecy or they cannot be attributed to any recognizable context.

## Comparisons in Haggai and Malachi

In Haggai 2.10–14 we meet a new kind of comparison:

V. 10: '. . . the word of the LORD came by Haggai the prophet:
V. 11: Thus says the LORD of hosts: Ask the priests
to decide this question:
V. 12: If one carries holy flesh in the skirt of his garment,
and touches . . ., does it become holy?
The priests answered: No!
V. 13: Then said Haggai, If one who is unclean by contact
with a dead body touches . . .'
does it become unclean?
The priests answered, It does become unclean.

V. 14: Then Haggai said,
So it is with this people . . . before me,
says the LORD; and so with every work of their hands;
and what they offer there is unclean.'

Here we meet a new kind of comparison in the context of a doctrinal argument. A legal or cultic issue is settled by means of a comparison. The structure of this section shows how this entirely different comparison emerges from the prophetic oracle. What remains is the framework of a prophetic oracle: vv. 10, 11a and the almost unrelated 'says the LORD' in v. 14. However, the content of this framework is priestly instruction, as defined in v.11b. There is also no real comparison here, because the two replies of the priest has no counterpart in v. 14.

In the prophecy of Malachi the doctrinal dialogue replaces the prophetic oracle in a different way. However, the oracles of Malachi, which are characterized by argument, do not contain any express comparisons. One could possibly regard 1.6 as a comparison; 'If then I am a father, where is my honour . . .?' But here the comparison is only hinted at, it is part of an argument.

## Comparisons in Later Additions

These have already been mentioned in part under the prophetic books to which they have been added. Here I confine myself to two groups which announce judgment upon Israel's enemies. In this context the comparison appears to take on a different function, for psychological reasons, viz. to express the powerless exasperation of those who have been defeated. This is also true of the related texts which announce that God's judgment of the nations shall be executed by Israel, Micah 4.11–13; Zech. 9.11–17; 12.2–6; Joel 4.12–13 and Obad. 18:

'The house of Jacob shall be a fire,
and the house of Joseph a flame,
and the house of Edom stubble;
they shall burn them and consume them.'

This announcement, that Yahweh will use his people Israel as a weapon to destroy the nations, is in stark contrast to the message of Deutero-Isaiah. To this we have to add a group of texts, again similar, in which the destruction of Israel's enemies is announced in more highly charged emotional language than anywhere else. This group is of particular importance for the history of comparisons, because such exaggeration is only possible by means of comparisons; this could not be expressed by any other form of speech:

> Zeph. 1.17: 'their blood shall be poured out like dust'.
> Zech. 9.15: 'they (subject uncertain) shall drink their blood like wine
> and be full like a bowl'.
> 10.5: 'trampling the foe in the mud of the streets'.

Similar expressions can be found in the songs of the wine press Isa. 63.1–6:

> '. . . I trod them in my anger.
> and I trampled them in my wrath;
> their lifeblood is sprinkled upon my garments,
> and I have stained all my raiment' (v. 3).
> 'I trod down peoples in my anger' (v. 6).

Isa. 34.1–6 expresses God's judgment upon Edom (and all the nations):

> 'For the LORD is enraged against all the nations,
> and furious against all their host . . .' (v. 2).
> 'The LORD has a sword; it is sated with blood, it is gorged with fat . . .
> For the LORD has a sacrifice in Bozra,
> a great slaughter in the land of Edom' (v. 6).

In all these passages – and we could easily cite a few more – God's judgment is depicted in comparisons; these are just as far removed from reality as those of the previous group. In Isa. 63 God's judgment on the nations is described as a trampling of the winepress, in ch. 34 as a sacrificial meal; both comparisons occur elsewhere. It is also true of this second group that its announcement is in stark contrast to the message of Deutero-Isaiah. In Isa. 63.1–6 it is even more obvious that the fate of the nations envisaged is different from Isa. 60–62. Hence this oracle can hardly be attributed to Trito-Isaiah, the prophet of chs 60–62. Even more striking is the remoteness from reality of the comparison in Isa. 63.1–6. The destruction of whole nations in individual combat is unrealistic. 'What we have here is a description such as is found in apocalyptic and couched in terms taken from myth' (C. Westermann, *Isaiah 40–66*, p. 384).

The oracle against the nations in Isa. 34 is equally full of emotion in its exuberant bloodthirstiness, which is manifest in its bizarre and grotesquely exaggerated comparisons. As in Isa. 63.1–6, the comparison is unrealistic. The idea of Yahweh sacrificing is inconceivable for ancient Israel; to whom could he sacrifice? The comparison is based on a purely superficial association. Neither text is a prophetic oracle, even though both are dressed up as such.

### The History of the Comparisons in the Prophetic Books

As long as the comparisons were understood as 'images' and correspondingly evalued as mere illustrations, it would not have occurred to anyone to inquire into their history. But once their independent function in their respective contexts, here in the context of the prophetic message, is recognized, then one would a priori expect them to have undergone changes in the course of the history of prophecy. As with the history of prophecy, so also with the history of the comparisons in prophecy, the exile represents the turning point. There is a clear difference between the comparisons in prophetic oracles before the exile and those after.

### Comparisons in Prophetic Oracles before the Exile

There is a clear division between the prophetic oracles before Amos – those transmitted in the historical books – and those from Amos onwards. In the former comparisons are quite rare, because the horizon of the prophetic oracle was more limited and as yet had no need of them. However, in special circumstances we meet comparisons expanded into parables, as in Judg. 9; II Sam. 12.1–13; (I Kings 22; vision); I Kings 20.39–43. The real function of comparisons in prophetic oracles only begins (from Amos onwards) where indictment and announcement of judgment are addressed to the whole people. Before Amos prophetic oracles and words of seers (Numb. 22–24) are still separate. From Amos onwards both occur together in the ministry of the prophets (vision). This also affects the comparisons.

The comparisons in the oracles from Amos to Jeremiah (only partly in the case of Ezekiel) have essentially the same function and the same (short) form. The differences between the comparisons in the individual prophets are not substantial. It is characteristic of the comparisons from Amos to Jeremiah that they are assigned to the prophetic speech forms, in particular to the announcement of judgment in its various parts. It is from this context that they derive their function: intensifying the announcement, the indictment, and the connection between the two. This process implies a strict and clear correspondence throughout between the subject and image of the comparison.

From Amos to Jeremiah we meet alongside the very frequent comparison the much rarer vision, consisting of content and its interpretation. Both remain separate, the vision having been taken over from the seers. From Amos to Jeremiah comparisons are concerned with the whole of reality human and cosmic, the whole of creation.

The comparisons are concentrated in the indictments, which for the prophets are the most important feature, and their consequences in the announcement of judgment: in Amos and Micah the social accusation, in Hosea Israel's unfaithfulness, in Isaiah her hybris, in Jeremiah the inconceivable character of her apostasy, and in Habakkuk the social indictment of the superpower.

The difference between the comparisons in the prophets of the 8th and 7th centuries respectively consists of the fact that in Jeremiah and to some extent in Ezekiel the prophet's person is much more involved in his message, a fact also reflected in the comparisons.

## Comparisons in Prophecy during the Exile

Comparisons in Deutero-Isaiah. The comparisons in Deutero-Isaiah are integrally connected with that prophet's message. Hence they have to be grouped according to his speech forms, commencing with the promise of liberation whereby the joyous message determines the whole of his prophecy. In their strict assignment to the speech forms the comparisons in Deutero-Isaiah agree with those of pre-exilic prophecy, and in this respect Deutero-Isaiah is closer to the pre-exilic prophecy of judgment than Ezekiel. The comparisons in Deutero-Isaiah's message of salvation are divided into those concerning the announcement of saving in chs 40–52 and those concerning the promise of blessing in chs 54–55. The novel feature in Deutero-Isaiah that the prophetic message is full of psalm language is also apparent in the comparisons.

Comparisons in Ezekiel. The radical difference between the comparisons in Ezekiel and those of the judgment prophecy before him is evident first of all in his explosive use of comparisons, but also in the fact that simple comparisons recede in favour of larger constructions. While the assignment to speech forms is retained, these tend to expand and often burst the bounds of the form; in this the combination of several motifs in a single comparison is more frequent than before. Characteristic of Ezekiel is the shepherd parable in ch. 34 which with its two parts (the wicked shepherds – the good shepherd) unites the two phases of the prophet's mission. Equally characteristic is the transition from comparison or parable to allegory in the allegories of the history of Israel. There is a concentration of symbolic actions in Ezekiel which often have an exaggeratedly baroque form. In the oracles against the nations the genre of the comparison takes on an independent character by means of pictorial expansions using borrowed motifs. These are secondary literary compositions. It is in Ezekiel's visions that the transition from prophecy to apocalyptic occurs; the transcendent is represented in images. In all this we can see the way the connection between the subject and the image of the comparison grows looser.

## Comparisons in Post-exilic Prophecy

The exile marks a significant watershed for the comparisons, too. The most important changes are:

(a) while up to the exile repetitions of comparisons are relatively rare (some frequent comparisons like the fire of the wrath of God come close to metaphor), from the exile onwards some comparisons are employed frequently, to some extent as stereotypes, and original comparisons seldom occur. To give one example: we often find the cup of wrath (or of staggering) as in Jer. 25; Hab. 3.15 f.; Obad. 16; Nahum 3.18; Zech. 12.2 or Obad. 4 = Hab. 2.9. This often leads to a change of function in the comparisons borrowed; e.g. the comparison with the lion occurs in many contexts.

(b) We often find accumulations of comparisons, as several times in Trito-Isaiah, e.g. 61.1–3. Such accumulations reduce the clarity and precision of the comparison, as the comparison generally becomes less powerful. In Isa. 59.7 this accumulation passes over into allegory.

(c) Correspondingly, the precision of the correspondence between the subject and the image of the comparison sometimes decreases. This can be observed first of all in the comparisons in Ezekiel's oracles against the nations, where the comparisons take on an independent character and thus distance themselves from the subject of comparison. Apart from Ezekiel this is particularly apparent in Joel, where firstly the call to lament in ch. 1 already presupposes the occurrence of the plague of locusts, and where secondly in ch. 2 the description of the approach of the locusts in 2.3b–9 is entirely independent of the framework 2.1–3a, 10–12, which announces the coming of the day of the LORD, and is only loosely connected with it.

The comparison in Hag. 2.10–14 is also inserted without any real link.

(d) Not uncommonly comparisons now reach the level of the grotesque and the bizarre.

# Comparisons in the Psalms

Since comparisons occur in the Psalms almost as frequently as in the prophets, they must be regarded as an essential component of the Psalms. Just as in the prophetic oracles the comparisons are determined by the prophet's commission and its execution, so too in the Psalms they are shaped by what happens in them between God and man, particularly in terms of lament and praise. Hence the comparisons automatically conform to the structure of the Psalms of Lament and Praise. When the same comparisons occur in different parts of the Psalm, this is usually due to motif migration.

Comparisons in the Laments. The comparisons are to be assigned to the three sections of the Communal and Individual Laments (details in C. Westermann, 'Struktur und Geschichte der Klage', in *Lob und Klage*, pp. 125–64).

Comparisons in the God-lament (accusation against God). Although the number of Communal Laments is much smaller than that of Individual ones, comparisons occur more frequently in the Communal Laments in the case of the God-lament (44; 79; 80; 89; Lam. 1.15) than in the Individual Laments (22; 38; 42; 88; 102; Lam. 3). The reason for this is that in the Individual Laments generally God-lament retreats into the background; it is often transformed into negative requests. All the comparisons accuse God of hostile and detrimental behaviour towards his people (in the Communal Laments):

> 'Thou hast made us like sheep for slaughter' (44.12, 23; EVV vv. 11, 22).
> 'Thou hast sold thy people for a trifle' (44.13; EVV v. 12).

'Thou hast given us wine to drink that made us reel' (60.6; EVV
v. 3).
'Thou hast fed them with bread of tears,
and given them tears to drink . . .' (80.6; EVV v. 5).

Cf. 89.40, 44; 80.13; 44.24; Lam. 1.12, 13, 15; 79.5; 44.20;
Lam. 3.44; 2.3; 4.11. The same applies to individuals in the
Individual Lament:

'thou dost lay me in the dust of death' (22.16; EVV v. 15).
'For thy arrows have sunk into me' (38.3; EVV v. 2).
'all thy waves and billows have gone over me' (42.8; EVV v. 7).

Cf. 88.8, 17 f.; 102.11; Lam. 3.1–16.
All these comparisons have the function of radicalizing the
indictment against God. The large number and the diver-
sity of the comparisons shows the passionate agitation
underlying the accusations, which cannot be restricted to a
single comparison. By strengthening the accusation against
God the comparisons themselves become indictments. Such
accusations against God can only be understood on the
assumption that God himself is behind everything that
happens and that this is self-evident to everyone and needs
no further reflection. It is the language of suffering and
pain which is being voiced here. To take such indictments
as objective statements about God would be to mis-
understand them. In them we hear pain crying out, the
cry of pain of those who are being beaten. This becomes
even more apparent when one realizes how the comparisons in both groups reflect the experience of the
people and of the individual respectively. In the Communal
Lament the lamenters accuse God of having become the
enemy of his people: 'He has bent his bow like an enemy',
Lam. 2.3–8; 'Thou hast breached all his walls', Ps. 89.40.
Cf. 80.13; 89.40, 44; Lam 3.5; these are not comparisons in
the strict sense, but they come close to them because in
them a complex historical process, the loss of a battle, is
concentrated into a single action. Instead of caring for his
people he abandons them: 'like sheep for slaughter', 44.12,
23 (EVV vv. 11, 22); 'sold . . . for a trifle', 44.13 (EVV
v. 12). Instead of giving his people glory he has 'defiled his
crown in the dust', 89.40 (EVV v. 39); cf. Lam. 3. 16, 45.

This presupposes the accusation that God has turned away from his people: Ps. 44.2; Lam. 3.44, that God has turned against his people in his wrath. In these accusations the wrath of God is repeatedly compared to the glow of a fire, Lam. 2.3 ff.; Ps. 79.5; Lam. 1. 12, 13.

The comparisons in the Individual Laments are completely different. We frequently find the accusation that God casts the lamenter into the depths of the waters (sea): Ps. 42.8; 88.8, 17 f., into darkness, 88.7; Lam. 3.2, into the grave or into death, Ps. 22.16; 88.7; Lam. 3.6; 3.1, 9. Here, too, God is accused of having become an enemy, but in relation to the individual: Ps. 38.3; Lam. 3.12, 13; Ps. 102.12. The Foe-lament, to which the comparison with wild beasts belongs, can be applied to the indictment against God: Lam. 3.10.

A synoptic view of these comparisons relating to the indictment of God in the laments shows more clearly than any summary, abstract concept the meaning of the accusation against God in the Psalms. Without the comparisons this would be inconceivable.

Comparisons in the I- (We-) lament. These occur predominantly in the Individual Laments. The I-lament is in the first instance a personal utterance of suffering. Only here do we meet a group of texts which describe the process of lamenting as such, 102.1: 'I pour (RSV: 'he pours') out my complaint before the LORD', and in particularly vivid language 42.3: 'My tears have been my food day and night', similarly 102.9 (here 'bread' and 'drink'). The rhythm of life is disturbed and threatened by the fact that tears have taken the place of eating and drinking. This comparison also occurs in Ps. 80.6 (EVV v. 5), perhaps as a result of motif migration.

The comparisons in the I-lament do not have the function of strengthening and intensifying as in the God-lament; this is evident from the kind of comparisons used. We notice immediately that wild animals do not appear in them, only sheep, deer, the worm, birds (doves, jackdaw, and owls). Common to most of these comparisons is their pointing to the creatureliness of the one who speaks in the

I-laments: the body and its members, eating and drinking, plants and animals. Through the use of all these images man, the suffering creature, confronts his creator with his threatened creatureliness. What these comparisons reveal is not passionate accusation, as in the God-lament, but plaintive pleading. Only the comparisons establish this subtle difference. It is the frailty of human existence to which most of these comparisons point; this is experienced as the suffering which afflicts the lamenter in his decline towards death, with death gaining power in the midst of life: 'I have passed out of mind like one who is dead; I have become like a broken vessel', Ps. 31.12; cf. 88.6; 55.5; 88.16 f. Such sentences understand death as a power which even reaches into life. This can be expressed in quite different ways, therefore 55.5 does not contradict 31.12 or 88.6. Similarly 44.26 (EVV v. 25): 'For our soul is bowed down to the dust; our body cleaves to the ground', cf. 119.25 or 28.1; '. . . like a deaf man . . . like a dumb man', 38.14 f. (EVV vv. 13 f.). The same decline towards death is represented as sinking in the floods, 69.1f.: 'For the waters have come up to my neck. I sink in deep mire . . ; I have come into deep waters, and the flood sweeps over me'. This text shows the tendency to expand comparisons in the direction of a narrative, similarly Lam. 3.54. In Ps. 38.5 (EVV v. 4): 'For my iniquities have gone over my head . . .'; the Confession of Sin has been combined with the I-lament. The power of death can also be described as disintegration, Ps. 22.15–16 (EVV vv. 14–15): 'I am poured out like water, . . . it is melted within my breast', cf. 102.4 f., 12 (EVV vv. 3 f., 11); 119. 83: 'like a wineskin in the smoke'. A few of these comparisons already manifest the transition to the Lament of Transitoriness, in which the I-lament has been expanded into a generalization about death as the fate of all human beings, also involving many comparisons: Pss 39.6, 7, 12, 13; 49.12, 13, 15, 21; 62.10; 90.5 f., 10; 144.4 and particularly in the Book of Job. This then is the charge brought by the lamenters against him who gave them life: it is you who gave us life – and now you allow it to vanish, sink, and break up! The use of so many different comparisons characterizes the situation precisely; this variety reflects the reality in which suffering grows out of the many pluriform individual destinies.

In another group the creatureliness which confronts the creator is expressed in comparison with and proximity to 'the whole creation groaning in travail': suffering is the cause of loneliness and humiliation, 102.7 (EVV v. 6): 'I am like a vulture of the wilderness, like an owl of the waste places'; cf. v. 8 (EVV v. 7); (55.3 f.); 119.176; 22.7; 55.17. Man's close connection with the other creatures is expressed in a particularly suggestive way in passages where the animal's desire for water is compared with the human desire for God's attention, 42.1: 'As the hart longs for fresh water (author's translation, RSV 'flowing streams'), so longs my soul for thee, O God', and 63.2; 143.6: '. . . like a parched land'. The animal comparisons used in this group show how frail humanity is conscious of its solidarity with the rest of creation (not only animals, but also the soil) and shares its suffering with 'creation groaning in travail'. The meaning of this comparison, 'I lie awake and complain like a lonely bird on the roof', cannot be rendered by one single expression, and only someone who himself suffers can really understand it. This group of comparisons already proves by itself that ancient Israel regarded the biblical statements about the creator and creation as a reality of which they were conscious every day.

Comparisons in the We-lament are few (mainly in Communal Laments outside the Psalter), but even so they allow us to recognize the time of their origin, viz. around the exile (Lam. and Deutero-Isaiah; Lam. 5 consists almost entirely of a We-lament expanded into a report). In Lam. 1.1–2 a lament is raised over Jerusalem as a lonely widow in grief: 'How lonely sits the city that was full of people! How like a widow has she become . . .'. This comparison with the childless widow occurs in many places in Deutero-Isaiah: '. . . and the reproach of your widowhood you will remember no more', Isa. 54.4 (also in 49.20, 21; 51.18, 20; 54.1, 6). Even their reflection in an oracle of salvation still allows us to recognize the comparisons in the lament which this oracle presupposes. It is characteristic of the We-lament that it is based on a comparison relating to a community. Equally typical of the time around the fall of Jerusalem is the way that in several places the shame of suffering is expressed in very striking comparisons, Lam. 3.45: 'Thou hast made us offscouring and refuse among the peoples', combined with the God-lament. Cf. Lam. 5.16; Isa. 64.5 f.; Lam. 1.8 f.:

> 'Jerusalem sinned grievously,
> therefore she became filthy;
> all who honoured her despise her,
> for they have seen her nakedness . . .,
> Her uncleanness was in her skirts'.

Just as characteristic of the lament of exilic times is its combination with the Confession of Sin, Isa. 64.5f.; Lam. 5.7, 16. This is also expressed, in combination with a God-lament, by an original comparison in Lam. 1.14:

> 'My transgressions were bound into a yoke;
> by his hand they were fastened together;
> they were set upon my neck'.

This comparison develops into a short story: God has found Israel out in her sins, now she experiences the consequences, now she is bound by them and has to bear these consequences.

The function of other comparisons is to describe the magnitude of the fall of Jerusalem, all of them intensify the We-lament, Isa. 59.9 f.:

> 'we look for light, and behold, darkness . . .
> We grope for the wall like the blind,
> we grope like those who have no eyes;
> we stumble at noon . . .' (cf. v. 14).

Comparisons express grief in the Individual Lament also: Lam. 3.10; 2.13; 5.15. And again very typical of the lament after the fall of Jerusalem is a contrasting comparison in two parts in Lam. 4.2–8:

'The precious sons of Zion, worth their weight in fine gold –
reckoned as earthen pots; even the jackals . . ., but the daughter of
my people . . ., like the ostriches in the wilderness.
Her princes were whiter than milk – blacker than soot.'

This, however, shows a significant difference from the
simple comparison in the We-lament: the lament has
turned into third person narrative, made strongly rhetorical by the contrast 'in former times – but now'. Its first
half (in former times) uses a different genre in the case
of the princes in v. 7, viz. the praise of beauty as in the
Song of Songs. Conversely, the comparison in Lam 1.6
is simple: 'Her princes have become like harts that find
no pasture.'

To sum up: while the comparisons in the We-lament
are assigned to the life of the people, those of the I-lament
relate to the life of the individual, to the personal sphere.
These two spheres are present in the lament addressed to
God in such a way that the elements which comprise these
two spheres are named in the comparisons and through
them receive a larger context, e.g. the sufferer is placed in
the circle of 'creation groaning in travail.'

If one eliminates the lament from prayer, as in the
Christian tradition, the comparisons, too, lose their place
and prayer takes on a more conceptual and abstract character. One might well ask whether this does not mean that
an essential element of biblical prayer has been lost.

Comparisons in the Foe-laments. They nearly all occur
in Individual Laments. The Communal Laments report
what the (political) enemies of Israel *have done*: this does
not require any comparisons. In the Individual Laments
enemies, the wicked and godless threaten the lamenter.
This threat is intensified in many comparisons which form
the strongest group numerically. (On the following cf. the
section on the Foe-lament in: C. Westermann, 'Struktur
und Geschichte der Klage', *Lob und Klage*, pp. 144–49).
The comparisons fall into three clearly distinct groups. All
three are concerned with the enemy threat.

(a) Threatened by wild animals. Ps. 22 contains a particularly detailed comparison in vv. 13 f. (EVV vv. 12 f.):

'Many bulls encompass me,
strong bulls of Bashan surround me;
they open wide their mouths at me,
like a ravening and roaring lion . . .',

further vv. 17, 21 f. All these sentences simply state a threat, v. 17b (EVV v. 16b) without a comparison: 'a company of evildoers encircle me'. Similar passages are: 'He sits in ambush in the villages; . . . His eyes stealthily watch for the hapless, he lurks in secret like a lion in his covert . . .', 10.9 f. (EVV vv. 8 f.) and 59.7, 15f.; 17.11 f. All these comparisons, which are very similar to each other, are apparently intended to paraphrase the same threat. It would be wrong to say that this group of texts describes the enemies of the worshipper by means of the image of wild beasts. Rather, the threat posed to the lamenter is compared to that posed by wild animals. He pleads for this threat to be averted: '. . . lest like a lion they rend me', Ps. 7.3 (EVV v. 2); cf. 58.7. Apart from the threat itself, the comparison makes no statements about the lamenter's enemies, except for their overpowering nature. In none of these sentences is there even any hint that the 'wild animals' have attacked the lamenter, fallen upon or seized him. It is noticeable that the wild animals do not appear in the section 'Request against the Enemies'. They designate the threat posed by the enemies, but not the enemies as such.

(b) A second group of passages adds a different aspect of the same threat. The threatening wild animal can be seen and heard; but the lamenters also feel threatened by dangers to their lives which they cannot see and which they always have to fear for this very reason. These invisible dangers are compared to the pit, the net, the snare, and the trap: 'For without cause they hid their net for me; without cause they dug a pit for my life', Ps. 35.7; 'they set a net for my steps; . . . they dug a pit in my way', 57.7 (EVV v. 6). We find the same or similar imagery in 7.16; 9.16; 10.2, 9; 64.6; 91.3; 104.6; 119.85 (without a comparison: 'They hold fast to their evil purpose; they talk of laying snares secretly . . . "We have thought out a cunningly conceived plot"', 64.6 f.; EVV vv. 5 f.). As in the comparison with wild animals, none of these laments actually goes beyond the threat itself; it is never stated that anyone has been caught by a snare or fallen into a pit. Both comparisons can also be combined with each other: 10.9; 57.5–7.

(c) The word as weapon. The first two kinds of comparisons do not mention the character of the threat. A faint clue is given by the third group: the weapons which threaten the lamenters are words. That the same threat is involved is shown by Ps. 57.5–7 in which all three groups follow one another. The lamenters have to live among people whose 'teeth are spears and arrows, their tongues sharp swords', 57.5 (EVV v. 4); cf. 5.10; 64.4; 52.4, also 12.3–5; 7.13; 11.2; 37.14; 64.4–9; 10.11; 42.11; 52.4, 6; 55.22; 59.8; 73.9; 140.4 (combined with wild animals). This largest group of comparisons shows on the one hand that it is not political enemies who are referred to; they live in the same community and in the same place as the lamenters. It further shows that those who threaten live under the laws of this community and this place, and that therefore they cannot simply remove the lamenters by force. It shows thirdly that their superiority enables them to attack the lamenters with words, to humiliate them, to hurt and insult them, to take away their honour.

The end of the wicked. While the comparisons in the first three groups express the threat to the lamenters directly, a fourth group adds an expansion which transcends it and no longer represents an integral element of the lament. For these sentences are no longer concerned with averting the threat, but with the wish or petition that the threatening enemy should die, namely as retribution for his behaviour towards the lamenter. Such a request for retribution is added several times to the other comparisons: that the one who has dug the pit should fall into it himself, 57.7; 7.16; 9.16; 10.2; 36.7 f.; 69.24; 'their sword shall enter their own heart', 37.15. 'May the LORD cut off all flattering lips', 12.3–5 (EVV vv. 2–4); 'because of their tongue he will bring them to ruin', 64.9 (EVV v. 8).

The majority of these comparisons express the wish that the wickedness of the enemies should fall back upon them. Their own curse shall come on them (109.18; EVV v. 17). This group of passages presupposes the magic act-consequence relationship which is alien to the thought and language of the Psalms. The comparisons of a further group wish for the end of the wicked; their function is to intensify this wish. '. . . they will soon fade like the grass, and wither like the green herb', 37.2, they are 'like the glory of the pastures, they vanish like smoke', 37.20, 35 f.; 50.8–9; 68.3; 73.20; 129.6. These comparisons, which are very similar to each other, originally belong to the lament of transitoriness, from which they have been adopted. Not unlike them are those comparisons in which God brings about the end of the wicked or is requested to do so: 'Let the wicked together fall into their own nets', 141.10; 58.7; 64.8 f.; phrased as a petition: 83.14–16; 119.119; 58.10; 11.6: fire and brimstone, taken over from the Communal Lament, as is the cup of wrath in 75.9. The end of the wicked is expressed differently in 52.7; 58.10; 73.18; 79.6.

To sum up: the first three groups of comparisons in the Foe-lament refer to three aspects of the accusation against the enemy; in all three the lamenter is threatened by enemies. The far-reaching similarity between the comparisons in these three groups points to the situation common to them all, viz. the distinction between the righteous and the wicked which is equally apparent in Proverbs and in the Book of Job. This is even more obvious in the development found in the fourth group, the end of the wicked, which can only be explained in terms of this situation and which is almost entirely lacking in original comparisons; they have all been borrowed from elsewhere. This fact is of theological significance because, on the basis of the comparisons, it can be proved that the petition against the enemies and thus also the cursing of the enemies are secondary additions to the Individual Lament, growing out of a recognizable and limited situation.

Comparisons in the Petition. We have to distinguish between the cry from distress, a major part of the Psalm of

Lament, and the transitive petition (request for something), which actually belongs to the blessing, as a request for blessing, and which in the Psalms of Lament only occurs in expansions. Comparisons are not usually part of the cry from distress. While they do occasionally occur, they are frequently borrowed; we find no fixed groups in use. We can only deduce that the comparison has no function in the cry from distress. The reason for this is that this part of the psalm was once an independent act, the call for help, the cry from the depths: *hōshiʻānāh*. The call for help, however, is so basic that it neither needs nor can it tolerate any comparisons. 35.1–3:

> 'Contend, O LORD, with those . . .
> Take hold of shield and buckler . . .
> Draw the spear and javelin',

is taken from the cry for help in an epiphany.

In 69.15–16 the plea for rescue, exemplified by one's being pulled out from the mire, deep waters, the well shaft, is combined with the lament, as the group of comparisons in the I-lament shows; cf. 71.2, 20; 142. 8. 35. 17, 'Rescue me from the ravages, my life from the lions', and 74.19 correspond to another group within the I-lament, that of the threat from wild animals. In Ps. 141.8 the request, 'do not pour out my life' (author's translation) refers to the lament, 'poured out like water' (Ps. 22.15; EVV v. 14), as well as the petition in 56.9 (EVV v. 8): 'put thou my tears in thy bottle!' Cf. also in the Communal Lament 126.4: 'Restore our fortunes, O LORD, like the watercourses in the Negeb', which refers to the late promise with the phrase *shūb shebūt*, e.g. in Isa. 64.1: 'O that thou wouldst rend the heavens and come down', a modification of the epiphany into a petition. Further in Ps. 60.4 (EVV v. 2): 'repair its breaches, for it totters', refers to a Communal Lament or to Isaiah's announcement of judgment in 30.13: 'shall be . . . like a break in a high wall'. These examples show clearly that in a few places the plea for rescue has been joined with a comparison, but such comparisons are approximations to the petition and their origin is in most cases clearly recognizable. The only notable exception is Ps. 123

where the gesture of pleading has been turned into a parable.

The transitive petition, added in some places as an expansion, consists predominantly of variants of the petition for blessing. Ps. 4.7 (EVV v. 6), 'lift up the light of thy countenance upon us', is a variant of Numb. 6.24–26, but in neither the one nor the other is 'light' still understood as a comparison. Ps. 17.8 is an expression of trust formulated as a request: 'Keep me as the apple of the eye: hide me in the shadow of thy wings . . .'; 90.16 (EVV v. 14) is a request for preservation: 'Satisfy us in the morning with thy steadfast love'. There is further the request for instruction and guidance in 25.4: 'Make me to know thy ways, O LORD, teach me thy paths'; cf. vv. 5, 10, 12; 27.11; 43.3: 'Oh send out thy light and thy truth; let them lead me, let them bring me to . . .', and 141.3: 'Set a guard over my mouth, O LORD, keep watch over the door of my lips!' But these are no longer comparisons in the strict sense. The language is that of Wisdom.

Comparisons in the review of God's previous acts of salvation. This section is peculiar to the Communal Lament; it is hardly ever found in the Individual type. Such comparisons refer to the beginnings of the history of the people.

> Ps. 44.3 (EVV v. 2): 'thou . . . didst drive out nations, but them thou didst plant;
> thou didst afflict peoples, but them thou didst set free',
> Ps. 74.2: 'Remember thy congregation, which thou hast gotten of old, which thou hast redeemed to be the tribe of thy heritage!'

and 80.9–12; Isa. 63.11–14. All these comparisons properly belong to the praise of God, in particular the praise of God who liberated Israel from Egypt and brought her into the promised land. But in the context of the Communal Lament they have the function of reminding God of his saving act at the beginning and moving him to help in the present. This is most powerfully expressed in Ps. 80 in which the comparison has been expanded into a parable. The result of this is that a sequence of actions, viz. those of the vine-dresser, is placed side by side with the sequence of historical processes then and now.

Comparisons in the Confession of Trust. To the Confession of Trust belongs the largest and in some respects most striking group of comparisons in the Psalter. This ultimately leads one to ask what the basis of this confession is. The vast majority of comparisons are expressions of trust in the God who saves from need and danger. In only a limited number of cases is reference made to the God who blesses, cares, and accompanies on the way. The boundary between comparison and direct description is often fluid. We frequently find the noun '$\bar{o}z$ = power, strength ('Yahweh is my strength'), which is no real comparison, but often occurs in parallelism with a word used in the comparison, as in Ps. 28.7: 'The LORD is my strength and shield; in him my heart trusts', see also 46.2; 59.10; 62.8, 12; 71.7; 81.2; 84.6; 86.12; Jer. 16.19 *et al.* The noun from the same root, *mā'ōz* (with *mem locale*), is a comparison. The *mem locale* occurs with several nouns of this group. It is not always possible to decide with certainty whether this local meaning is still prevalent, but it is always the etymological basis of such words: *maḥaseh* = a hiding place; *mānōs* = a place of refuge. In profane usage *maḥaseh* represents a place of refuge for humans and animals: Job 24.8; Ps. 104.18, cf. Isa. 25.4; 28.15, 17. Apart from this, the word only occurs in the Confession of Trust or its derivatives. Ps. 61.4 (EVV v. 3) shows this original local meaning: 'thou art my refuge, a strong tower against the enemy', as does 91.2: 'My refuge and my fortress; my God, in whom I trust', and Jer. 17.17: 'thou art my refuge in the day of evil'. In all passages the meaning is essentially the same: Pss 14.6; 46.2; 62.8, 9; 71.7; 73.28; 91.2, 9; 142. 6; 94.22; Joel 4.16; Prov. 14.26; Isa. 4.6. This comparison has to be understood on the basis of its place in the structure of the Psalm of Lament, at the transition from the lament to the petition. Reaching a place of refuge only has a point in the kind of emergency situation such as is expressed here. This situation gives the comparisons their function: they are intended to confirm one's trust. This is due to the exalted significance which the centre of the Psalm of Lament has for man's relationship with God in the OT. The 'indispensability' of God finds its strongest expression in this centre, in which the worshipper, having poured out his heart, turns away from his distress to God as his helper. Here it becomes apparent what God means for him. The comparisons speak of this indispensability: there is a place where one can hide in the hour of oppression. The experience of rescue shared by so many offers these comparisons as an open possibility.

A small group employs *mānōs* (= refuge) in a similar sense: Ps. 59.17; II Sam. 22.3 and Jer. 16.19. Closely related to these two terms is *mibṭāḥ* (= place of safety, confidence and trust). Ps. 40.5 (EVV v. 4): 'Blessed is the man who makes the LORD his trust'=Jer. 17.7; Ps. 65.6 (EVV v. 5): 'who art the hope of all the ends of the earth', and 71.5 f.

The comparisons of God with a rock or a fortress form a group closely akin to the first one, often in parallelism with a word from the latter. God is called a rock (*ṣūr*) in 26 places; often he is invoked as rock: 'To thee, O LORD, I call; my rock . . .', Ps. 28.1; 'O LORD, my rock and my redeemer', 19.15 (EVV v. 14), cf. 73.26; 92.16; 89.27. The following use the word *sala‘* for rock: 18.3; 31.4; 42.10 (in the 3rd person 18.3, 4, 7). Yahweh is called 'my rock' and 'my fortress' in 62.3, 7, 8 (EVV vv. 2, 6, 7): 'He only is my rock and my salvation, my fortress . . .', cf. 32.31; 76.6 (LXX); II Sam. 23.3; Isa. 30.29; Ps. 94.22. The term 'rock' is associated with the praise of God in Isa. 26.4; Ps. 18.32 (EVV v.31): 'And who is a rock, except our God?' Isa. 44.8: 'Is there a God besides me? There is no rock . . .'; Deut. 32.4, 37; II Sam. 23.3; Isa. 30.29; Ps. 144.1: 'Blessed be the LORD, my rock'; Ps. 95.1: 'let us make a joyful noise to the rock of our salvation!' The term is used as a petition in 31.3; 71.3, and as a review in 78.35 and Isa. 17.10. The comparison of God with a rock has the same significance and the same function as that with a place of refuge, indeed a rock is a possible place of refuge, a place which means shelter and safety in the face of deadly danger. The modified version of this, involving God placing the worshipper on a rock (Ps. 27.5: 'he will set me high upon a rock'), shows that it is not a matter of comparing state with state here, but process with process (the same in 40.3 with *sala'* and as a petition in 61.3). The continuation of this comparison in the praise of God, the review, and the cry for rescue shows how central it is to the Psalm of Lament.

God is called a fortress (*misgāb*) seventeen times, a hill fortress (*meṣudāh*) five times, and a bulwark (*mā'ōz*) six times. God is invoked as a fortress in 59.10, 18 (EVV vv. 9, 17): 'for thou . . . art my fortress', cf. 144.2; 31.3; 91.2; 31.5; 43.2; 18.3 with an accumulation of comparisons; 46.8, 12; 59.17 f. and 94.22 in the review. The 3rd person is used in Ps. 27.1, 'The LORD is the stronghold (refuge) of my life', and in 62.2, 7. The image occurs in the praise of God in 48.4 (EVV v. 3): 'Within her citadels God has shown himself a sure defence', cf. 28.8; 37.39 and in the petition in 31.3 (EVV v. 2): 'Be thou a rock of refuge for me, a strong fortress to save me' (=71.3). It can be found as Wisdom exhortation in 52.9 (EVV v. 7): 'See the man who would not make God his refuge'. There is no difference in meaning between 'refuge' and 'fortress', the fortress is a place of refuge. This does not mean the security offered by power, but rather a place of shelter (the original meaning of the word in German). What was said with reference to the previous group ('refuge') also applies here. A dwelling can also provide shelter, as in Ps. 27.5: 'For he will hide me in his shelter in the day of trouble; he will conceal me under the cover of his tent, he will set me high upon a rock'. This sheltering house can also be the temple (84.4; 65.5; 61.5; 23.6).

In seventeen places God is referred to as a shield, the third largest group of comparisons, as in 144.2: 'My shield and he in whom I take refuge'. God means to the worshipper what his shield means to the warrior in battle: protection against arrows and blows. It is worth noting that in the Confession of Trust the comparison of God with an offensive weapon is absent. A sentence like 'God is my sword' never occurs; consequently the comparison does not imply that God is my supporter in battle (this can, however, be said elsewhere, e.g. in Ps. 18). But in connection with the expression of confidence the comparison implies that God is my protection, and this comparison is then not limited to the context of battle. God is invoked as a shield in II Sam. 22.3: 'my shield and the horn of my salvation', and in Ps. 3.4 (EVV v. 3): 'thou, O LORD, art a shield about me, my glory . . .', cf. 18.36; 119.114; 144.2. The motif is used in the 3rd person in Ps. 7.11 (EVV v. 10): 'My shield is with God' (cf. 28.7; 33.20), concerning the king in 84.10 and 89.19, as praise of God in II Sam. 22.31: 'he is shield for all those who take refuge in him' (cf. 84.12; 115.9, 10, 11), in the form of a promise of salvation in Gen. 15.1: 'I am your shield', and in Wisdom, Prov. 2.7: 'he is a shield to those who walk in integrity' (cf. Prov. 30.5). In some of these passages the use of the word 'shield' comes close to being a metaphor for the abstract noun 'protection', but it is significant for the language of the Psalms that 'shield' nowhere becomes a complete metaphor; the form of the comparison – even without any comparative particle – is always adhered to. They all talk of events in which someone experiences this kind of protection. It is from such experiences that the comparison derives, in it they are preserved and transmitted.

Akin to the comparisons involving the shield are those with the noun *sēter* ( = shelter, cover, hiding place), e.g. Ps. 32.7: 'Thou art a hiding place for me, thou preservest me from trouble'. Human beings provide protection in Isa. 16.4; 28.17; 32.2. This motif appears as an address to God in Pss 31.21; 32.7; 119.114, and in the 3rd person in 27.5 and 91.1: 'He who dwells in the shelter of the Most High', and applied to the petition in 61.5. It is used in parallel with 'shield' 119.114, with 'hut' (RSV 'shelter') in 27.5; 31.21 and 'tent' in 61.5 ('shelter of thy wings'), and 'shadow' in 91.1. Hence we find 'shelter' several times in parallelism with 'tent' and 'hut', but never with 'rock' and 'fortress'. Not the place but the act of sheltering is the subject in 57.2 (EVV v. 1): 'in the shadow of thy wings I will take refuge, till the storms of destruction pass by'. A young bird shelters in the shadow of its parents' wings, a most picturesque comparison (cf. Judg. 9.15; Isa. 30.2;

Ruth 2.12; Pss 61.5; 63.8). This recalls the larger context of animal comparisons in Proverbs. Judg. 9.15 presupposes a metaphorical usage. In the Book of Ruth this image is applied to God. The comparison is so impressive that it has found its way into a German hymn: 'Wie ein Adler sein Gefieder über seine Jungen reckt . . .' (as an eagle spreads its feathers over its young).

All comparisons so far deal with trust in God as the saviour. Their concern is with God's saving acts and the process underlying them is confined to a moment of time. The following groups, however, exhibit a transition to God's continuous activity. Hence the Confession of Trust contains both: the first group (a) talks about God as leader, guide and keeper, while the other (b) expresses trust in God who provides and blesses.

(a) God as shepherd (Pss 23; 80.2; 28.9; 78.52; Isa. 40.11; 63.11). The comparison of God with a shepherd is almost exclusively applied in the OT to his relationship with his people. Of the examples only Ps. 80.2 and the review in Isa. 63.11 are close to the Confession of Trust. It frequently occurs in prophecy, in particular in the indictment of the bad shepherds (the leadership) and in the promise of a good shepherd as in Ezek. 34. This is one of the few comparisons which prophets and Psalms have in common. In connection with the Confession of Trust by an individual, the comparison with the shepherd occurs only in Ps. 23; in this case it is expanded into a parable. This Psalm, too, still retains a hint of the idea that comparisons primarily refer to the saving acts of God, 23.4, as with comparisons in prophecy. It is the expansion which adds God's continuous activity.

(b) In a small group of texts Yahweh is referred to as 'my portion' (ḥeläq) or gōrāl): 'the LORD is my chosen portion and my cup; thou holdest my lot', Ps. 16.5 f.; 'but God is the rock of my heart and my portion for ever', 73.26, cf. 119.57; 142.6; Lam. 3.24. Further, the name ḥilqiyāhū means: my portion is the LORD. This small group is the only one which speaks of God's provision in the Confession of Trust by means of a comparison. But these passages imply more than just ordinary day to day provision, as Ps. 73.26 in particular shows, in which the worshipper confesses that Yahweh is for him the only one who preserves life.

Both groups (a) and (b) come together in Ps. 23. This whole Psalm is in fact a Confession of Trust. The comparison with the shepherd includes guiding, protecting and providing. This happens only in this Psalm. Conversely, in most of the Psalms the comparisons point to the acts of the God who saves.

To sum up: if we look at the above comparisons together, we find that in terms of usage they fall into groups which only occur here in this particular form. The comparisons occur in the invocation of God in these prayers, in the 3rd person as a transition to the praise of God applied to the petition, and in the review. This serves to confirm the thesis that the Confession of Trust forms the centre of this type of Psalm. The comparisons share in this to the extent that they can be involved all the way through from petition to praise of God. This demonstrates the special significance of comparisons with regard to this motif. Whereas Western European theological thinking reduces these manifold experiences to a single concept and dissolves them into it, Hebrew thought insists on retaining the essential multiplicity of individual experiences which can never be reduced to an abstract term. The full range of individual experiences of being saved, preserved, and heard by God is in fact retained by the comparisons with the place of refuge, the fortress, the rock. Once terms like 'trust' and 'confidence' are cut loose from individual experience they inevitably become petrified. Trust and confidence exist only in the context of the individual experiences out of which they grow and on which they are based. The significance of these comparisons lies in maintaining this link. The implication of this for our understanding of the parables of Jesus in the NT would be that any reduction of the meaning of the parables to an abstract concept would constitute a misinterpretation of them.

The function of all these phrases of comparison in the

Confession of Trust is to confirm and strengthen man's sense of being safe with God. This includes a process of transmission insofar that those who have experienced God as refuge will tell their contemporaries and future generations that God will remain like this. It is also of theological significance that few comparisons occur in statements in the form: 'God is . . .', whereas those in the form: 'God is to me . . .' contain comparisons in plenty. The God of whom the Psalms speak is not God as such, but the God who is concerned with humanity.

Comparisons in narrative praise (Psalm of Thanksgiving). One might expect that in narrative praise comparisons would not have any specific function and be infrequent, corresponding to the scarcity of comparisons in the narrative texts of the OT. However, contrary to this expectation, we meet a not inconsiderable number of them in the Narrative Psalms of Praise (Psalms of Thanksgiving). An explanation of this can be found if one takes a closer look at the groups of comparisons which occur here. They cannot be divided up according to the various sections of this Psalm because they all refer to the turning-point between distress and rescue. This can occur in a single sentence which summarizes distress and saving, as in Ps. 4.2 (EVV v. 1): 'Thou hast given me room in distress', and also 9.14; 56.14; 30.2; 40.3 *et al.* This sentence normally forms the introductory summary. Alternatively, the description of distress is followed by the report of the saving, both involving several sentences. Here, too, the comparison can embrace both.

The review of the distress, which precedes and is combined with the report of saving, presents that distress in terms of being overwhelmed by water or by floods, Ps. 18.17 (EVV v. 16): 'he drew me out of many waters'; cf. 18.5; 40.5; 86.13; 116.8; 124.4 f.; 93.3; 66.12; Jonah 2.4, 6. Alternatively it can be described as rescue from the pit, the depth or the mire, 40.3 (EVV v. 2): 'He drew me up from the desolate pit, out of the miry bog'; 30.2 (EVV v. 1): 'thou hast drawn me up'; 18.17 (EVV v.16): 'He reached from on high, he took me'; Jonah 2.4, 7 (EVV

vv. 3, 6): 'thou didst cast me into the deep . . . I went down to the land whose bars closed upon me for ever; yet thou didst bring up my life from the Pit'; the worshipper is placed on a rock in Pss 30.8; 40.3; 103.4; 116.16, or saved from the snares of death, 116.3: 'The snares of death encompassed me, the pangs of Sheol laid hold on me'; 18.5 (EVV v. 4): 'The cords of death encompassed me . . .'; 30.4 (EVV v. 3): 'Thou hast brought up my soul from Sheol . . .'; 9.14 (EVV v. 13): 'O thou who liftest me up from the gates of death'; Ecclus 51.2, 5; Lam. 3.53, 55. From a confined state into open space (liberation): Ps. 4.2 (EVV v. 1): 'Thou hast given me room when I was in distress'; 18.20 (EVV v. 19): 'He brought me forth into a broad place'; 18.37; 31.9; 55.19; 66.12; 71.2. Sometimes the rescue is described as bodily restoration, e.g. in 30.2; 32.4; 73.2.

All these groups of comparisons, however, can also be found in the Laments, in particular the I-laments, in part with identical wording. This implies that the Narrative Psalm resumes in the Review of the Distress the same comparisons which were used to intensify the lament and develops them further in the Report of Rescue: 'thou hast drawn me up', 30.2 (EVV v. 1). This shows on the one hand that the Narrative Psalm does not form any comparisons which are peculiar to it; on the other, the comparisons provide express proof that the Psalms of Lament and Praise belong together. This clearly proves the polarity of lament and praise (a fact which escaped me in my earlier study, 'The Praise of God'). If one were to understand these particular comparisons as pictorial language on the part of the Psalms (as Gunkel and most interpreters have done), this would not express the proper function of these comparisons. J. Pedersen, and following him C. Barth, had already noted with regard to the terms used of saving from death: 'The distinction between 'pictorial' and 'real' or 'inauthentic' and 'authentic' is of little relevance here' (C. Barth, *Die Errettung vom Tode*, 1947, p. 114). These phrases refer to the actual effect of death as a power pervading life. But what appear to be comparative speech forms – which refer in the same sense to floods of water, the pit, the mire, the depth, the dust, the gates and bars, and the snares of death – cannot be regarded as pictorial or inauthentic speech. All these phrases indicate real experiences. These experiences are complex, hence the need for different comparisons. These manifold comparisons have the special function of representing the individual experiences in such language that many can recognize their very own experiences in them. An example of this is Ps. 107 which lists several reports of rescue, but in this case as short stories. Such experiences are also the subject of the comparisons when they speak of the pit, the mire, and the depth. Sometimes we catch a glimpse of this when some Psalms hint at the tension caused by the threat of death, like Ps. 93 and Jonah 2. The Narrative Psalms of Praise can probably enable us to observe in part the origin of such comparisons. They are formed when typical experiences, like being overwhelmed by floods of water, are repeated by other people. Even if their experiences were only similar, they are comparable all the same. This is immediately evident in a sentence like: 'He brought me forth into a broad place', 18.20 (EVV v. 19), an expression of liberation which originally reflected a definite individual experience, and which was then able to reflect many similar experiences. This is confirmed by comparing the above-mentioned groups of comparisons, which virtually all belong to the report of the rescue of individuals, with sentences which describe the saving of the people, 93.3 (?); 124.4–7; 66.10–12; 77.21; 78.52; 81.7. In the case of the latter typical elements recede in the face of unique ones – even if these are only hinted at, as in 81.7 (EVV v.6): 'I relieved your shoulder of the burden; your hands were freed from the basket'; 66.12: 'thou didst let men ride over our heads . . .'. Here, too, the distress, insofar as it was that of a group, is recounted quite differently from that in the case of an individual human life. This is a clear, yet important clue that the process of transmission must be different in both cases.

Particularly characteristic is a small group of passages in which the comparison in the Report of Rescue does not describe the saving act itself, but its effect on the person saved, e.g. 30.12 (EVV v. 11): 'thou hast loosed my sack-cloth and girded me with gladness', cf. 4.8; 92.11. With astonishing power the sequence of events leading from lament to praise has here been concentrated into a single sentence. A comparison is also able to express an interpretation of suffering derived from reflection, 66.10: 'For thou, O God, has tested us; thou hast tried us as silver is tried', cf. Gen. 22.1.

To summarize our discussion of the Narrative Psalm of Praise, the comparisons, largely derived from the lament, have on the one hand the function of expressing the link between the events of distress and rescue, but at the same time the function of reducing the many and manifold experiences of rescue from distress to what is common to and typical of them all.

Comparisons in the Descriptive Praise of God (*Hymnos*). Although one might expect a particularly rich display of comparisons when God in his majesty and goodness is the recipient of praise, this is not what one finds. Comparisons are not particularly frequent, and distinct groups cannot be recognized among them. Ps. 113, a typical descriptive Psalm of Praise, but which contains no comparisons, can serve to explain this fact. At the centre of this Psalm we find the sentence: 'Who is like the LORD our God . . .?' (v. 5). The subject of God's incomparability is also raised in other contexts in the OT, especially in Isa. 40.12–31. V. 18 reads: 'To whom then will you liken God, or what likeness compare with him?' When it comes to speaking about God comparisons fail and fall silent. This, too, reflects the second commandment. Ps. 113.5 continues: 'who is seated on high, who looks far down . . .'. These two sentences sum up the essence of God's divinity. The first sentence is unfolded in v. 4: 'The LORD is high . . ., and his glory . . .', the second in vv. 7–9: 'He raises the poor from the dust . . .'. Here we note a difference with regard to the comparisons; what is incomparable is God's majesty, God *in* his majesty. For this divine predicates are used, but no comparisons. God's mercy is incomparable, but his condescension from his height to our depths can be experienced, it touches our earth, and for this aspect comparisons are possible.

Predicates in the Praise of God. In contrast to the custom in the religions of the Near East, such predicates are rare in the OT, although they do still crop up. Only 'king' occurs frequently as a divine predicate, less often 'judge'. The former is very significant for the praise of God, e.g. Ps. 5.2: 'my king and my God'; 9.8 (EVV v. 7): 'But the LORD sits enthroned for ever'; 2.4; 9.8 f.; 9.12; 10.16; 11.4; 22.29; 24.7–10; 26.8; 47.1–10; 55.20; 74.12; Pss 95–99; 103.19 *et al.* Sometimes it is combined with the predicate 'judge', as in 9.8–12; Isa. 33.22: 'For the LORD is our judge, the LORD is our ruler (*meḥōqeqēnu*), the LORD is our king; he will save us'. (All relevant passages can be found in G. Liedke's article on *špt* 'to judge', THAT II, cols. 1007–09). Both are divine predicates like *'adōnai*, 'LORD'. They can, of course, be called metaphors, they no longer feel like comparisons. The predicate 'king' was regarded as a term directly denoting the majesty of God, as can be seen from the fact that it never occurs in the Confession of Trust. In addition, the description of God is meant as a form of direct speech referring to the special activity of God in question. While we do find sentences such as 36.7 (EVV v. 6): 'Thy righteousness is like the mountains of God', we never come across sentences like: God speaks justly like a judge. And elsewhere, too, we never find a divine predicate which is an unequivocal comparison. This can also be seen from the typical divine predicates *kābhōd* and *qādōsh*; both directly express God's majesty. In contrast, it is all the more noticeable that in the praise of God's mercy comparisons have an evident function. This comes out particularly clearly in Ps. 103, a deliberately one-sided praise of God's mercy, with the two related comparisons in vv. 11–12 and 13 from the realm of creation and that of human society:

'For as the heavens are high above the earth,
so great is his steadfast love toward those who fear him;
as far as the east is from the west,
so far does he remove our transgressions from us' (v.11 f.).

The effect of God's mercy is praised by making it great and exalted in height and breadth, as in Ps. 108.6; 36.6 f.; 57.11. The two statements are interconnected: because God's mercy is so high above human actions – including their failings – their sins can be forgiven in such a way that they are in fact removed, i.e. rendered ineffective. This suggests that God's mercy is greater than can be conceived of by our criteria for guilt and punishment. This is a profound comparison insofar that God's majesty (height and breadth) serves to demonstrate the extent of his mercy. In Ps. 103.13 this is supplemented by the comparison taken from human society:

> 'As a father pities his children,
> so the LORD pities those who fear him'.

The fact that parents and children belong together makes possible a kind of mercy which transcends the normal criteria for guilt and punishment. The comparison with the father also occurs in Ps. 68.6; Isa. 63.16; cf. Ps. 92.2; 97.2. These two comparisons in Ps. 103 show the possibilities of a comparison and the weighty theological function it can have. The second comparison also shows how the OT comparisons can become the roots of the parables of Jesus: the parable of the Prodigal Son in Lk. 15.11–32 is a development of this comparison in Ps. 103.13 (as Lk. 15.4–6 develops the statement in Ps. 119.176). The same comparison as in 103.11–12 occurs with only slight differences in Ps. 36.6f.; cf. 57.11. It continues in v.8 (EVV v. 7): 'How precious is thy steadfast love, O God! The children of men take refuge in the shadow of thy wings'. This comparison originally belongs to the Confession of Trust. With regard to this motif we were able to observe an occasional transition of its statements into the form of the praise of God (see above p. 129). Correspondingly, for the purpose of praising God's mercy, a series of comparisons were taken over into the context of the praise of God, as in Ps. 36.8; cf. 18.32 (EVV v. 31): 'And who is a rock, except our God?'; v. 47 (EVV v.46): 'The LORD lives; and blessed be my rock', or 31.21 (EVV v. 20): 'thou holdest them safe under thy shelter . . .'. Most comparisons used there recur in the praise of God: fortress 9.10; rock 18.32, 47; shield 18.31, 36, 47; refuge 27.1; shelter 31.21 and 36.8 (EVV v. 7): 'in the shadow of thy wings'. This striking fact shows that both Psalm motifs coincide in this aspect: the expression of trust can suddenly turn into the praise of God. But this also demonstrates that descriptive praise has not developed any fixed groups of comparisons of its own. The original function of these comparisons is to be found in the Confession of Trust; they can be utilized in the praise of God, but they do not have to be.

Ps. 33.4 summarizes the activity of God, unfolded in his praise: his word – his actions, similarly 18.31. No comparison is used here. Ps. 12 (parallel to 18.31) further develops a statement from Ps. 33.4 ('the word of the LORD is upright') in v. 7 (EVV v. 6): 'Silver refined in a furnace . . purified seven times'. This sentence comes close to the praise of the Torah as the word of God in Pss 19b and 119: 'More to be desired . . . than fine gold, even much fine gold', 19.11 (EVV v. 10): 'Thy word is a lamp to my feet and a light to my path', 119.105, cf. vv. 14, 72, 103, 111, 127 and 162. Here we can see clearly how the praise of the word of God, the Torah, develops from the praise of God and becomes an independent element; the comparisons reflect this process. Ps. 33 unfolds the activity of God (summarized in v. 4), frequently in both directions, God's activity in creation and his acts in history. When reference is made to creation, the comparison becomes necessary because the individual works of creation can only be expressed by means of a comparison with human activity.

> 33.7: 'He gathered the waters of the sea as in a bottle;
> he puts the deeps in storehouses',

or 104.1–2:

> 'O LORD, my God, . . .
> who coverest thyself with light as with a garment'.

Ps. 139.13: 'thou didst knit me together in my mother's womb', cf. especially the comparison in Job 38 and Isa. 40.12–31.

The praise of God's eternity is contrasted with comparisons of temporality, as in 102.26–28 (EVV vv. 25–27):

'Of old thou didst lay the foundation of the earth,
and the heavens are the work of thy hands.
They will perish, but thou dost endure;
they will all wear out like a garment,
but thou . . .'.

Similarly, Ps. 103.14–17 confronts man's temporality with the eternal nature of grace. In Ps. 36 the comparison 'shadow of thy wings' in v. 8b (EVV v. 7b) is followed by the praise of the God who blesses, again with a comparison, vv. 9–10 (EVV vv. 8–9):

'They feast on the abundance of thy house,
and thou givest them drink from the river of thy delights.
For with thee is the fountain of life;
in thy light do we see light'.

Light and shield also occur together in the praise of God in 84.12 (EVV v. 11): 'the LORD God is a sun and shield'. The proximity of rescue (help), blessing, and trust in the praise of God is shown by 27.1:

'The LORD is my light and my salvation;
whom shall I fear?
The LORD is the stronghold of my life;
of whom shall I be afraid?'

It is characteristic of descriptive praise that God is praised in the fulness of his divinity; this praise is directed to the saving as well as the blessing God. Therefore the comparison with the light (sun) is particularly apt, firstly, because the sun makes possible all life, growth, and increase, secondly, because it has the dominant role described in Ps. 19, and thirdly, because its rising means the end of the night = distress. Because the Psalms of Praise contain the praise of the saving as well as of the blessing God, there is a partial overlap with the description of blessing (particularly 65.10–14; 85.9–14). The latter has its original setting in the promise of blessing, especially in the words of seers (Numb. 22–24), and has frequently been adopted by prophecy. In post-exilic times it is particularly common in the promise of blessing to the pious. This in turn is an expansion of the motif of the confrontation between the wicked and the pious, which has entered the Psalter from pious Wisdom as an addition, as in Ps. 1 which is a kind of Introit to the Psalter. This confrontation is emphasized by a comparison:

> 'He is like a tree planted by streams of water,
> that yields its fruit in its season;
> and its leaf does not wither.
> In all that he does, he prospers' (v. 3).
> 'The wicked are not so,
> but are like chaff which the wind drives away' (v. 4).

In unfolding the comparison in three sentences and with the contrast in v. 4, the description of blessing in v. 3 approximates to a parable in which the whole emphasis lies on the promise of blessing to the pious, similarly 92.13–15. This shows the function and effect of the comparison in contrast to Ps. 112 which, while also dealing with the righteous and the wicked, does not contain any comparisons. The same contrast is frequently employed in the friends' speeches in the Book of Job. Akin to the description of blessing are Pss 127, 128 and 133 with their many comparisons, which in terms of their origin belong to proverbial Wisdom:

> 'Like arrows in the hand of a warrior
> are the sons of one's youth.
> Happy is the man who has his quiver full of them!' (127.4 f.).
> '. . . your children will be like olive shoots around your table'
> (128.3).

In addition we ought to mention the descriptions of blessing relating to the people, especially in 65.10–14; 85.9–14; 72.5 f., 16; 65.12 (EVV v. 11): 'Thou crownest the year with thy bounty . . .'; v. 13 (EVV v. 12): 'The pastures of the wilderness drip, the hills gird themselves with joy'; v. 14 (EVV v. 13): 'the meadows clothe themselves with flocks . . .'; 85.11: 'Faithfulness will spring up from the ground, and righteousness will look down from the sky';

72.3: 'Let the mountains bear prosperity for the people, and the hills, in righteousness!'; v. 16: 'and may men blossom forth from the cities like the grass of the field'. That the comparisons which articulate God's blessing activity are drawn from the realm of plants is the result of the distinctly aesthetic function of the comparisons here, based on the fact that beauty is part of creation (Gen. 1), that beauty has its origin in God's blessing activity. It is the function of the comparisons in the description of blessing to enliven the whole of creation, to which beauty belongs, by means of the image and subject of comparison – the whole of creation insofar that God's blessing affects plants and animals just as much as man the creature and his community. 'Faithfulness will spring up from the ground, and righteousness will look down from the sky.' There could be no finer expression of man's unity with the rest of creation.

To summarize the comparisons in the Psalms: comparisons occur in the Psalter roughly as often as in the prophets; they form an essential part of the Psalter. They are determined by what happens in the Psalms between God and man, in pleading with God (lament) and in praise. They follow the structure of the Psalms of Lament and Praise. To each part of the Psalms of Lament and Praise belong quite different comparisons, linked to each particular part of the respective Psalm. Thus in the We-lament, for example, the comparisons relate to the community, while those in the I-lament refer to the life of the individual. The comparisons in the Foe-lament only involve wild animals, those in the I-lament only tame ones; the sufferer is set in the circle of creation groaning in travail (as generally the unity of man with the other creatures dominates the comparisons in the Laments and in the Praise of God). Different comparisons are employed in the case of the saving of the people as compared to the saving of the individual. The Foe-laments distinguish between a threat which is visible (wild animals), and one which cannot be perceived (snares). In the case of the pleading petition from distress and the report of rescue, the comparison has, for different reasons, no specific function. In descriptive praise comparisons occur mainly in the praise of God's mercy, rarely in the praise of his majesty; the praise of the creator is uttered almost exclusively in comparisons.

The function of the comparisons in the Psalms is determined by their allocation to the respective parts of these Psalms; e.g. the comparisons in the indictment of God intensify this accusation. In the Praise of God they serve to exalt him; in the Review of the Distress in the Narrative Psalm of Praise the comparisons take up the lament and thereby bind together lament and praise.

The comparisons in the Confession of Trust form the largest and most striking single group. Their function, to confirm trust, is evident; by means of this they point to the indispensability of God, thereby allowing us to recognise the origin of the comparisons: typical experiences are repeated by other people and this linguistic expression becomes a means by which they in turn can voice their own experiences. In other words, these comparisons form a tradition.

## Comparisons in the Book of Job

The Book of Job is a poetic work based on the author's design, which is reflected in the book's structure. The comparisons, too, are part of this poetic design, a fact which distinguishes them from those in the Psalms. Not only do the comparisons belong to the respective motifs in which they occur, but they are at the same time part of the overall design, something which has to be kept in mind when attempting to define their function. In many places they have a pronounced poetic character, which is particularly apparent in their elaboration, but also in their distribution. Above all, in the Book of Job (as in Deutero-Isaiah) the boundaries between direct speech and comparison are often fluid.

Corresponding to the structure of the book, the comparisons in its individual sections are also clearly different: in Job's laments, in the speeches of his friends, in the divine speeches, and in the Wisdom chapter (28).

*Comparisons in Job's laments.* These contain the largest number of comparisons; the greatest accumulation occurs in the indictment of God. This is also the group which shows the strongest power of expression and is the liveliest. This group again is the most clearly structured and shows no sign of petrified formulae. The special character of this group is based on the design of the entire book, whose individuality is most apparent here. Whereas in the Individual Laments the indictment of God and the relevant comparisons are rarely found, in this case it forms the most important part of the lament with particularly striking comparisons. This was the main concern of the author of the Book of Job. The comparisons in the indictment of God display a clearly recognizable structure:

(a)   God has become Job's enemy: 'For the arrows of the Almighty are in me; my spirit drinks their poison', 6.4; 'thou dost renew thy witnesses against me . . .' (opponents), 10.17; 'He has torn me in his wrath, and hated me; he has gnashed his teeth at me; my adversary sharpens his eyes against me', 16.9; v. 12: 'he set me up as his target'; v. 13: 'his archers surround me. He slashes open my kidneys, and does not spare'; v. 14: 'He breaks me with breach upon breach; he runs upon me like a warrior.'

'He has kindled his wrath against me,
and counts me as his adversary.
His troops come on together;
they have cast up siegeworks against me,
and encamp round about my tent' (19.11 f.).

'Thou hast turned cruel to me; with the might of thy hand thou dost persecute me', 30.21. The same can be expressed in mythic language: 'Am I the sea, or a sea monster, that thou settest a guard over me?', 7.12.

(b) Even harsher are the comparisons in which God attacks Job like an elemental power or a wild beast: 'For he crushes me with a tempest', 9.17; 'And if I lift myself up, thou dost hunt me like a lion', 10.16; 'I was at ease, and he broke me asunder; he seized me by the neck and dashed me to pieces', 16.12; 'He breaks me down on every side', 19.10; 'God has cast me into the mire', 30.19; v. 22: 'Thou liftest me up on the wind, thou makest me ride on it, and thou tossest me about in the roar of the storm'.

(c) God afflicts Job with pain and suffering: '. . . and multiplies my wounds without cause', 9.17; v.18: 'he will not let me get my breath, but fills me with bitterness'; v. 23: 'When disaster brings sudden death, he mocks at the calamity of the innocent'; v. 34: 'Let him take his rod away from me'. 30.11: 'Because God has loosed my cord and humbled me' (v. 19: '. . . and I have become like dust and ashes'); v. 23: 'I know that thou wilt bring me to death, and to the house appointed for all living', cf. 14.20.

(d) God takes away Job's future and hope: '. . . to a man whose way is hid, whom God has hedged in', 3.23; 'Thou puttest my feet in the stocks, and watchest all my paths; thou settest a bound to the soles of my feet', 13.27;

'But the mountain falls and crumbles away,
and the rock is removed from its place;
the waters wear away the stones;
the torrents wash away the soil of the earth;
so thou destroyest the hope of man' (14.18–19).

'He has walled up my way, so that I cannot pass, and he has set darkness upon my paths', 19.8; v. 10: 'my hope has he pulled up like a tree'.

(e) God ties Job down to his sins and takes his honour away:

'If I wash myself with snow,
and cleanse my hands with lye,
yet thou wilt plunge me into a pit,
and my own clothes will abhor me' (9.30).
'Remember that thou hast made me of clay;
and wilt thou turn me to dust again?
Didst thou not pour me out . . .?
Yes these things thou didst hide in thy heart . . .;
If I sin, thou dost mark me, . . .
And if I lift myself up, thou dost hunt me like a lion' (10.9–17).

In this passage and in 10.4 f. ('Hast thou eyes of flesh? Dost thou see as a man sees? Are thy days as the days of man?') the suffering Job recalls the activity of the creator, who by rights should be dealing differently with his creature. The same is the case in 13.25: 'Wilt thou frighten a driven leaf and pursue dry chaff?' God has taken away dignity and honour from his creature: 'know then that God has put me in the wrong', 19.6; v. 9: 'He has stripped from me my glory, and taken the crown from my head'; 16.11: 'God gives me up to the ungodly, and casts me into the hands of the wicked'.

In all these reproaches the creature charges his creator with not treating him in the way appropriate to such a relationship. To the indictment that God has become his enemy (a) is now added (e) the reflection about how this could possibly have happened; this is an expression of the desperation of the creature who can no longer understand his creator. In all five groups the comparisons have the same function, i.e. to intensify the indictment against God. This is entirely in line with the conception underlying the Book of Job; hence it is not to be understood only in terms of the lament motif, but also on the basis of the author's intention. There is probably in the whole of world literature no religious work which raises such a passionate and manifold accusation against God. This could not be done without the comparisons. This then is one context in which their significance is crystal clear. The author is concerned to expose the incomprehensibility of God's actions in the face of the attempt by Job's friends to fix God's activity among men in the form of a doctrine which would be at man's intellectual disposal. Ch. 12.13–25 extends the same point to God's acts in history, v. 14: 'If he tears down, none can rebuild; if he shuts a man in, none can open'; v. 21: 'He pours contempt on princes, and looses the belt of the strong'; v. 16: 'the deceived and the deceiver are his'; v. 23: 'He makes nations great, and he destroys them'. Strictly speaking, these are not proper comparisons; complex historical processes are here depicted as rather more simple processes in the life of the individual.

This, too, focusses on the incomprehensibility of God's acts in history.

Comparisons in the I-lament. The second largest group of comparisons comprises those in the I-lament. One might have expected it to be dominated by references to illness, but this is not the case and such references are few and do not include comparisons. The I-lament falls almost entirely into two groups, viz. the description of the lament and its expansion into a collective lament of transitoriness.

(a) 'For my sighing comes as my bread, and my groanings are poured out like water', 3.24; 'O that my vexation were weighed, and all my calamity laid in the balances! For then it would be heavier than the sand of the sea', 6.2 f.; vv. 5–7:

> 'Does the wild ass bray when he has grass,
> or the ox low over his fodder?
> Can that which is tasteless be eaten without salt,
> or is there any taste in the slime of the purslane?
> My appetite refuses . . . is loathsome . . .'.

'I am a brother of jackals, and a companion of ostriches', 30.29. Tracking down the function of each of these comparisons requires a good deal of careful thought. It is the parallelism of bread and water which determines 3.24: the lament has taken the place of the eating and drinking essential to life; in 6.2 the lament is appropriate to the severity of the suffering, it cannot be denied to the sufferer (aimed at the friends). 6.5 and 30.29 say the same thing in a different way, here the lamenter is conscious of being part of the suffering creation.

(b) In the Lament of Transitoriness comparisons are richly developed. This is due to the structure of the work. The poet emphasizes the link between Job's personal suffering and the suffering of everyman subject to death. This is the occasion for the poet to display something of his art in expanding the lament of transitoriness, especially in 7.1–10 and 14.1–12. These are beautiful, self-contained poems which are brought totally to life by the comparisons. They really demand a thoroughgoing process of interpretation which, however, cannot be offered here. We have comparisons with the service of the soldier and that of the slave in 7.1–3 (14.14), and the comparison of human hope with that of a tree in 14.7–11. Transitoriness can be expressed in the comparisons as a breath (7.7), a weaver's shuttle (7.6), a vanishing cloud (7.9), and as a flower and a shadow (14.2).

> 'My days are swifter than a runner;
> they flee away, they see no good.
> They go by like skiffs of reed,
> like an eagle swooping on the prey' (9.25 f.).

This is poetic language: the sufferer's life is devoid of joy and events. His life is sometimes described as an almost imperceptible decline, but then again as a terminal collapse. This is a profound observation derived from bitter experience, but it can only be articulated by means of comparisons.

The Foe-lament. In Job's speeches the Foe-lament is very much in the background, because it is raised by his friends as an indictment of the wicked, the godless. For Job's laments only a partial aspect of the Foe-lament is relevant, viz. that the sufferer's friends turn into his enemies. Job expresses this directly to his friends, mostly without any comparisons, as in 13.12: 'Your maxims are proverbs of ashes, your defences are defences of clay'; 19.2: '. . . and break me in pieces with words'. Job states this pointedly in the single comparison developed in the direction of a parable, in which he compares his friends with treacherous torrent-beds:

> 'My brethren are treacherous as a torrent-bed . . .
> The caravans turn aside from their course;  ₵
> they go up into the waste, and perish.
> The caravans of Tema look . . .,
> they . . . are confounded.
> Such you have now become to me' (6.15–21).

It is a genuine parable insofar that an event in one sphere has been juxtaposed with one from another; the audience are left to draw their own conclusions.

The fact that the comparisons are assigned to the same three parts of the lament as we find in the Psalms is confirmation that the author of Job presupposes the same lament structure. Further comparisons in other parts of the lament have been omitted here.

Comparisons in the speeches of the friends. Most of the comparisons in the friends' speeches belong to the dominant motif, the doctrine of retribution. There are several variants.

(a) Punishment strikes the culprit: 'Those who plough iniquity and sow trouble reap the same', 4.8; 'Surely vexation kills the fool, and jealousy slays the simple', 5.2; 'They conceive mischief and bring forth evil and their heart prepares deceit', 15.35; 'He swallows down riches and vomits them up again; . . . He will suck the poison of asps; the tongue of a viper will kill him', 20.15 f.; 'Drought and heat snatch away the snow waters; so does Sheol those who have sinned', 24.19; v. 20: 'wickedness is broken like a tree'.

(b) The rise of the wicked is followed by their fall: 'I have seen the fool taking root, but suddenly I cursed his dwelling', 5.3 (Hebrew uncertain); 'Can papyrus grow where there is no marsh? Can reeds flourish where there is no water?', 8.11; v. 12: 'While yet in flower and not cut down, they wither before any other plant'; v. 13: 'Such are the paths of all who forget God', cf. 8.16 f.; 20.6–8:

'Though his height mount up to the heavens,
and his head reach to the clouds,
he will perish for ever like his own dung; . . .
He will fly away like a dream, and not be found;
he will be chased away like a vision of the night'.

All these comparisons are intended to make the doctrine of retribution impressive. This didactic tendency is apparent in the frequent conclusion: 'Behold . . .', in the introduction 8.10, where the didactic purpose is pronounced, and in the educational questions in 8.11 f. The weakness of these comparisons derives from the fact that all of them already presuppose that Job is one of the wicked. In no case is the slightest attempt made to show and prove to the addressee that he is one of the godless. Moreover, the comparisons are also weak in themselves. If it is the purpose of a comparison to juxtapose a process from one sphere with that from another, then the comparing process ought to have a structure corresponding to that of the subject of comparison, it should also demonstrate cause and effect. All these parallel processes are unable to demonstrate a cause which would point to a crime or sin. In all these comparisons the decline, the collapse, the trespass can be shown, but not the reason for it. This is probably also the reason why in the speeches of Elihu, added later in chs 32–37, comparisons are almost completely absent.

In the friends' speeches comparisons occur in the (rare) promise of blessing, which completely corresponds to the traditional structure, 5.18: 'For he wounds, but he binds up; he smites, but his hands heal'; v. 21: 'You shall be hid from the scourge of the tongue'; v. 26: 'as a shock of grain comes up to the threshing floor in its season'; 22.25: 'if the Almighty is your gold, and your precious silver'.

Comparisons in the divine speeches chs 38–41. While in Job's speeches the comparisons are assigned to elements of the lament, the divine speeches by contrast are based on a part of the praise of God taken from the Psalms, the praise of the creator. The first part (38.1–38) is indirect praise of the creator, a speech in the first person in which God asks Job: Were you the creator then? Vv. 4–11: 'Where were you when I . . .?' There follows the indirect praise of the creator in vv. 12–28, resembling the praise of the creator in the Psalms. Here we now find something similar to the comparison in a peculiar and unique form. Whereas in the history of the transmission of the creator and creation motif the earlier discourse employing concrete verbs such as *yāṣab* (to form), which describe human activity, was replaced in the Priestly Writer by the abstract verb *bārā'*, a term reserved for God's creative acts alone, the author of the Book of Job again employs a wealth of concrete verbs in talking about creation. God's creation and his dominion over his creatures is depicted in a human, and hence inappropriate, way in that it is equated with human actions; with begetting (38.28–29), with a craftsman's work (38.31 binding), with governing, guiding, instructing, and leading (38.32–39), with the bestowing of wisdom and acting with wisdom and moderation (vv. 36–38 using the analogy of natural law). Human works and actions become a parable of the creator's activity in this question put by God to a human being; in addressing human beings God can only speak in this fashion. The author of the Book of Job thus explains why there is no other way of talking about creation except in human terms. For in 38.4–11, where God is the subject of creation, the same human language is used with regard to it: he determined its measurement and stretched the measuring-line (v. 5), sunk its bases, laid its cornerstone (v. 6), shut doors (v. 8); the sea burst forth from the womb (v. 8); he made into garments and swaddling bands (v. 9), prescribed bounds and set bars and doors (v. 10), and commanded (v. 11).

In the relation between God and man there are contexts in which it is not possible to speak about God except by means of comparisons. The term 'anthropomorphic' is usually applied to this, but this is improper and misleading. For such discourse is not concerned with God's or man's *morphē*, but rather the comparison is between divine and human activity. This is also the case when the OT speaks of God's arm, as in 40.1–9; the 'arm of God' moreover does not so much refer to a part of his body as to a way of acting, the strength of his actions. When Job 38 speaks of God as sinking posts and laying cornerstones, then God's actions are being equated with human actions in these sentences in such a way that this equation is limited *ab initio* by the opposition between God and man, which is strongly emphasized in this chapter. The comparison serves, precisely through this equation, to articulate the opposition between God and man: God is the creator, man the creature. By speaking in the comparison of God's creational activity in terms of human actions, the author indicates the disparity all the more clearly. By emphasizing the contrast between creator and creature, God is exalted and praised as the creator. Such comparative discourse about the creator implies his praise; this is the real function of the comparisons in Job 38.

Ch. 28 represents the expansion of a riddle, consisting of question and answer, the question in vv. 12–20 and the answer in v. 23. Juxtaposed with the positive answer in v. 23 is the negative one in vv. 13–21. The reason for the positive answer is given in vv. 24–27: God knows the place of Wisdom because he is the creator. The negative answer denies two possibilities of acquiring Wisdom. It cannot be purchased (vv. 15–19). The other possibility would be to look for it. This possibility is rejected by means of a contrast parable: while humans have been able to force access to subterranean treasures (vv. 1–11), no human technical skill can force access to Wisdom. Only God the creator knows the way to Wisdom. This word is spoken as the friends depart. The friends thought that they themselves were in possession of Wisdom and therefore felt able to convict Job of wickedness. The purpose of ch. 28, a Wisdom speech, is to reject this position (cf. C. Westermann, *The Structure of the Book of Job*, pp. 135–38). Job. 28.1–11 is a contrast parable of particular poetic beauty. This contrasting comparison is here clearly expanded into a parable, an independent unit. This contrasting comparison functions on several levels. On the surface it represents praise for man's technical abilities and potential, i.e. a positive and encouraging word on the development of technology. However, at a deeper level resulting from the context of this chapter, it is a denial of man's capacity to reach Wisdom or the place of Wisdom by himself. Here his searching and his potential have reached their limit. Indirectly, this represents praise of the creator who alone knows the place of Wisdom.

In sum: the author of the Book of Job has assigned the comparisons as a powerful poetic tool various functions in the structure of his work: in Job's speeches as a means of intensifying the lament in its three parts, in the friends' speeches as confirmation of the doctrine of retribution in terms of instruction and argument, and in the divine speeches as well as in ch. 28 as indirect praise of God.

# Epilogue to the Investigation of Comparisons in the OT

I am acutely conscious that this study only marks a beginning. This, what might be termed, 'vertical' investigation following through the books of the OT would have to be supplemented by a 'horizontal' one. The latter would first have to summarize the functions of the comparisons in the OT, and then investigate the comparisons as such in their respective areas. An investigation using these two steps could formulate much of what I have discovered more precisely, develop it further, and perhaps to some extent correct it.

I should like, in conclusion, to emphasize a few points arising from my survey:

(1) The comparisons form an essential element of what the OT says about God and about what happens between God and man respectively. They have theological relevance.

(2) This relevance is already evident from the fact that these comparisons do not just occur anywhere, but that they have their specific significance in dialogical texts, especially in prophecy and the Psalms (as well as in several groups of profane texts), but not in narrative or legal passages.

(3) The occurrence and use of the comparisons in the OT contradicts the view that all comparisons have an illustrative function, that they can therefore be described as 'images'. Rather, the comparisons receive their function from their particular contexts; this function is derived from the context.

(4) Since the comparisons belong to dialogical texts, this context in every case is something which happens between the partners in this dialogue. The relation in which the comparison is involved is not one of image and subject

matter, rather, in the comparison an event from one sphere is juxtaposed with an event from another (with the image serving the subject matter).

(5) Such a context, however, is still part of a larger structure, e.g. a prophetic oracle or a Psalm. The comparisons are meant to ensure that the Psalm or prophetic oracle is listened to, even each individual part to which they belong. Comparisons in the indictment of God intensify it, as do those in the I-lament, while comparisons in the Confession of Trust confirm what the worshipper puts his trust in, and those in the Praise of God are meant to exalt God. The same is true of the prophetic oracles.

(6) Because of this intensifying function neither the language of prophetic oracles nor that of the Psalms can do without comparisons; without them prophetic oracles and Psalms would not be able to convey their message.

(7) The subject matter of these comparisons takes in the whole of human reality and that of the world. In the comparisons the whole reality of the created order, the entire dimension of creation speaks in harmony with the words in which they are expressed. This gives the biblical statements about creation a significance which cannot be divorced from what God says to humans and they to God.

# CONSEQUENCES FOR OUR UNDERSTANDING OF THE PARABLES

The Consequences of our Investigation of the Comparisons in the OT for our Understanding of the Parables of Jesus in the NT

(a) We found from our investigation of the comparisons of the OT that they receive their function and meaning from the contexts in which they occur.

(b) The OT comparisons only occur in dialogical texts (with some exceptions for which there are very good reasons). They form part of the address or assist it; they derive their function from the context of address. To the degree and extent that parables are expansions of comparisons, the same is also true of them.

(c) In the parable, as in the comparison, one process is juxtaposed with another which it is intended to comment upon. The intention of this juxtaposition is the same as the function of the comparison as well as of the parable. Just as the comparisons (and in some cases the parables also) belong to a part of a Psalm or prophetic oracle, the parables, too, have their place and their function in a constituent part of the message or ministry of Jesus, or in the development of the life and activity of the original Christian community.

(d) Just like the comparisons in the OT, the comparisons and parables in the preaching of Jesus can only be explained from their overall context. In both Testaments we find texts which represent a transitional form between comparison and parable. Our first step then would have to be a survey and analysis of the NT parables. Like the OT comparisons, the Gospel parables have different functions in different contexts.

(e) Like the OT comparisons, the parables of Jesus do not appeal to faith, but demand independent judgment. The instructions of Jesus, for example, like the words of the prophets, are not supported by a power, office or institution; the speaker can only appeal to the understanding and inner agreement of his audience.

(f) The scope of comparisons in the OT and in the preaching of Jesus is similar; in both cases we encounter in the comparisons potentially the whole of human and extra-human reality, i.e. the whole of creation. As in the OT comparisons, the addressee of the parables of Jesus is capable of judging the comparisons as a creature, equipped by his creator to come to terms with his world and to find his way in it. This gives an increased significance to the statements about creation in the parables of Jesus as well as in the OT comparisons: what happens in creation is reflected in the relationship between God and man.

# The History of Parable Interpretation in NT Research

(a) R. Bultmann, *Geschichte der synoptischen Tradition*, 1931, [8]1970, pp. 179–222: 'Gleichnisse und Verwandtes' (ET: *The History of the Synoptic Tradition*, 1963, pp. 166–205: 'Similitudes and Similar Forms'). – Bultmann's investigation of the parables is fundamental for modern research. He proceeds from 'figures' which paint a picture (pp. 181–83); similitudes are distinguishable from them by their detail (pp. 184–88); such a similitude can have been developed from a figure or a comparison. From the similitude he with Jülicher distinguishes the parable (pp. 188–92) – the former being a typical recurrent event, the latter an interesting particular situation – and the exemplary story (pp. 192–3). This is followed by 'Form und Geschichte des Stoffes', pp. 193–222 (ET: 'Form and History of the Material', pp. 179–205).

We can agree with Bultmann's distinction between short figures which paint a picture and the more detailed similitudes which can be understood as expansions of the former. But what is problematic is the designation 'figures' and their distinction from metaphors (p. 193), which, as opposed to the 'concrete comparison', lack the comparative term. Among the figures Bultmann mentions Lk. 6.39: 'Can a blind man lead a blind man?' But this saying does not so much paint a picture as juxtapose one process with another which it is meant to comment upon. Bultmann counts as metaphors among others Mt. 5.13, 14, 16: 'You are the salt of the earth . . .', because there are no comparative terms present. But their absence does not alter the fact that we are dealing here with a comparison in a single sentence; they are equally lacking in Lk 6.39 which Bultmann calls a figure (= comparison). The activity of the disciples in the world is compared to the effect of salt in food. On the contrary, in v. 16 'light' is used as a metaphor, as a single word with a figurative sense. This figurative sense has arisen out of a comparison, viz. v. 14. In the same way 'fruits' in Mt. 7.16 is used as a metaphor: 'You will know them by their fruits'. Behind this metaphorical usage there lies a comparison. However, the saying Mt. 7.3–5 (Bultmann: 'The saying about the mote and the beam can be counted as such') is clearly an expanded comparison. Mt. 7.1–5 is a warning against wrong actions. Vv. 3–5 add a reason for the warning in a comparison from which the addressee is meant to draw his own conclusions. Such a reason has at the same time the function of strengthening the warning given in v. 1. The passage Mt. 7.1–5 confirms that the term 'figure' is inappropriate because, wherever in the Gospels a comparison such as this one in vv. 4–5 is expanded, this is done through verbs, almost like a short story, but never in the manner of painting a picture.

When one surveys the texts listed by Bultmann (pp. 181–84) under the headings 'figures', 'metaphors' and 'comparisons', which does not thereby make the particular classification clear, one gets the impression that extremely varied passages have been juxtaposed. The result of this is that assigning them to one of these particular headings is not sufficient to determine coherent groups. This confirms that it is impossible to form these groups without determining the function of these figures of speech. In pp. 184–93 Bultmann groups the similitudes which he defines as follows: '. . . such formulations . . . are distinguished from comparisons or figures only by the detail . . .'. But the main difference is that while the comparison has the form of a sentence, the parable has that of a story. Fundamental to the parable is the fact that it is a *sequence* of acts formed into a narrative. But it is only in the section 'Technique of Telling a Similitude' that Bultmann (pp. 203–10), following Olrik, refers to the parable as a story. Here, too, he only deals with elements of the story, not the narrative structure as a whole.

The result is that the ensuing treatment of the individual parables (pp. 184–193) according to purely formal criteria is not convincing. Bultmann lists such diverse parables one after another that we are unable to recognize clearly distinct groups among them. Correspondingly, while Bultmann in the section 'Form and History of the Material' (pp. 193–222) treats in detail the introduction (p. 193), the conclusion (p. 198), and individual elements of the parable, he has nothing to say about the whole narrative and its structure. Following Olrik, he convincingly shows (pp. 203–10) that the same kind of multiform narrative art can be found in the parables as in the old popular narratives of oral tradition. But the obvious conclusion, that the parables belong as regards their form to the larger genre of these oral narratives, Bultmann has failed to draw. The question of how then the parables relate to the narratives in the sense established by Olrik (who was not thinking of parables at all) has also not been posed by him. Therefore Bultmann was also blind to the fact that the majority of parables are abbreviated stories, not complete ones, but sections of stories; complete narratives are only found in the small group of exemplary stories. What is narrated in the remaining parables is only what is essential for the context and with it the function of the parable, everything else has been omitted. Bultmann notes with exactitude the introduction and conclusion of the parable (pp. 193–95, 197–202, 208–10). However, when paying attention to the whole narrative structure, one must distinguish between the introduction and conclusion of the story as a whole and the introduction and conclusion of the parable as a section of a larger narrative context. This distinction alone enables us to identify the context from which the parable receives its function. It further serves to help us distinguish different groups of parables according to their functions.

(b) J. Jeremias, *Die Gleichnisse Jesu*, 1947, ⁹1977 (ET: *The Parables of Jesus*, rev. ed. 1963). – In Part I 'The Problem' Jeremias deals under 'the recovery of their original meaning' (p. 9) briefly and sketchily with the history of previous research; he mentions A. Jülicher, A. T. Cadoux, B. T. D. Smith, C. H. Dodd, but not R. Bultmann. Part II 'The Return to Jesus from the Primitive Church' is an attempt to enable us 'to hear once more the original tones of the utterances of Jesus'; 'to meet with him can alone give power to our preaching'.

In Part III 'The Message of the Parables of Jesus' (pp. 115–226) Jeremias (p. 115) anticipates one of the results of his enquiry: 'We shall find that many parables express one and the same idea by means of varying symbols', therefore only 'a few simple essential ideas stand out'. They fall almost automatically into ten groups, and 'as a whole these groups present a comprehensive conception of the message of Jesus'. Jeremias, too, takes it for granted that the parables consist of images which are meant to express ideas (so on p. 91), and that a message consists of ideas. In fact, a message proclaims that something has happened (Lk. 7.22; Mt. 11.5, quoted by Jeremias at the beginning of this chapter). But even apart from this, the assumption that the ten main ideas fall automatically into ten groups which 'as a whole . . . present a comprehensive conception of the message of Jesus' (p. 115), remains a pure hypothesis, which is not borne out by his treatment of the ten points.

Section 1 'Now is the Day of Salvation' (p. 115) as well

as section 8 'The Via Dolorosa and Exaltation of the Son of Man' (p. 217) contain no parables, only comparisons, similarly section 9 'The Consummation'; section 10 deals with parabolic actions. This leaves only sections 2–7 for the treatment of parables. Only section 2 'God's Mercy for Sinners' consists of a group of parables with the same function and addressees: in it 'Jesus vindicate(s) the gospel against its critics' (p. 125). Section 3 combines 'growth parables' with entirely different ones. The parables in sections 4–7 are also of very diverse kinds, assembled – one gains the impression – according to theoretical and subjective criteria. Some parables occur twice; one of them is expressly designated a parable of judgment, but also crops up in another group.

Jeremias' attempt to group the parables is right and necessary, because it gives the individual parables a firmer context and thereby sets their interpretation on more solid ground. But the attempt fails to gain momentum because safe criteria are lacking.

Bultmann's and Jeremias' investigations of the parables are plainly opposed to each other. For Bultmann the form alone is decisive, for Jeremias the content. It has become clear that in both cases one-sidedness leads to difficulties. However, Bultmann's precise investigation of individual detail supplies the necessary foundation for further research. Jeremias' hypothesis that his 10 (9) groups represent the whole message of Jesus is untenable, but his positive contribution is to have correctly defined some groups according to their functions and addressees.

(c) C. H. Dodd, *The Parables of the Kingdom*, 1935. – The first chapter 'The Nature of the Gospel Parables' defines the parables as the natural expression of a way of thinking that sees truth in concrete pictures rather than in abstractions. Dodd distinguishes on formal grounds between metaphor, elaboration of a simple metaphor into a picture, and elaboration into a story. Each of these forms has a *single* point of comparison. The realism of the parables is based on the fact that the Kingdom of God is intrinsically like the processes of nature and of human life:

'since nature and supernature are one order'. The parables relate to the critical situation in which Jesus and his audience find themselves; this implies that we have to distinguish between the original meaning of the parables in the situation of Jesus and his disciples and that after the death of Jesus when the parables were transformed for parenetic or eschatological purposes.

Chapters II and III are intended to elucidate the theological background against which the parables have to be understood: 'The Kingdom of God' and 'The Day of the Son of Man'. Chapter IV 'The Setting in Life' sorts the parables into those which are situated in the ministry of Jesus and those which arose in the community or were modified by it after the death of Jesus. Chapter V 'Parables of Crisis' distinguishes from the later expectation of Jesus' Second Coming the crisis caused by his first coming. Chapter VI 'Parables of Growth' sees the crisis brought about by the coming of Jesus as the climax of a long process, the history of God's acts with his people before Christ. In his conclusion (Ch. VII) Dodd calls the parables 'comments upon an historical situation'. Now is the hour of decision, 'realized eschatology'. This applies to all parables: 'The parables represent the interpretation which our Lord offered of His own ministry'.

Dodd's attempt to explain the parables from the ministry of Jesus and on the basis of that ministry is to be welcomed. It is, however, questionable whether Jesus' ministry can be reduced in this way to a single concept, viz. the Kingdom of God, as Dodd presupposes. For the Gospels do not so much develop a concept as tell a story. The consequence of this is that Dodd is limited from the outset to the purely conceptual question: whether and to what extent the parables of Jesus reflect Dodd's own understanding of the Kingdom of God as 'realized eschatology'. This limitation makes it inevitable that the author is particularly interested in what all the parables have in common: they *all* refer to the crisis which occurred in the ministry of Jesus – even where the later reworking no longer allows us to recognize this. This is true e.g. of the parables of growth, which are so clearly distinct from all the rest, where he is not interested in what they all have in common; rather he places the whole emphasis on the culmination of the development described in them, which has the effect of turning them too into parables of crisis. In his introduction Dodd says that the parables have the character of an argument. But he does not ask whether in fact all the parables have this character or only a single group whose argumentative character can be proved.

Following the majority of interpreters of the parables, Dodd understands them as images. They are 'the natural expression of a mind that sees truth in concrete pictures rather than conceives it in abstractions'. But parables are narratives, and not images.

In Ch. IV the author defines the setting in life of the parables as the situation of Jesus' ministry; sometimes he refers to it as an historic situation. But what is meant here by situation? The Gospels tell a story of the ministry of Jesus. This story contains a number of different situations in which he could have told parables. The parables would have to be grouped according to such possible situations. This implies not least the question whether we can distinguish between those parables in which Jesus addresses opponents and those in which he speaks to his disciples or to a willing audience in a wider sense. This question has been entirely overlooked by Dodd. To this we would have to add further distinctions which the text of the parables justifies, without thereby already embarking on an interpretation. Such distinctions are also lacking. The reason for this is Dodd's fixation with the single question whether a parable belongs to the time before or after the death of Christ.

When the author again emphasizes in the conclusion of his book (ch. VII) that the parables all have the same meaning and that this is unfolded in the course of Jesus' ministry as a whole, the question becomes inevitable: why then this rich, moving variety of Jesus' parables, what then remains of the function which is peculiar to them alone and of their special message?

(d) G. Eichholz, *Gleichnisse der Evangelien* (Einleitung, Sprache und Struktur der Gleichnisse. Eine kleine Methodenlehre der Gleichnisauslegung), 1971, [3]1979. – 'Parable' is a kind of collective term; in each case what is being said is expressed in a pictorial form. But to speak of the 'language of images' is only a starting-point. The distinction between *Bildhälfte* (the aspect relating to the image) and *Sachhälfte* (the aspect relating to the subject-matter) can still retain some limited value. The *Bildhälfte* does not actually present an image, but rather a sequence of images, or even better: the course of an event. This is a necessary corrective to any reference to the 'language of images'. We agree with the author's statement that the synoptic parable has the natural fall of a story line, the point in question is primarily an event, because in the message of Jesus God is always the acting God and man is called by it to action. These two aspects often correspond with one another. In the end, all parables demand to be told as stories. Even the images used still reflect the character of the events in question.

The author's criticism of the definition of the parables as the 'language of images' and of the distinction between *Bildhälfte* and *Sachhälfte* is completely justified, one cannot but agree with it, as well as with its being based on the message of Jesus. But then it remains incomprehensible why the author insists on sitting on the fence and asserting that the distinction between *Bildhälfte* and *Sachhälfte* can still retain some limited value. Either the parable is an image or it is a story; an image is not a story! Either the *Sachhälfte* deals with a thing or with an event. This alternative requires an unambiguous answer!

Hence, in the exposition of the parables in the second part of the book, it becomes evident that the correct understanding of the parable as an event has also not really been applied. If it had been, the author could not have failed to notice that what is related in the parables of growth (pp. 65–84) is an event essentially different from those narrated in parables which are based on events. But for Eichholz the point is the same in both cases: the parable expresses a promise of God's eschatological action: 'the action of God the creator becomes a parable of his eschatological action' (p. 76). Differences are being levelled out, the proper character of the parables of growth is being misunderstood.

One would have expected that the insight that the parables are not concerned with image and subject, but with an event, would have had obvious consequences for their exposition. Rather, we still find in the latter an uncritical use of the distinction between *Bildhälfte* and *Sachhälfte* (e.g. pp. 84 and 120). The author does not draw the necessary conclusion from his insights that, if the parable is an event, a story, then what the parable is meant to express or explain must also be an event. Instead the *Sachhälfte* is reduced to a concept. The author correctly asserts: 'In the case of the Kingdom of Heaven we have to do with something essentially like an everyday event' (p. 115). Does this not necessarily imply that the Kingdom of Heaven must also refer to an event, and not to an abstract concept? In concluding his fine exposition of the parable of the Good Samaritan Eichholz states: 'The event of love meets us in this parable'; 'we are concerned with the heart of the good news'. But this parable does not talk about love; it is far too sober for that. And when Eichholz describes the parable in sum as 'the heart of the good news' then he has perhaps forgotten that it was a Samaritan who showed himself merciful, a Samaritan who knew nothing of the good news. Once it has been recognized that in the parables an everyday event is being compared to an event between God and man then the expositor ought to endeavour to allow this everyday event to be heard, and one ought to be more cautious in one's use of general theological terms.

(e) Eta Linnemann, *Gleichnisse Jesu*, 1961, ⁴1966 (ET: *Parables of Jesus*, 1966). – Part I of this book deals with 'The Basic Principles of Parable Interpretation' (pp. 13–54). In section 1, 'Similitudes, Parables, Illustrations, Allegories', the author adopts the standard division, but she fails to achieve a clear delimitation of several genres, just as much as Bultmann. In what follows we find these distinctions more or less abandoned. In the next two sections, 'The Narrative Laws of Similitudes and Parables' (2) and 'Introductory Formulas and Applications' (3), she follows Bultmann.

In section 4, 'The Parable as a Form of Communication', Linnemann stresses that the origin of the parable lies in dialogue, in conversation (like G. Eichholz). 'Whoever tells a parable intends to influence others'. Here the author could have pointed to comparisons and parables in the prophets. The situation of such dialogue can be very different; the parable can serve the purposes of instruction (as used by the rabbis) or of exhortation (also rabbinical), scholarly argument (likewise), conviction of a culprit (II Sam. 12), as a weapon in disputation, and in order to reach a decision (Menenius Agrippa). With regard to the parables of Jesus, Linnemann simply states that they do not serve any of these purposes, with the occasional exception of exhortation. They predominantly address opponents and are attempting to gain their agreement. The author does not go beyond these vague hints; no attempt is made to group the parables of Jesus according to their functions.

Section 5, 'The Structure of the Parable', begins with a refutation of the customary designation of the parables as images or illustrations: 'Parables are something different from pictures. They are neither illustrations nor communications in pictorial language' (p. 31). We could not agree more. But what then are they? The author's own positive contribution is somewhat disappointing: 'The parable is a means of proof'; 'the intention of parables is to prove a point'. Is this meant to be true of all parables? Can the parable of the Prodigal Son be regarded as a means of some proof? Furthermore, the expression is inappropriate; the point is made more clearly in section 4. Since they are regarded as means of proof they only have one point of comparison, the *tertium comparationis*. It 'is the pivot which unites the parable and its subject matter, *Bildhälfte* and *Sachhälfte*, with each other. The terms *Bildhälfte* and *Sachhälfte* or image and subject matter make the distinction between what the narrative portrays and what it means' (p. 32). Just before we were told: 'Parables are something different from pictures'. While in what follows the use of the terms image and subject matter is restricted to 'later readers and commentators', who are no longer aware of the situation, this careful distinction is again later dropped. Although Linnemann, like Eichholz, recognizes the inappropriateness of the terms image and subject matter, nevertheless she goes on using them uncritically, despite her insight.

In her summary the author surprisingly limits her results to 'those parables which are intended to bridge over an opposition between the narrator and the listeners' (p. 37). Such a restriction has not been mentioned before. This is a sign of considerable uncertainty, caused by the fact that most expositors of the parables start out intending to make methodical or factual statements about the whole genre, but then become aware of the fact that these statements only apply to a certain number, and not all of the parables. This again automatically gives rise to the demand that they be grouped according to their functions.

Using the comparisons (and parables) in the OT as a starting-point, this pre-history shows that they occur here in contexts which allow us to recognize their functions. On the assumption that the parables of Jesus must be regarded as expanded comparisons, which, as such, originally belong to a particular context, the situation in which they were spoken, one could at least attempt a grouping of them according to what they have in common, even if much of this remains questionable.

(f) Art. 'Gleichnis und Parabel' (similitude and parable) in *RGG*[3] vol. I cols 1614–21: in the history of religion: C.-M. Edsman (1614–15); in the Bible: in the OT: G. Fohrer (1615–16); in Judaism: E. L. Dietrich (1616–17); in the NT: N. A. Dahl (1617–19).

The authors all agree in understanding comparisons and parables as pictorial phrases. Edsman: 'Similitude and parable belong to general as well as religious pictorial language, in which they are particularly apt for representing spiritual reality'; 'image and subject matter'; 'pictorial language'. Fohrer: 'The actual parable is a pictorial comparison, which has to be distinguished from simple pictorial language'. Dahl: 'The word 'parable' is only used where a sequence of events is described in images'; 'the way of using images'; '*Bildhälfte* – intended subject matter'. It is particularly noticeable that Edsman retains the old supernatural formulation: 'for representing spiritual reality'. Edsman hardly says anything about the significance of comparisons and parables for the history of religion; for him the parable is an almost exclusively literary phenomenon. In this regard he stresses: 'Similitudes . . . and parables have been favoured by an epic form of presentation'. This may be true of Homer, but is not true of the Bible; in the 'epic' parts of the OT, viz. narrative and historical report, comparisons are almost completely absent, whereas in the prophets and in the Psalms they are richly developed. Fohrer deals with the 'pictorial comparison', but only in a few remarks on a handful of passages, which prevents us from recognizing the predominant significance of the comparison in the OT, viz. the symbolic actions of the prophets and the seven extended parables. Edsman rightly states: 'The parable is an expanded comparison', which also seems to be Fohrer's opinion, but he does not discuss the relationship of the two genres to each other, nor their functions. Dietrich (Judaism) regards the parable as a stylistic form of the *midrash*: 'the rabbinic parable is of value not only for life, but also for forming a theory'. It is part of the doctrinal teaching of the scribes. Later it is pushed into the background by allegory. Dahl says of the NT parables: 'In contrast to the often complicated Jewish parables, to which they are akin, they show simplicity and spontaneity'. This and their Palestinian origin is a reason for investigating their roots. There seems to be general agreement that the underlying basis of the parables belongs to those words of Jesus which have been most faithfully transmitted. But all we get is a vague enumeration: 'As regards detail, however, much remains uncertain'.

   (g) M. D. Goulder, *Midrash and Lection in Matthew*,

1974, ch. 3: 'The Midrashic Parable', pp. 47–69. – Goulder intends to prove that the author of the Gospel of Matthew had Mark as his only source and that the remainder of Matthew (with a few exceptions) was created by the author of the Gospel himself. The parables, which he treats in ch. 3 of his book, form a major part of his argument. It is typical of Matthew to expand the Marcan text by means of parables, the parallels to which are to be found in rabbinic literature (Goulder lists 100 of these on pp. 66–69). With regard to the parables, the three Gospels exhibit remarkable differences (cf. Goulder, 'Characteristics of the Parables in the Several Gospels', *JTS* 19/1, 1968, pp. 51–69). From the demonstration that these Matthean parables differ from the others by their rabbinic style and considerable proximity to rabbinic parables, he concludes that they were composed by Matthew himself, a Christian-rabbinic writer.

On the basis of these rabbinic parallels Goulder understands the parable from the outset as a story, and not as an image or pictorial speech. Goulder supplies the following definitions: 'The parable is a comparison . . . in form of a story, however slight' (p. 47); and 'They are about God's action in inaugurating his kingdom and man's response' (p. 49). He briefly comments on five OT parables: Judg. 9; II Sam. 12; II Kings 14; Isa. 5 (he omits Isa. 28.23–29) and Ezek. 17 (an allegory; Ezek. 34 is missing). The parables, like the rabbinic ones, are all indicative, and none are imperative parables: 'They are concerned to demonstrate the world's situation in the perspective of the action of God' (p. 48). They usually arise from a text that needs explaining or from a question of doctrine. Their subject is most commonly Israel, but other subjects include the Fathers, the Torah, the soul and the body etc. (further examples). With regard to the Gospels, there is a striking difference between Matthew and Mark, on the one hand, whose parables are all (or nearly all) indicative, and Luke, on the other, almost all of whose parables are imperative, 'a direct suggestion of what the Christian should do'. Luke introduces an almost unbroken element of imperative parables into an almost unbroken tradition of indicative parables. Here Mark and Matthew stand in the Jewish tradition while Luke does not.

This is also apparent in the introductory formulae. Most rabbinic parables are introduced by: 'I will relate a parable to you. With what shall the matter be compared? It is the case with it as with . . .'. Two of the Marcan parables (4.26, 30) begin like this. The others all have the word *parable* to introduce them. Similarly Matthew begins: 'The kingdom of heaven may be likened to . . .'. Luke on the other hand never uses introductory formulae, except when he takes parables from previous tradition. Otherwise he goes straight into the story: 'A certain man . . .'.

There are further differences insofar that the OT parables are essentially comparisons between the divine–human situation and an analogue in nature. The Marcan parables follow this tradition. Such nature-parables are alien to the rabbinic parabolic tradition (only ten out of 100). Matthew's parables stand in this rabbinic tradition; he even personalizes two of Mark's nature-parables. The only nature-parable that is added by Matthew is that of the Leaven. Luke also here essentially follows the rabbinic tradition. Of the rabbinic examples 51 out of 100 are contrasts of some kind. Such contrasts rarely occur in Mark and Luke, but are very striking in Matthew whose 13 long parables are all black-and-white contrasts. Stock figures are particularly characteristic of the rabbinic parables, e.g. the king. The same is true of Matthew, while Luke's characters are highly individual. Allegories are predominant in Matthew, rare in Mark, and almost totally absent in Luke. Here, too, Matthew follows the rabbinic tradition.

An appended interpretation is also part of the rabbinic tradition; 97 out of the 100 examples end in sentences such as: 'Even so will the Holy One, blessed be He . . .'. Here, too, Luke is the most remote from the rabbinic tradition.

The rabbinic parables give preference to those of high rank, often dealing with the king, his court, and the rich with their extensive lands. Of 90 parables 50 deal with the king and ten with people of exalted rank. Among the Gospels this clearly corresponds to Matthew's usage, while Mark's parables are concerned with village life. Luke, standing halfway between the two, prefers the country gentry and the middle class.

The central doctrines of Matthew are the same as in Mark. But some of them receive a special emphasis in Matthew: instead of 'Kingdom of God' Matthew says 'Kingdom of Heaven' like the rabbinic parables. In line with rabbinic teaching he stresses hell and its torments, eternal punishment, darkness, unquenchable fire, wailing and gnashing of teeth. This is far less obvious in Luke, and is mentioned only once in Mark. Angels are of great significance for Matthew, more than for Mark or Luke. This too corresponds to rabbinic teaching.

Goulder summarizes his conclusions in a parable: three rooms are full of paintings. The paintings in all three have been attributed to Leonardo, but critics have discovered that they have all been worked over by pupils. We are unable to remove the layer of overpainting by the pupils without destroying the originals; as a result of the overpainting each of the three rooms has its own character. Similarly, Matthew's parables differ by their rabbinic character from those of Mark and Luke; they are Matthew's own composition, their author Matthew 'the Christian scribe'. He teaches in parables in the name of Christ, as a rabbi in the name of his own teacher.

Comparing Goulder's investigation of the parables with those previously mentioned we are struck by a difference: he studies the parables themselves in terms of their literal meaning, and not on the basis of their interpretation. The reason for this is Goulder's intention to determine the relationship of the NT parables to the rabbinic ones right down to the minutest detail. The author does not proceed on the basis of an already established interpretation of the parables (i.e. one formed in the Christian tradition), but regards them as texts to be compared with another similar group, which in terms of the time of their origin are also relatively close to them. In consequence Goulder is able to recognize and evaluate the textual elements of the parables in a much more precise way than a tradition of interpretation in which the meaning of general terms such as 'Kingdom of Heaven' is already predetermined for the expositor, or in which 'the parables' as a whole have already been subordinated to a concept such as 'eschatological, eschatology'. Such general conceptual classifications of parables do not occur in his work and this new approach gives Goulder's interpretation of the parables its special significance. The author's new approach is quite independent of his results; this is already clear from his starting point, the considerable difference between the parables in the three Gospels. The demonstration of the different nature of the parables in the three Gospels, combined with the proof that Matthew's parables are closest to the rabbinic ones, is conducted on the basis of individual features which allow for an objective distinction between individual groups of parables. In Matthew (but also in Mark) all parables are indicative, in Luke (almost) all are imperative (see below on this distinction). Matthew is in the rabbinic tradition with regard to the following; the introductory formulae (never in Luke!), the predominance of personal over against nature parables, the frequent use of contrast parables, preference for stock figures in contrast to Luke whose characters are more highly individual, and the predominance of personages of high social rank; in accordance with rabbinic doctrine 'Kingdom of Heaven' is used in preference to 'Kingdom of God' and the significance of angels and hell with its torments is emphasized. Further observations add up to the overwhelming conclusion that the parables of Matthew are particularly close to those of the rabbis.

One might expect some of the author's observations resulting from comparing the NT parables with the rabbinic ones to agree with (or approximate to) my own made by comparing the NT parables with the comparisons in the OT. This would be true of Goulder's distinction between indicative and imperative parables, which is similar to mine between parables of proclamation and those

which call for action. While I am of the opinion that
Goulder's distinction requires more precise definition and
differentiation, I agree with it in principle. Since Goulder
and I have reached this conclusion by different routes and
independently of one another, it would be worth pursuing
it further; its significance lies mainly in the fact that it is
now no longer possible to make all-embracing statements
about the parables of Jesus without taking this distinction
into account.

My questions about Goulder's investigation on matters
over which we disagree arise from our different starting
points.

Thus Goulder also mentions the OT parables, but only
those five usually cited in this context. It is my conviction,
however, that these five OT parables cannot be isolated in
the way they have been up till now, because parables are
expanded comparisons and because we find in the OT a
whole series of transitional texts. These as well as the
comparisons have to be included in our investigation. This
would result in our being able to achieve a much more
precise grouping of the parables corresponding to that of
the comparisons in the OT.

A further consequence would be that one could not
only take note of the striking correspondence between
Matthew's parables and the rabbinic ones, but also the
marked differences between the two. Goulder quite rightly
says of the rabbinic parables 'They usually arise out of a
text that needs exposition, or a question of doctrine'. But
it is precisely at this point that we find a basic difference
from the parables of Matthew – as also those of Mark and
Luke. Jesus' parables refer neither to a next that needs
exposition nor to a question of doctrine; rather, they
acquire their function from the ministry of Jesus as a
whole. The rabbinic parables have essentially an explanatory function, with the explanations referring to an
established item of the doctrinal tradition. But the function
of Jesus' parables is that of proclamation or instruction,
which precisely do not refer to traditional doctrine but are
given authoritatively: '. . . he speaks with authority, and

not like the scribes'. This is not to deny the close proximity of Matthew's parables to the rabbinic ones, but the differences have to be noted as well. The explanatory function of the rabbinic parables is well illustrated by the examples quoted by Goulder on p. 48. But his distinction between indicative and imperative parables (pp. 48–50) requires a much more precise definition. Goulder's claim (p. 49 f.) of a marked contrast between Mark and Matthew, whose parables are almost all indicative, on the other hand, and Luke, whose parables are almost exclusively imperative, on the other, is simply not true. One of the most important groups of Lucan parables, that in ch. 15, is clearly indicative: the three parables announce the superabundant mercy of God, who seeks and accepts the lost.In the case of the imperative parables one has to distinguish between instruction to act in the present time and such instruction as concerns the future. According to their function, the three parables in Mt. 24–25, which Goulder quite appropriately considers further developments of the Marcan parable of the doorkeeper, are instructions to act, but relating to an event in the future. They are clearly imperative parables. Here again the difference from the rabbinic parables has to be pointed out: such parables, which call their hearers to be awake and ready in the future (when the Lord comes again), do not have even the remotest parallel in the rabbinic parables.

Goulder summarizes his conclusions in an ingenious comparison (see above p. 167). Here for the first time in the chapter on parables the question is raised as to how the parables in the three Gospels relate to the parables of Jesus. But the question is consequently rejected as inappropriate. We cannot remove the pupils' overpainting of the master's pictures. This implies that we cannot even pose the question which of the parables can be attributed to Jesus (this is the precise opposite of Jeremias' position). But even if the situation were such as Goulder implies in his comparison, is it not just as dangerous and uncertain to attribute all the synoptic parables without exception to the three writers of the Gospels, who would then be at the same time the authors of the parables? Would this provide any kind of credible explanation at all of the origin of these parables? I do not think so. Goulder's fundamental error seems to me to be that he basically only recognizes a literary explanation for the origin of parables. For him Matthew is a writer. However, the parables which, as Goulder himself admits, are all short stories, clearly display the characteristics of oral origin. This had already been incontrovertibly proved by Bultmann with reference to Olrik. These parables have been told as stories, and the differences between the parables in the three Gospels point unmistakably to a process which includes an oral stage prior to their being committed to writing. The one-sidedness of Goulder's conclusions is based on the fact that he has failed to inquire into the oral origin of the parables of Jesus and into the first stage of the oral transmission of these narratives.

# The Parable as Metaphor

(a) Paul Ricoeur, 'Stellung und Funktion der Metapher in der biblischen Sprache', in: P. Ricoeur and E. Jüngel, *Metapher*, *Ev Theol* Sonderheft 1974, pp. 45–70. – Ricoeur investigates the metaphor as a phenomenon of language in general, and then of religious language in particular. 'We are dealing with the ability of the metaphor to constitute meaning' (p. 46).

I. The Semantics of the Metaphor. Ricoeur rejects the traditional understanding of metaphor as a 'pictorial mode of expression'. Metaphors are not words used pictorially, but metaphorical statements (p. 47). They do not consist of clothing ideas with images but in allowing a relationship to become visible which ordinary vision would not perceive. 'Good metaphors are those which constitute a similarity rather than describing it' (p. 48). 'They are not a form of speech decoration but carry with them some new information' (p. 49).

II. Metaphor and Reality. This section deals with the function of metaphor in poetic language.

III. Metaphor and Parable. 'The parable is a mode of speech which applies a metaphorical process to a narrative form' (p. 55: 'The metaphorical mode of functioning of a story'). At several points Ricoeur follows D. O. Via's understanding of parables (*The Parables. Their Literary and Existential Dimension*, 1967). Via understands the parable on the basis of its dramatic structure as either 'tragic' or 'comic', built on the pattern of beginning – middle – end, with a definite assignment of main and subordinate characters. Our understanding of the parable does not depend on its 'point' (the *tertium comparationis*, in contrast to A. Jülicher), but on the structure of the narrative as a whole; 'the action as such is the bearer of the metaphorical process' (p. 60). Ricoeur comments: 'We need to forget the dualism of "subject matter" and "figure of speech", its transformation as "thought" and "image"' (p. 62).

IV. Parables and Borderline Expressions. To the previous definition of the parable as 'the combination of a narrative form with a metaphorical process' (p. 65) has to be added its intentionality, which is expressed by the fact that it deals with the 'Kingdom of Heaven' (p. 66). This intentionality is more apparent in other kinds of words, in eschatological sayings and proverbial expressions: Mk 1.15; Lk. 11.20; 17.20; Mt. 11.12. These are all borderline expressions, transgressing into another genre. This 'transgressing into another genre' constitutes the nature of religious language (p. 66). This is also evident in the feature of intensification, based on paradox and hyperbole (p. 67): Lk. 17.33: 'Whoever seeks to gain his life will lose it'; Lk. 6.27 (love of enemies). 'The function of borderline expressions is in this case their intention to give new orientation to life by first disorienting it' (p. 67). In the parables this is achieved by the extravagance of the action itself: in the parables of the Wicked Husbandmen (Mk 12.1–12), the Great Supper, the Labourers in the Vineyard, the Prodigal Son and others.

We cannot but agree with Ricoeur's rejection of the

traditional understanding of 'metaphor'. To emphasize a few points: the metaphor is not a pictorial mode of expression, it does not consist of clothing an idea with an image, it is not a form of speech decoration. Following Via: what matters in the parable is not the *tertium comparationis* but the narrative structure as a whole. The definition of a parable in terms of *Bildhälfte* and *Sachhälfte* should be abandoned altogether. Ricoeur, after defining the metaphor and thereby also the parable in his first three chapters as 'the combination of a narrative form with a metaphorical process' (p. 65), adds in ch. IV an element not mentioned previously: 'the intentionality of the parable' (is this what he had previously called its 'function'?): it deals with the 'Kingdom of Heaven'. Surprisingly he finds this intentionality more clearly expressed in other speech forms in the Gospels. It is therefore not something specific to the parables. This intentionality, however, is not apparent in the parables as such, but only in a certain feature, their 'extravagance', which again is confined to just one group of them. While it is no doubt important and valuable to note this special feature, nevertheless it remains just one special feature in one section of the parables.

This difficulty is caused by the fact that Ricoeur starts out from a concept of metaphor which, in spite of all protestations to the contrary, is still the same as in Aristotle, i.e. a phenomenon of language, timeless and ahistorical, abstract and objectified. Such an objectified metaphor is a purely mental concept, it does not really exist in language itself. In language such transformation (in verbal, not in nominal form) occurs only in historically conditioned speech forms and contexts. A 'metaphor' divorced from its context is a pure abstraction (cf. C. Stoffer-Heibel, 1981, below).

In ch. IV Ricoeur does recognize the significance of the context for the parables of Jesus, but at this juncture this rather has the effect of an appendix with little connection with what has gone before. A further difficulty arises from the fact that Ricoeur leaves open the question of the metaphor's linguistic form. Initially, in opposition to earlier

views, he states with some justification that the metaphor
does not relate to single words, but to statements (meaning:
sentences). With regard to religious language he does
mention comparisons in sentence form, but only of narrative type, viz. the parables: 'the combination of a narrative form with a metaphorical process'. This 'metaphorical process', i.e. the comparison (in the verbal sense),
takes place in the Bible in three forms: in single words
which have taken on a figurative sense ('cup', 'arm of the
LORD'), in sentences ('the LORD is my rock'), and in
narratives = parables. Such a narrative is special insofar as it
consists of the expansion of a comparison in sentence
form, and can only be understood as such.

A third difficulty lies in the fact that Ricoeur, following
the old tradition, understands 'metaphor' as a form of
statement. Comparisons in the Bible, however, are, with a
few exceptions, forms of address and receive their function
in each case from this address.

(b) E. Jüngel, 'Metapher', in P. Ricoeur and E. Jüngel,
*Metapher*, *EvTheol* Sonderheft 1974. – In contrast to the
tradition of Western thought which regards the metaphor
or metaphorical speech as figurative speech, above all as
decoration (*ornatus*), more recent developments in linguistics and theology (in expounding the parables) regard the
parable as a special genre of direct speech, a basic process
of language: 'The language of faith is constituted by
metaphors'. 'The metaphor is an excellent way for language to deal with existing things, it leads to the gaining
of knowledge, there is a flash of recognition of the similar
in the dissimilar'.

The familiar metaphors in our language are a reminisc-
ence of the metaphorical character of language. It is incumb-
ent on us to recognize metaphor as the occurrence of
truth. The language of faith is metaphorical through and
through; 'God' is a meaningful term only in the context of
metaphorical discourse. 'God' can only be voiced meta-
phorically. Human language as such has the character of
address; even talk about God has this form. God is a word
which addresses, and man a being to be addressed. The

fundamental metaphor is the identification of the risen Lord with the crucified man Jesus.

The following questions would occur to the exegete:

(1) According to the dictionary, *metaphora* has the meaning of 'translating', i.e. the term clearly refers to a process. If the term is used as Jüngel uses it, as an ontological term, one would have to point out that this is not the proper meaning of the word. While Jüngel occasionally speaks of the metaphor as a process (p. 73: 'a process fundamental to human language', cf. pp. 77, 89, 101), nevertheless what predominates is his understanding of the metaphor as an ontological statement, as on p. 113: 'Metaphors make plain the "As-if-structure" of being', or when he talks about the 'metaphorical character of language' on p. 105 etc.

(2) What is awkward is that Jüngel claims on the one hand that language as such has a metaphorical character, while on the other particularly emphasizing the metaphorical character of religious language: 'The language of faith is metaphorical through and through; "God" is a meaningful term only in the context of metaphorical discourse' (p. 110). If language as such is metaphorical, then not only the word 'God', but any other word is only meaningful 'in the context of metaphorical discourse'. When Jüngel abandons the basic difference between the generally prevailing language and metaphor (against Aristotle), the specific sense of the word 'metaphor' is lost. He also never clearly indicates what he means by the 'metaphorical character of language'. Are all speech forms as such metaphorical? He says at one point: 'Strictly speaking, metaphors are not words but statements' (p. 112). In that case, strictly speaking, the word 'God' would not be a metaphor! But in contrast to Aristotle the author is not interested in the form of language. At one point he connects the metaphorical character of language with its 'address character' (p. 108), whereby he identifies address and statement: 'The language of faith is an address in statement form'. If, however, the language has evolved different forms for address

and statement, does this not imply that it intends to make a distinction between statement and address?

(3) As he says on p. 73, Jüngel is concerned with a 'fundamental consideration of the function of metaphor'. This apparently presupposes that metaphor only has one function, which is the same everywhere (e.g. pp. 113, 119 point 3). This assumption is incorrect; metaphors and comparisons have different functions depending on the contexts in which they occur. But Jüngel never inquires into the context of a metaphor. Initially he quotes as an example of a metaphor: 'Achilles is a lion', an example to which he frequently returns. He explains this sentence as follows: 'Part of the essence of the lion is attributed to Achilles, the statement reveals something of Achilles' being' (p. 113). Here he has Homer's epics in mind, in which comparisons have an aesthetic function. But this is only one of many possible functions. This comparison with the lion occurs frequently in the Bible. In the tribal sayings Gen. 49.9 a tribe of Israel is compared to a lion (see above p. 7); its function here is the praise of the tribe of Judah. What is attributed to Judah is not part of the lion's essence but of its actions. This comparison has a different function in prophecy, where in Hos. 5.14 God who intervenes destructively against his own people is compared to a lion. The function of a comparison (or metaphor) can only be determined from its context.

(4) Finally the exegete would have to ask the systematician whether it makes sense to talk of the metaphor without taking into account its background in the history of literature and culture. Jüngel says: 'Language could actually exist without metaphors, but such language would clearly be unattractive' (p. 91). Hence Jüngel attributes an aesthetic function to the metaphor, referring to metaphors in stories: '. . . so that the narrative . . . only comes to life through the comparison' (p. 101 f.). This sentence is a quotation from B. Snell's work on the Homeric epics (*Die Entdeckung des Geistes*, [2]1955). In saying this Jüngel ignores the fact that the function of comparison can be different in different cultures and at different times. In contrast to

Homeric epics, the epic narratives of the OT are almost entirely lacking in comparisons (see above p. 5 f.), whereas the Psalms and prophets have them in great numbers. The handful of comparisons occurring in narrative and report have, with a few exceptions, an explanatory function.

These few suggestions may suffice to illustrate the fact that in any investigation of the function of comparisons (metaphors) one needs to take account not only of the context, but also of the cultural and literary background. Cf. on this C. Stoffer-Heibel, *Metaphernstudien*, 1981.

(c) H. Weder, *Die Gleichnisse als Metaphern*, 1978. – In his first part 'On the Theory of Parable Interpretation' Weder deals with the 'Approaches in Recent Research': Jülicher, Bultmann, Dodd, Jeremias, Linnemann, Fuchs, Jüngel, Funk, Via. His own comments follow in: 'Some Remarks on the Theory of Parable Interpretation'. In the second part there follows an investigation of individual parables which he summarizes in part 3. In his understanding of the parables Weder is strongly dependent on Fuchs and Jüngel, the latter of whom is quoted again and again throughout the work and from whose interpretation Weder hardly ever departs. It is Weder's intention to understand the parables of Jesus on the basis of 'the essence of the metaphor'. What is difficult is Weder's initial admission that in general language usage 'metaphor' is a single word, whereas he, following others, employs it to refer to a sentence: 'However, it has to be maintained that the metaphor is part of the semantics of the sentence' (p. 59). The structure of this sentence he defines as follows: subject – copula – predicate ('Achilles is a lion', cf. Jüngel). Weder considers this basic form of the metaphor on the analogy of the parables of Jesus, with the parable story as the 'predicate'. However, this analogy conceals a further problem: it is a simple fact that the metaphor (according to Weder) has the structure of a sentence, the parable on the other hand that of a story. Jüngel's example of a metaphor, 'Achilles is a lion', runs through Weder's whole investigation. This sentence cannot be compared to the parables of Jesus because in it the essence of a lion is compared to the essence of Achilles (as in Jüngel), whereas the parables of Jesus relate a happening (cf. p. 160 above). When Weder identifies the parable story with the predicate of a sentence, he is still, without noticing it, clinging to Jülicher's distinction between image and subject matter. While thesis 1 of his summary (p. 97) asserts: 'The distinction between *Bildhälfte* and *Sachhälfte* ... ought to be abandoned', thesis 3a says: 'The story then is to be interpreted as a representation of the Kingdom of God'. A story is no picture, it cannot depict anything!

My main objection is directed against Weder's tendency, on the basis of an abstract concept of parable, to relativize the differences between various kinds of parables as far as possible, and to refer throughout to *the* parables of Jesus, as if they all said more or less the same thing. The new literary research on metaphor recognizes that a metaphor can only be understood from its context, and since contexts differ, so too do the functions of metaphor. The question of the different contexts in which parables occur in Jesus' message is almost entirely ignored by Weder; such a question would have necessitated a grouping of the parables according to these contexts. Too often we find him making statements about '*the* parables of Jesus' which clearly only apply to certain, but by no means all of them. For a precise exposition one could not avoid dividing the parables up according to their contexts, so that it would be clear which parables were being referred to at any point. The high degree of abstraction of what Weder says about 'the parables of Jesus' consistently pushes the variety and pluriformity of these parables into the background.

If I may be permitted to make an observation as an expositor of the OT: the parables of Jesus have in common with the comparisons in the OT the fact that they are simple and convincing in their simplicity. In my opinion, the interpretation of a text has at least to correspond closely to it. In Weder's interpretation of the parables the distance between the language of his interpretation and that of the parables is so considerable that the simplicity of the parables is no longer recognizable in the lofty heights of the abstract language of his interpretation.

The book's second part, the interpretation of individual parables, is fruitful and valuable. Weder's careful traditio-historical exposition, which isolates the different stages of the origin of the parables, employs an entirely different language from parts 1 and 3. In contrast to them, the special message of each individual parable clearly emerges.

(d) N. Frye, *The Great Code: The Bible and Literature*, 1982, chs III-VI on metaphor. – The Bible is full of explicit metaphors. To them have to be added implicit ones in the juxtaposition of words and images. The metaphorical is identical with the spiritual. The primary and literal sense of the Bible is the poetic one; this poetic sense expresses itself in a world of images. Since he understands the metaphor in an extremely broad sense, the author does not refer to comparisons and parables, except in occasional brief remarks.

(e) C. Stoffer-Heibel, *Metaphernstudien*; Stuttgarter Arbeiten zur Germanistik 96, 1981. – In the first part of her book the author deals with metaphor and the theory of metaphor, in the second with the metaphor in modern poetry. In her preface (pp. I–VI) she points out the basic change in the understanding of metaphor in semantics and literary criticism: the traditional criteria of metaphor, its figurative character, clarity, and analogous structure, do not suffice to comprehend this concept and phenomenon. Above all, 'the deeply rooted idea of metaphor as an "image of speech" still haunts literary-critical theory and prevents an adequate new definition'.

The first part of her study provides a valuable survey of the theories of metaphor in various disciplines. They have led to the insight 'that the metaphor is a semantic phenomenon which can only be understood as part of a text' (p. 4 f.). This dependence of the metaphor on its context renders meaningless from the outset any treatment of isolated metaphors; we can only gain access to the phenomenon via its function in the text.

In the first chapter of her book the author provides a

historical survey of the problem, starting from Aristotle's classic theory of metaphor in his 'Poetics' and 'Rhetoric', which for centuries determined the Western understanding of metaphor. 'It was Aristotle's definition of metaphor as a *single word* which had the effect right up to the present time of treating it in isolation, and not in its respective context' (p. 4). Following Aristotle, Cicero in the third book of his *De oratore* defines metaphor as a stylistic device '*ad illustrandum atque exornandum orationem*'. He, too, defines metaphor as a single word, as does Quintilian in book VIII of his *Institutiones oratoriae*.

It was only in modern semantics that the understanding of metaphor was thoroughly reconsidered. It is now considered a phenomenon of the semantic level of language, relevant in terms of communication. This puts a stop to the conception of the figurative character of metaphor and the understanding of it as a single word (p. 94 f.); metaphor has to be understood as part of a text. So for example H. Weinreich: 'A metaphor is never just a simple word, but always a piece of text, however small' (*Semantik der Metapher*, 1970, p. 271). As part of a text the metaphor is embedded in a context, which on the one hand is a condition of its existence, but which it influences on the other. 'The function of a metaphor can only be defined in terms of its context' (p. 95 f.). The understanding of metaphor as an image cannot be reconciled with its definition as a semantic phenomenon. While the traditional metaphor based on the analogy between two model images of reality, 'issuer' and 'receiver' of images, construes the *tertium comparationis* as a heuristic analogue, modern semantics abandons this function of metaphor as an image. Metaphor is rather a model which does not derive from images and reality (p. 100 f.).

While I only came across this understanding of metaphor after having completed my own work, it has been confirmed by my investigation of comparisons in the OT. However, the interpreters of the parables of Jesus will have to take note of it as well.

## The Interpretation of the Parables and our Understanding of Metaphor

(a) The equation of parables with images or with pictorial language, i.e. the claim that the function of the parables as a whole is to illustrate and clarify (Bultmann, Jeremias, Dodd, Eichholz (I), Linnemann (II), Edsman, Fohrer, Dahl etc.) has to be abandoned. This is the conclusion not only of the study of the comparisons in the OT, but also of modern linguistics, particularly semantics, which has abandoned talk of the image function or the clarifying function of metaphor as the sole criterion, all along the line (Via, Ricoeur, Stoffer-Heibel etc.).

(b) This positive thesis of modern semantics, that a metaphor can only be explained from its context (Stoffer-Heibel), must be consistently applied to the parables of Jesus; even where we no longer have the original context of many parables, these questions still have to be asked.

(c) This makes it necessary to begin the exposition of the parables by sorting them into groups. Previous interpreters of the parables have so far failed to solve this problem. While some have not even seen this as a problem, others tend to make statements about *the* parables as a whole, without taking any notices of the differences (Jüngel and Weder), and others still have not yet got beyond the initial stages of such a grouping (Linnemann). Comparing the studies by Bultmann and Jeremias, we find that criteria of form and content must be equally applied in determining such groups. That definitions based solely on the thought content are not sufficient is shown by the contributions of Jeremias and Dodd, and that purely formal criteria are inadequate is plain from Bultmann's study.

(d) The tendency of most scholars to encapsulate the meaning of a parable in an abstract theological concept extracted from that parable, the so-called *tertium comparationis*, does not accord with the parable's narrative form. The story itself must be allowed to speak, not an abstract idea distilled from it, this means the narrative as a whole, whose structure has to be investigated in each case (Via and Ricoeur).

That the parables are stories and also remain such in their function as parables is especially stressed by more recent authors (Via, Ricoeur, Goulder: Bultmann had already emphasized the narrative technique). They either have to be understood as images *or* as stories. Sitting on the fence in this case (Eichholz, Linnemann) will not do! If it is a story, a parable cannot be pinned down by an abstract theoretical interpretation. The event depicted in a parable as such remains fundamentally open (Ricoeur). While this permits a history of interpretations, as is already shown by the Gospels, there can be no final one. A parable can never be identified with its interpretation to such an extent that this fixing renders the parable story redundant. The story lives on even after all the interpretations given to a particular parable.

(e) The introduction to some parables: 'The Kingdom of Heaven is like . . .' is often interpreted on the assumption that parables are concerned with image and subject matter, in such a way that the Kingdom of God is the 'subject matter' which is clarified by means of many images. If that were the case, then all the parables of the Kingdom would have the same subject matter. Dodd, for example, first defines in two chapters what the Kingdom of God is, and then merely uses the parables to illustrate something which he knows already! But the Kingdom of God in the Old Testament as well as in the New is not a thing but a happening. It refers to God's manifold activity. A king cannot always be doing the same thing. The variety of what the parables have to tell corresponds to the variety of God's activity. When one reduces this Kingdom of God to an abstract concept ('eschatological' or 'realized eschatology') in a one-sided fashion, one deprives the parables of something essential, viz. that each has its own particular message, and one thereby fails to recognize what is characteristic of the office of a king.

(f) The philosophical and systematic studies (Ricoeur, Jüngel and, following him, Weder) proceed from a timeless and unhistorical linguistic phenomenon called 'metaphor', which they are intent on applying to the biblical texts. But this cannot succeed, they all run into difficulties in this attempt. If 'metaphor is a semantic phenomenon which can only be understood as part of a text' and if therefore 'an isolated treatment of metaphors is a priori meaningless' (Stoffer-Heibel), then, as part of a text, it always belongs to the historical setting and form of that text. 'Metaphor' then does not have a 'nominal' but a 'verbal' structure in its three possible speech forms, of which the middle one is the comparison in the form of a sentence. The comparison can be expanded into a story (= parable) or reduced to a single word ('metaphor' in the narrower sense). The comparison is only timeless and universal in its abbreviated form as a 'dead comparison'. However, if one uses this term as a generalization by talking of a 'metaphorical character of language' (Jüngel), then, as a result, the comparison loses its specific meaning.

Frye goes even further in generalizing metaphor in chs III and IV of his book: the whole Bible has a poetic sense represented in a world of images. Comparisons and parables he does not even mention in this context.

## The Structure of the Parables

To begin with, in order to determine the function of a parable it is necessary to assign all the parables to groups so as to find their connection with the message or ministry of Jesus, to which each individual parable belongs. Each individual parable is thereby given its context. To illustrate this point, I offer a somewhat sketchy grouping of the parables, which does not claim to be more than a preliminary attempt. This analysis differs from its predecessors by not taking the interpretation of parables as its starting point, but simply following their wording. However, it is not necessary to assign all the parables in the Gospels to these groups. Some cannot be assigned to any group, and with others it is questionable whether they even belong to the parables. The distinction between the parables of Jesus and those formulated by the early church is largely ignored at this stage, since it represents a second step.

I. Stories involving sudden change (parables of proclamation)

       (a) Lost and found

       (b) Merciful acceptance

       (c) Mercy is incalculable

       (d) From the petitioner's position

       (e) Treasure and pearl

       (f) Subordinate motifs in other parables

II. Parables of growth

III. Announcement of judgment in a parable

       (a) against Israel

       (b) Exclusion from the feast

       (c) Verdict of rejection

IV. (A) Instruction for present action

       (a) in exemplary stories

       (b) as a subordinate motif

       (c) in expanded comparisons

       (B) Instruction for future action

I. Stories involving sudden change (parables of proclamation)

(a) Lost and found: Lk. 15.4–7, 8–10, 11–32; cf. Mt. 18.12–14; Gospel of Thomas (= Gosp. Thom.) 107.

These parables undoubtedly correspond to a definite context in the gospel report of the ministry of Jesus: the reversal of the destiny of those who were lost occurs when Jesus turns to those who suffer, the sinners and outcasts. This action of Jesus reflects the turning of God in his mercy, who looks down from his heights into the depths referred to in the Praise of God's Mercy in the Psalms (e.g. Ps. 113). The story of the Prodigal Son is an exposition of Ps. 103.13: 'As a father . . .'. This comparison has been expanded in Lk. 15 into a parable. The joyful exclamation of the woman in Lk. 15.9: 'I have found the coin which I had lost', corresponds to narrative praise in the Psalms.

(b) Merciful acceptance. Other parables speak in differing ways of God's merciful acceptance of sinners, and those who are despised, which causes a sudden change: the parable of the two debtors, Lk. 7.41–45, two very different sons, Mt. 21.28–32, the barren fig tree, Lk. 13.6–9, Pharisee and tax collector, Lk. 18.9–14, and the first part of the unmerciful servant parable, Mt. 18.23–35.

(c) Mercy is incalculable. A special aspect of God's mercy is shown in the parable of the labourers in the vineyard in Mt. 20.1–16: the mercy in this story is incalculable, as in the praise of God's mercy in Ps. 103: '. . . as the heavens are high above the earth . . .' (v. 11). In contrast to what Jesus has to say about God's mercy, his opponents insist on his righteousness being calculable. The expansion in Lk. 15.25–32 presupposes the same objection.

(d) The two parables of the importunate friend, Lk. 11.5–8, and the persistent widow, Lk. 18.1–8, reflect God's merciful acceptance as seen from the point of view of the petitioners and sufferers. The message of both parables is that the apparently hopeless petition is eventually heeded. This is based on the Certainty of Hearing in the Psalms of Lament.

(e) Treasure and pearl. To this section (I) perhaps also belong the two parables of the treasure and the pearl, Mt. 13.44–46; Gosp. Thom. 109 and 76. For here, too, the overabundance of what fell into the finder's lap causes a sudden change. The two people who are the subject of the parables are prepared to give up everything they possess for this overabundance which transforms their lives. This would represent a further aspect in addition to the sudden change.

(f) Subordinate motifs in other parables. It is quite possible that the Indirect Praise of God's Mercy in the message of Jesus can be found in a few more parables which really belong to other groups. This is firstly the case in the story of the Good Samaritan, Lk. 10.31–37, in which the victim experiences the saving mercy of God through the help of a stranger, secondly in the parable of the dishonest steward, Lk. 16.1–8, who nevertheless is given a chance, and thirdly in the story of the rich man and poor Lazarus, Lk. 16.19–31, in the motif that the sufferer and the sick person receives God's merciful accept-

ance even after death. This interpretation is made possible
by the fact that all three are Lucan parables, and that Luke
has most texts in this group.

To sum up: all these parables deal in such a way with
God's merciful acceptance of the sufferers, the sinners, and
those who are despised, that each of these stories makes
this point in its own particular way. This special contribution of each story could not be made by means of a single
term, but only by means of narrative in all its variety. The
group 'lost and found', for example, contains three aspects:
an object – an animal – people.

II. Parables of growth. They speak of a continuous –
not a 'one-off' – happening, a creaturely process of growth.
What happens here does not primarily happen between
persons. Humans do not influence this process of growth
at all, the power of growth comes from God the creator.

(a) The process of growth as such is the subject of the
following parables: the sower, Mk 4.3–8; Mt. 13.3–8; Lk.
8.5–8; Gosp. Thom. 9; the seed that grows by itself, Mk
4.26–29; mustard seed and leaven, Mt. 13.31–33; Lk.
13.18–21; Gosp. Thom. 20; 96.

In Mk 4.3–8 the call to hear at beginning and end can
only refer to the process as a whole, from seed to harvest.
It is meant to speak for itself, the parable contains no hint
of an interpretation, which in fact would be quite unnecessary. The same applies to the remaining parables of
growth. The fact that only one of them, the parable of the
mustard seed, is introduced as a parable of the Kingdom,
does not affect its understanding at all. Again, special
aspects of growth are each depicted in particular narratives:
on the one hand the power of growth causes upward
growth, on the other growth permeating the whole. While
it is *possible* to relate these parables to certain events in the
ministry of Jesus or in the early church, e.g. the effect of
his preaching, one must, however, not confine them to
this single line of interpretation.

(b) In the parable of the wheat and the tares, Mt. 13.24–
30, yet another aspect is added: here, too, we are concerned
with the effect of God's blessing evident in the growth

process, but the stress in this case is on the fact that humans should not interfere with this process, even when bad seed grows up together with the good. This corresponds to Mt. 5.45, a saying which also deals with God's blessing. This parable, too, must not be confined to one single form of interpretation.

Similar to this is the parable of the fishing net, Mt. 13.47 f., which this time deals with fruits from the sea.

(c) Growth occurs as a subordinate motif in the parable of the fig tree in Mk 13.28–29. The text is closer to a comparison than to a parable. It resembles a parable of growth in that it is able to say something to the person who observes this growth process. The text is intended as a call to be on one's guard; Lk. 13.6–9, the barren fig tree, merely touches on the motif of a tree which bears no fruit.

To sum up: both groups belong to the context of God's acts of salvation; they are, however, clearly different insofar that the first group of parables refers to the saving acts of God or Jesus respectively ('I have come to seek and save what was lost'), while the second deals with God's blessing activity, which precisely in these parables is distinct from his saving acts. (On this distinction cf. my *Theologie des Alten Testaments in Grundzügen*, 1978; ET: Elements of Old Testament Theology, 1982, parts II and III.)

III. Announcement of judgment in a parable. One can only speak with some reservation of a group of such parables. Groups I and II, both dealing with God's acts of salvation, have no counterpart in a roughly equivalent group dealing with God's acts of judgment. All one can say is that the motif of God's judgment also occurs in a few parables.

(a) The parable of the wicked tenants of the vineyard, Mk 12.1–11, is concerned with an announcement of judgment against Israel corresponding to the prophetic announcement. This announcement in the parable has to be seen in the context of Jesus' oracles of judgment against Israel, spoken elsewhere without a parable (Mt. 23.37–39; 24.1–2; Lk. 19.41–44; 21.5–6).

This parable is meant to explain why judgment has to

come, and therefore deliberately refers back to Isa. 5.1–7: the reason is the people's rejection of God's loving care. The same is true of the parable of the unmerciful servant (cf. I(b)). Judgment becomes necessary when God's merciful care is rejected. In this respect this parable is close to group I.

(b) Exclusion (of individuals) from the (eschatological) feast. The parable of the closed door, Lk. 13.24–30: its text is difficult, probably composite; vv. 24b and 29 belong together. Vv. 25–29 describe the householder's rejection: those who demand admission are rejected as evildoers. Many from the people of Israel shall not take part in the eschatological banquet, while those who have come from a distance are admitted. Exclusion from the banquet is also the subject in Mt. 22.11–13, the wedding garment, an addition to the parable of the wedding feast, Mt. 22.1–10.

Exclusion from the feast serves only as a subordinate motif in the parable of the ten virgins, Mt. 25.1–13, in vv. 11–12 which are similar to Lk. 13.25–29. On the basis of its main motif, Mt. 25.1–13 would have to be attributed to group IVB.

(c) Verdict of rejection in the additions. It is particularly noteworthy that the harsh and uncompromising verdict of rejection ('wailing and gnashing of teeth', execution) never occurs as an organic part of parables, but only in texts which are definitely or probably additions. This is definitely the case for Mt. 22.11–13 (an addition already dealt with under IIIb) and Mt. 25.29–30 (an addition to 25.14–30, money entrusted); this is probably the case for the wicked servant parable (Mt. 24.48–51 and Lk. 12.45–47), according to Goulder.

(d) Mention should also be made of the condemnation of the rich man, Lk. 16.19–31, which is not a parable.

Summarizing group III we find that the announcement of judgment against Israel, occurring in one parable only, clearly corresponds to group I. This allows us to conclude that this parable was spoken by Jesus himself. The exclusion of individuals from the eschatological meal (IIIb) and the verdict of rejection of individuals (IIIc) is quite different from the announcement against Israel (IIIa) and only really becomes meaningful in the period after Jesus. These features do not occur as a main motif in parables which are all of a piece, but predominantly in additions. This, too, points to their origin in the situation of the Christian church after Jesus. This implies that, in addition to a multitude of parables which deal with God's or Jesus' acts of salvation, only one parable is concerned with God's judgment of Israel, while the oracles of judgment against individuals have not formed parables of their own.

IV. Instructions for present/future action. The parables in this group are based on instructions on the part of Jesus or imply such instructions. They are meant to encourage action or behaviour or to pass judgment on such. Hence their function is fundamentally different from that of the first two groups. Goulder distinguishes between imperative and indicative parables. Making statements about *the* parables of Jesus without observing this distinction can only confuse the issue.

For the same reasons a further distinction has to be observed with regard to group IV: the behaviour to which the parables refer can have no temporal reference, as in the parable of the servant's wages, while in other texts such behaviour refers to a precise point in the future, e.g. the return of the Lord. This distinction has to be gleaned from the texts before any interpretation is attempted.

A: Instruction for present action.

(a) The parable of the Good Samaritan, Lk. 10.30–37, is a complete narrative (exemplary story). It implicitly demands merciful behaviour which is not limited by any boundaries. Similarly, in Mt. 25.31–46, which is not a parable, an appeal for merciful action is dressed up as a story of the Last Judgment. The parable of the rich fool, Lk. 12.16–21, an exemplary story, is intended as a warning against making future plans. It is assumed that the audience will be able to judge the rich fool's future plans from their own experiences of life and act accordingly. The dishonest steward, Lk. 16.1–8, is also an exemplary story. The convicted dishonest steward uses the only option still open to him, to make friends by giving presents. Such behaviour is praised. The deposed crook is not held up as an example, rather, this praise implies that even he was still given a chance, which he took. In the parable of the servant's wages, Lk. 17.7–10, the audience is called upon to take a stand on a particular issue. This parable is a warning not to derive claims from having carried out the master's commands. The people addressed are those who lay claim to a special rank on the basis of their obedience to the Law.

(b) In addition we should mention parables which contain instruction as a subordinate motif. The parables of the importunate friend, Lk. 11.5–8, and of the persistent widow, Lk. 18.1–8, are implicit exhortations to persist in asking when in distress. The parable of the unmerciful servant, Mt. 18.23–35, gives tacit encouragement to remit the debt of one's fellow servant, motivated by the remission of one's own debt. The parable of the two debtors, Lk. 7.41–43, indirectly demands forgiveness without limits. We may even include the story of Mary and Martha here.

(c) There are a couple more texts which can only be considered as parables in a restricted sense. Both are expanded comparisons, containing instructions on how to behave. Mt. 7.24–27 on house building is an exhortation to act according to what one has heard and forms the redactional conclusion to the collection in chs 5 to 7. A similar text is Lk. 14.28–32 on tower building and warfare. This doubly expanded comparison is meant to encourage a particular action on the part of those addressed. It then refers in v. 33 to the decision to be a disciple; but both comparisons remain open to many further interpretations. They are meant to warn against rash decisions.

The story about the places at the feast, Lk. 14.7–11, is not a parable but advice on prudent behaviour. If this text has been transmitted as a word of Jesus, then it has to be considered in the context of his championing the cause of humble folk. It is particularly addressed to those who are always trying to seize the places at the top. It is a simple piece of advice, which in this context takes on an element of criticism of the leadership's code of honour. A similar piece of advice based on an example is given in Mt. 5.23–26 (Lk. 12.57–59), on the way to court: it is more sensible to reach an agreement with your opponent before you come to the judge.

To conclude this group IVA, we find it characterized by the sentence with which Lk. 12.58–59 is introduced: 'And why do you not judge for yourselves what is right?' (v. 57). Those addressed in this exhortation should be quite capable of judging the situation for themselves and acting accordingly. Experiences which are obvious to everyone can enable people to come to the right decision. This is also true of a group of comparisons which are again instructions, but for future actions or behaviour (see below). Both groups closely resemble the proverbial sayings of comparison in Proverbs, which characterize behaviour by means of a comparison. The texts referred to as 'exemplary narratives' belong to this group, which characterizes them more precisely according to their function.

B: Instruction for future action.

The tradition-history of Matthew's Gospel already confirms that this group of parables belongs together. Since all these texts are grouped together in Mt. 24 and 25, they could once have formed an independent collection. As regards content, they are dominated throughout by the exhortation to stay awake (24.42, 44; 25.13), due to the fact that the time of the Lord's return is uncertain (Mt. 24.27, 36). The parables in Mt. 24–25 support, each in its own way, the call to be watchful and ready:

24.27: Comparison with the flash of lightning
  32–33: The sign of the sprouting fig tree
  37–42: As in the days of Noah . . . watch!
  43–44: The thief in the night . . . you must be ready!
  45–51: The good servant and the wicked one
25.1–13: Ten virgins
  14–30: money entrusted
(25.31–46: The Last Judgment)
and parallels.

The further fact that several parables have the common motif that the Lord's departure is narrated in a way corresponding to his return also clearly demonstrates that this group belongs together. They all deal with the return of the Lord who has gone away from his disciples (cf. the disciples' question in 24.3). This one group of parables alone agrees to such an extent as regards content, this one alone deals with Jesus himself, viz. his death and return. As regards the other parables, the comparison of the sprouting fig tree, Mt. 24.32–33, in this context is a call to watch attentively for signs of that return; 24.37–42 compares it to the sudden occurrence of a flood; 24.27 to a flash of lightning; 24.43–44 to a break-in by a thief in the night. The faithful steward is praised because during his master's absence he administers the latter's estate conscientiously (vv. 45–51 are probably a later addition). Then there follow in ch.25 the three longer parables. The subject of 25.1–13 is participating in a wedding feast, again involving the motif of the absence and return (of the bridegroom). The parable calls for watchful readiness: 'for you know neither the day nor the hour'. While 25.14–30 has the same basic structure, it adds, however, a new aspect, namely the reckoning on the master's return involving reward and punishment (v. 28; the punishment in v. 30 is a later addition). 25.31–46 has been included here because it has been dressed up as a story of the Last Judgment (see above under IVA). But the motif of separation in this story corresponds to 25.1–13 and 14–30.

But there are variants of this in other Gospels, too. The doorkeeper (Mk 13.33–37/Lk. 12.35–38) is an expanded comparison intended to strengthen a call for watchfulness. Here, too, the reason given is that the master of the house may return at an unknown time. In the variant, Lk. 12.35–38, the master returns from a feast.

This, to conclude, is the most compact group of parables and the only one to deal with the Lord's return. However it is not his return as such which is the subject of the comparisons, but rather the watchful readiness of the servants in awaiting the return of their master, for which these comparisons call. They are therefore strictly speaking not parables of the return (as many term them), but, as exhortations to watchfulness (in view of the expected return of the Lord), they correspond to the instructions to action or behaviour in IVA. The many diverse instructions for the present (in IVA) have now been replaced by the single exhortation to be ready for the return of the Lord. The only possible explanation for this must be that both groups have a different origin; IVB is intended for the time after the Lord's departure.

Summary of the structure of the parables:

1. We have found groups of parables which are clearly recognizable and have plainly different functions. There are on the one hand groups of parables which, since they say something about God's activity, are to be assigned to the message and ministry of Jesus, and on the other, clearly distinct from the former, those which are concerned with or implicitly contain instructions for human action or behaviour.

2. The parables dealing with God's activity are assigned in one group to the saving acts of the God who condescends to sufferers and sinners; in this they reflect the ministry of Jesus in his helping, healing, and forgiving. In the other group they are assigned to the blessing activity of God, which is equally embodied in Jesus' speeches and actions. God's judging activity recedes right into the background, in contrast to his saving and blessing.

3. With regard to the instructions for action, we have to distinguish between actions or behaviour which are pluriform and relate to the present and those which refer to the sole future event, the return of the Lord.

4. It is probable that many texts from groups III and IVB only originated after the death of Jesus and acquired their function in the light of the background of that time. The main bulk of the parables, the majority of which at least go back to Jesus, reflect on the one hand the saving and blessing activity of God, and on the other the activity

of the people with their present day concerns among whom Jesus' ministry took place.

5. This sketch of how the parables of Jesus may be structured does not claim to be the last word on the subject. My intention has only been to demonstrate that for our understanding of the parables of Jesus such a grouping is necessary because it points to the different contexts and thereby the different functions of these parables. It would have to be supplemented by a traditio-historical investigation which would have to include the relationship of the parables in the three Gospels to one another. In the exposition of the parables of Jesus up till now there has been too ready a tendency to say too much about *the* parables of Jesus, and to press this into general and abstract terms which cannot be valid for the parables as a whole. There is no single message of the parables of Jesus. Equally, one cannot say that all parables of Jesus are to be understood 'eschatologically' or 'christologically' etc. The parables of Jesus are only taken seriously when one asks each one individually in the light of its special character what it has to say. Only then will one be able to recognize the context of each individual parable within those groups which clearly belong together.

Observations on the Comparisons in the Synoptic Gospels

I.   Instructions for action
        (a) Instruction for action in the present
        (b) Instruction for entering the Kingdom of God
        (c) Instruction in the context of the mission of the disciples
        (d) Warning against a rash decision on discipleship
II.  (a) Jesus' commission: mercy on sufferers and sinners
        (b) Refutation of opponents
III. Announcement of the Passion and return
IV. Comparisons in scriptural quotations

If one is entitled to see parables as expansions of comparisons, and if some texts can assume an intermediate position between parables and comparisons, i.e. provide a transition between both, then comparisons will also have to be included in our investigation.

Introduction. Mark has around 23 comparisons, Matthew 60, and Luke without the Matthean parallels around 22. As in the OT, they do not just occur at random. They are entirely or almost entirely absent in reports (Mt. 1–4; 26–28; Lk. 1–2; 22–24) and in stories, i.e. the speech form which takes up more space than any other in the Gospels. They are only to be found in dialogue, as in the OT, i.e. they derive their function from address.

The fact that the distinction between comparisons (one or two sentences) and parables (stories) is fluid is evident from the hesitation of expositors over whether some texts are to be regarded as comparisons ('pictorial speech') or as parables, e.g. Mt. 5.13–16 (salt, city, light); Mt. 7.5–11; 7.16–23; 11.16–19 et al. This hesitation is unnecessary if one regards them as expanded comparisons. Since comparisons consisting of one sentence only belong to a single context, the function of the comparison in question can normally be determined from that context (as in the OT). And since they occur in different contexts, their function must needs be different accordingly. In order to understand the comparisons it is necessary to determine the groups of texts which form a common context. While I am only able to provide a rough overall sketch which would require more precise elaboration, I have found the following contexts:

I. Instruction for action. By far the largest group of comparisons in the synoptic Gospels forms part of instruction for action or occurs in or as such instruction. They all have the function of intensifying this instruction, only in different ways. They never have the functions of clarifying or illustrating, therefore the term 'pictorial speech' (Bultmann, Jeremias et al.) is not appropriate. This classification yields three sub-groups:

(a) Comparisons in the instruction for present action. This is the largest of these sub-groups. In it the *whole* audience is addressed, not just the disciples or opponents. This type is most concentrated in the Sermon on the Mount (Mt. 5–7 par). The instructions in the Sermon on the Mount are not specifically addressed to the disciples, as is clear from Mt. 5.1. Examples of this type are: the speck and the log, Mt. 7.3–5; 'the measure you give', 7.2; pearls before swine, 7.6; the eye as the lamp of the body, 6.22 f. Typical of the function of these comparisons is that they appeal to common sense, i.e. they mean to give instructions for sensible action which are obvious to everyone, as in Mk 2.21 f. ('new wine in old wineskins') or Mt. 6.24 ('no one can serve two masters'). In this way Jesus' instructions correspond to a high degree with those in the Book of Proverbs, which appeal to common sense in the same way.

These instructions refer on several occasions to God's activity in creation: freeing from anxiety, Mt. 6.25–34, which points to the lilies of the field and the birds of the air; Jesus makes the same point separately to his disciples in Mt. 10.29–31: the sparrows and 'the hairs on your head are all numbered'. The command to love one's enemies is grounded in the activity of the creator: '(who) sends rain on . . .', Mt. 5.45. The parables of growth point to the creator's activity in a similar way.

(b) Instruction for entering the Kingdom of God. This group, too, is addressed to the *whole* of Jesus' audience, not just to his disciples. All these comparisons represent reaching the Kingdom of God (or in a few places 'life') as something difficult, something which requires hard sacrifice or radical change. It is so difficult for the rich man that a camel could go through a needle's eye more easily, Mk 10.25; one would have to resign adult status and become like a child, Mk 10.14 f.; one would have to be prepared to sacrifice a limb or an eye for it, Mk 9.43–48 (this is not meant literally, but as a comparison); one has to enter by the narrow door, Lk. 13.24; and it is not those who are close to the Kingdom but those who are distant who will enter it, Mt. 8.11; 19.30.

While these are only a few texts, they nevertheless agree in defining the Kingdom of God (Heaven) as the goal of each individual human life. None of these passages even hints that entering the Kingdom of God is in any way connected with the person or the ministry of Jesus or with faith in him; it also has nothing to do with the history or the fate of the people of God.

(c) Instruction in the context of the disciples' mission. This is the only group containing instructions which are exclusively addressed to the disciples. The few comparisons we encounter here have the one and only function of preparing and strengthening the disciples for their intended task. They are meant to know that this task is dangerous: '. . . as sheep in the midst of wolves', Mt. 10.16a; therefore they are warned to 'be wise as serpents and innocent as doves', v. 16b. The fate of the disciples will be no better than that of their master, 10.24 f.; they will have to share in his passion. But at the same time he takes away their fear of this difficult task, e.g. in Lk. 12.32: 'Fear not, little flock!', for their master will take care of them, Lk. 10.19: '. . . authority to tread upon serpents and scorpions'; their 'names are written in heaven', v. 20. Here the comparisons have the same function as in the call of Jeremiah, Jer. 1. The comparison in Mt. 10.26 f., which underlines the necessity of preaching, also serves to strengthen the disciples: '. . . proclaim upon the house-tops'. To this context also belongs the request for further messengers: 'the harvest is plentiful, but the labourers are few', Mt. 9.37. The disciples, too, are the subject of the call to readiness and watchfulness: 'Let your loins be girded and your lamps burning', Lk. 12.35. The word to Peter: 'you are Peter . . .', Mt. 16.18, is a wordplay which implies a comparison.

(d) Warning against a rash decision for discipleship. It is noteworthy that the Gospels contain no comparisons underlining the call to discipleship, but several warning against a rash decision to be a disciple, Mt. 8.20: 'Foxes have holes . . .', and Lk. 9.62: 'No one who puts his hand to the plough . . .'. The double parables of house building and warfare should also be mentioned here, listed above as expanded comparisons (cf. p. 190).

IIa. Jesus' commission: mercy on sufferers and sinners. The execution of Jesus' commission to those to whom he was sent is presented in narrative speech form; no comparisons are used. This is evident in Jesus' reply to John's question in Mt. 11.5. Where Jesus speaks about his commission we encounter comparisons, but ones taken over from the OT only: 'He saw a great throng, and he had compassion on them . . . like sheep without a shepherd', Mk 6.34 (cf. Ezek. 34 and elsewhere); 'For the Son of man came to seek and save the lost', Lk. 19.10 (cf. ch. 15).

One can also include here comparisons in the 'invitation to salvation': '. . . who hunger and thirst for righteousness', Mt. 5.6; the saviour's call in Mt. 11.28–30 and the promise of being heard in 7.7–8, 9–11 with the contrast comparison 'bread–stone', 'you–your Father in heaven'; also his acceptance of the children, Mk 10.14 f.

IIb. Refutation of opponents, disputations and oracles of judgment. But Jesus does speak about his commission in comparisons when he is attacked in his ministry and replies to these attacks, in a way similar to the disputations (refutations) in the prophets. That the comparisons here function as part of the refutation of such attacks, whereas the stories of Jesus' ministry have no need of such comparisons, clearly shows the dialogical function of the comparisons. When Jesus is attacked in his ministry of healing and helping, he replies in Mk 2.17: 'Those who are well have no need of a physician, but those who are sick: I came not to call the righteous, but sinners'. Plucking ears of grain on the sabbath, Mt. 12.1–8: Jesus refers to David's behaviour (I Sam. 21) and the work of the priests on the sabbath: 'Something greater than the temple is here': 'I desire steadfast love and not sacrifice' (Hos. 6.6). The following section is similar, Mt. 12.9–13, healing on the sabbath; like saving a sheep on the sabbath, one may do good on that day.

In Mk 2.19 f., the question of fasting, Jesus replies to the attack of the Pharisees by calling his presence a time of feasting and by pointing ahead to its end: then is the time for his disciples to fast. – To the charge that he casts out Satan by Beelzebul, Mk 3.23–27, Jesus replies with the comparison: 'No one can enter a strong man's house', thereby claiming that in his work of salvation the power of Satan is being broken. Responding to another accusation, Jesus (Mt. 15.11) tells his opponents in a contrast parable what it is that really makes people unclean.

While in the passages mentioned so far Jesus defends his ministry, in others he attacks the activities of his opponents. These accusations he bolsters up by the use of comparisons, as the prophets do in their indictments. Mt. 15.14: the blind leading the blind; there follows an oracle of judgment: 'both will fall into a pit'. 23.4: 'they bind heavy burdens . . . and lay them on men's shoulders', further v. 13: '. . . because you shut the kingdom of heaven against men', v. 24: gnat–camel, v. 27: 'whitewashed tombs', v. 33: 'brood of vipers'. The woes in ch. 23 closely resemble the prophetic oracles of woe. The indictment uttered in Jeremiah's temple speech has been taken up in Mk 11.17: house of prayer–den of robbers. Mt. 15.13 is an announcement of judgment against Jesus' opponents in form of a comparison: 'Every plant . . .'.

Group IIb, refutation of the opponents who attack Jesus' ministry, is after Ia the largest group of comparisons in the Gospels. It corresponds to the refutations in the parables. This implies that both groups were of outstanding significance in the ministry of Jesus, in the same way as the intensifying function of the OT comparisons points to their outstanding significance.

III. Announcement of the Passion and return. In Mk 2.18–20, the question of fasting, the comparison of the presence of Jesus with a feast is followed by the announcement: '. . . the days will come, when the bridegroom is taken away from them'. As in the OT prophets, two processes which follow each other have been joined together in a single comparison (e.g. Isa. 5.1–7). This shows how close the comparisons of Jesus can come to those of the OT. Lk. 12.50 announces Jesus' Passion by means of a comparison: 'I have a baptism to be baptized with . . .'; Mk 9.49f., 'salted with fire', has probably the same meaning. Alternatively, OT passages point to his Passion: the sign of Jonah in Mt. 12.38–42 (16.1–4); 'I will destroy this temple', Mk 14.58. His saying, 'I will strike the shepherd and the sheep will be scattered', Mk 14.27 (cf. Ezek. 34), summarizes his Passion and that of his disciples. Both are referred to in Mt. 10.24f.: 'A disciple is not above his teacher . . .'. Both are in view in the question to his disciples: 'Are you able to drink the cup that I drink?', Mk 10.38, and in the saying to Peter: 'Satan . . . that he might sift you like wheat', Lk. 22.31. The saying about lightning, Mt. 24.37 f. and Lk. 10.18, may perhaps refer to Jesus' return. In the announcements of the Passion the comparisons also have a concealing function.

IV. Comparisons in scriptural quotations. The comparison with shepherd and flock (Ezek. 34 and elsewhere) occurs in several places: Mt. 15.24; Mk 6.34; 14.27. The reception of this comparison and the repeated quotation of the Servant Songs in the healing stories, Mt. 8.14–17 and 12.9–21, show how deeply rooted the ministry of Jesus is in the OT, according to the Gospels. The other passages which take up an OT comparison have already been referred to.

In conclusion, it must be pointed out once again that what has been said about the comparisons in the Gospels is just a sketch which simply quotes examples; an extensive study would have to consider all the comparisons. This would also include some which have so far evaded an authoritative exposition, such as Mt. 13.52; Lk. 12.4 f. Such a more precise study would also have to include a more detailed comparison of groups of parables with those of comparisons. Looking at both together we find:

1. The two main groups can be found in both parables and comparisons. The Gospels talk in parables and comparisons of the commission of Jesus who in his saving ministry represents the mercy of God condescending to sufferers and sinners. There is a difference insofar that God's mercy is related primarily in parables, while comparisons are more frequent in connection with the refutation of opponents who resist the saving ministry. Needless to say, such refutation can also occur in parables. Both parables and comparisons feature the blessing activity of God as well as his saving one.

While the announcement of judgment is more prominent in the comparisons connected with the refutation of Jesus' opponents, in the parables it recedes into the background. But in the – probably later – motif 'exclusion from the feast and rejection' it is again more apparent.

2. The other main group 'instructions for action or behaviour' occurs just as frequently in the parables as in the comparisons. This is particularly true of the sub-group 'instruction for the present'; in the case of the parables this would involve exemplary stories, while this forms the largest group of comparisons. In both parables and comparisons instructions are addressed to the audience as a whole. They are most concentrated in the Sermon on the Mount, which illustrates their significance. The two subgroups 'instruction for entering the Kingdom of God' and 'instruction in connection with the mission of the disciples' occur in connection with the comparisons only, there is nothing corresponding to them in the parables. The same applies to the group 'announcement of the Passion and return'. Hence it is clear that only the comparisons are connected with the actual ministry of Jesus (mission of the disciples, announcement of the Passion, return), not the parables. What conclusions are to be drawn from this will have to be looked at in a larger context.

## Conclusions

The conclusions I have already stated at the end of the individual sections of this investigation will not be repeated here.

1. We have found that comparisons and parables form an essential part of the Bible, both in the Old Testament and in the New (the metaphors not investigated here would also have to be considered, see above p. 3 f.). All three linguistic forms in which they occur (the single word – the sentence – the story) are connected with each other. It is the same process of comparing which has fashioned all three.

2. We have further noted that comparisons do not occur at random in the Old and New Testaments, but only

(with well founded exceptions) in dialogical texts. It is from address that the comparisons and parables in the Old and New Testaments derive their functions.

3. The function of comparisons and parables differs according to the context in which they are found and from which in turn they derive their function. The comparisons are not images and the parables are not pictorial speech.

4. Through the use of comparison and parable the image influences the subject of comparison. If the subject is an event between God and man, the image, something which happens in the world as creation and between creatures, influences what happens between God and man. Since all comparisons and parables refer to events in creation and between creatures, these comparisons and parables assign great significance to God's creation in the context of what the Bible says about God.

5. Going beyond the limits of our study, we may conclude that the understanding of the term 'instruction' in the Gospel has to be corrected insofar that in all passages containing comparisons and in all parables this term 'instruction' does not refer to a doctrinal statement, but to an address.

6. There remains the further task of comparing the comparisons in the Gospels with those of the NT epistles. One would be surprised how much they differ from one another. The reason is simply that they have different functions in each case. Whereas the comparisons in the epistles belong more to the tradition of early Jewish instructional parables and comparisons, the comparisons and parables in the Gospels stand rather in the tradition of the OT comparisons and parables.

# INDEX OF BIBLICAL REFERENCES

| | | | | | |
|---|---|---|---|---|---|
| 9.8–12 | 134, 136 | 30.2, 4 | 130 f. | 47.1–10 | 134 |
| 9.14 | 130 f. | 30.8 | 131 | 48.4 | 126 |
| 9.16 | 119 f. | 30.12 | 133 | 49.12 f. | 115 |
| 10.2 | 119 f. | 31.3 | 103, 125 f. | 49.15, 21 | 115 |
| 10.7, 9 f. | 119 f. | 31.4 | 125 | 50.8 f. | 121 |
| 10.11 | 120 | 31.5 | 126 | 52.4, 6 | 120 |
| 10.16 | 134 | 31.9 | 131 | 52.7 | 121 |
| 11.2 | 120 | 31.12 | 115 | 52.9 | 126 |
| 11.4 | 134 | 31.21 | 127 f., 135 f. | 55.3 f. | 116 |
| 11.6 | 121 | 32.4 | 131 | 55.5 | 115 |
| 12.3–5 | 120 | 32.7 | 127 | 55.17 | 116 |
| 12.7 | 136 | 32.31 | 125 | 55.19 | 131 |
| 14.6 | 124 | 33.4 | 136 | 55.20 | 134 |
| 16.5 f. | 128 | 33.7 | 136 | 55.22 | 120 |
| 17.8 | 123 | 33.20 | 127 | 56.9 | 122 |
| 17.11 f. | 119 | 35.1–3 | 122 | 56.14 | 130 |
| 18 | 18, 20, 25, 88, 126 | 35.7 | 119 | 57.2 | 127 |
| 18.3 f. | 125 f. | 35.17 | 122 | 57.5–7 | 119 f. |
| 18.5 | 130 f. | 36.6 f., 8 | 135, 136 f. | 57.11 | 135 |
| 18.7 | 125 | 36.7 f. | 120, 134 | 58.7, 10 | 119, 121 |
| 18.17 | 130 | 36.9 f. | 137 | 59.7 f. | 119 f. |
| 18.19 | 44 | 37.2 | 121 | 59.10 | 124, 126 |
| 18.20 | 131 f. | 37.14 f. | 120 | 59.15 f. | 119 |
| 18.31 | 136 | 37.20, 35 f. | 121 | 59.17 f. | 125 f. |
| 18.32 | 125, 135 f. | 37.39 | 126 | 59.18, | 126 |
| 18.36 | 127, 136 | 38 | 112 | 60.4 | 122 |
| 18.37 | 131 | 38.3 | 113 f. | 60.6 | 113 |
| 18.47 | 135 f. | 38.5 | 115 | 61.3, 5 | 125 f., 127 f. |
| 19 | 136 f. | 38.14 f. | 115 | 61.4 | 124 |
| 19.15 | 125 | 39.6 f. | 115 | 62.2, 7 | 126 |
| 22 | 112, 118 | 39.12 f. | 115 | 62.3, 7–9, 12 | 124 f. |
| 22.7 | 116 | 40.3 | 125 f., 130 f. | 62.10 | 115 |
| 22.13 f. | 118 | 40.5 | 125, 130 | 63.2 | 116 |
| 22.15 f. | 115, 122 | 42 | 112 | 63.8 | 128 |
| 22.16 | 113 f. | 42.1 | 116 | 64.4–9 | 119 f. |
| 22.17, 21 f. | 119 | 42.3 | 114 | 64.8 f. | 121 |
| 22.29 | 134 | 42.8 | 113 f. | 65.5 f. | 125 f. |
| 23 | 128 f. | 42.10 | 125 | 65.10–14 | 137 f. |
| 23.4 | 44, 128 | 42.11 | 120 | 66.10–12 | 130–33 |
| 23.6 | 126 | 43.2 f. | 123, 126 | 68.3 | 121 |
| 24.7–10 | 134 | 44 | 112 | 68.6 | 135 |
| 25.4 f., 10, 12 | 123 | 44.2 | 113 | 69.1 f. | 115 |
| 26.8 | 134 | 44.3 | 123 | 69.15 f. | 122 |
| 27.1 | 126, 136 f. | 44.12 f. | 112 f. | 69.24 | 120 |
| 27.5 | 125–127 | 44.20 | 113 | 70.20 | 121 |
| 27.11 | 123 | 44.23 | 112 f. | 71.2 | 122, 131 |
| 28.1 | 115, 125 | 44.24 | 113 | 71.3 | 125 f. |
| 28.7 | 124, 127 | 44.26 | 115 | 71.5–7 | 124 f. |
| 28.8 | 126 | 46.2 | 124 f. | 71.20 | 122 |
| 28.9 | 128 | 46.8, 12 | 126 | 72.3, 5 f., 16 | 138 f. |